THE TOWN in Ireland

THE TOWN in Ireland

Edited by **David Harkness**
and **Mary O'Dowd**

HISTORICAL STUDIES XIII
Papers read before the Irish
Conference of Historians

BELFAST
30 May–2 June, 1979

G. MacNIOCAILL
R. J. HUNTER
M. MURPHY
P. FROGGATT
S. GRIBBON

G. H. MARTIN
L. CLARKSON
P. J. JUPP
C. O'LEARY
M. DALY

APPLETREE PRESS

First published in 1981 by
The Appletree Press Ltd
7 James Street South
Belfast BT2 8DL

©

G. MacNiocaill, G. H. Martin
R. J. Hunter, L. Clarkson
M. Murphy, P. J. Jupp
P. Froggatt, C. O'Leary
S. Gribbon, M. Daly

1981

British Library Cataloguing in Publication Data
Irish Conference of Historians (*1979: Belfast*)
The town in Ireland.—(Historical studies;
13)
1. Cities and towns—Ireland—History—
Congresses
I. Title II. Harkness, D. W.
III. O'Dowd, Mary IV. Series
941.5'009'732   HT145.17

ISBN 0-904651-72-X

Printed in Northern Ireland by Appletree Press Ltd

Contents

Preface

The Irish Committee of Historical Sciences inaugurated a series of biennial conferences of historians in July 1953. Since then the 'Irish Conference of Historians' has circulated among the Irish universities and university colleges, and the papers read since 1955 have been published as *Historical Studies*. Since 1975 the conferences have been devoted to a single theme, the full list being as follows:

volume	conference	editor	date of publication
I	Trinity College and University College, Dublin, 11–13 July 1955	T. D. Williams	1958
II	The Queen's University of Belfast, 22–23 May 1957	Michael Roberts	1959
III	University College, Cork, 27–29 May 1959	James Hogan	1961
IV	University College, Galway, 25–27 May 1961	G. A. Hayes-McCoy	1963
V	Magee University College, Londonderry, 30 May–1 June 1963	J. L. McCracken	1965
VI	Trinity College, Dublin, 2–5 June 1965	T. W. Moody	1968
VII	The Queen's University of Belfast, 24–27 May 1967	J. C. Beckett	1969
VIII	University College, Dublin, 27–30 May 1969	T. D. Williams	1971
IX	University College, Cork, 29–31 May 1971	J. G. Barry	1974

The Fourteenth Conference of Irish Historians, the bulk of the proceedings of which constitute this volume, attracted more than one hundred participants to hear eleven papers spread over four days. The Irish Committee of Historical Sciences wishes to pay tribute to the hospitality of the Queen's University, not alone for the provision of facilities and services for the Conference itself, but also for a generous grant towards the publication of this volume.

Note: Abbreviations used in this volume conform to those recommended in *Rules for Contributors to Irish Historical Studies* (Supplement 1, January 1968).

Introduction

The papers published in this volume are both a reflection of an increasing scholarly concern with Irish urban history and a response to a demand. The study of the town in Ireland has too long been neglected, distinguished though a few limited studies have been. The present volume does not itself provide the answers to all the questions currently being asked but it is the belief of authors and editors alike that it represents a serious response to the basic questions and should provide a stimulus to the research and the publication of answers to others. Here, then, is both a framework to be consulted and a map of the way to further progress in the historical investigation of urban Ireland.

One of the most basic problems facing Irish urban historians concerns the origins of urban life in Ireland. It was for long assumed that the Vikings were responsible for introducing towns to Ireland and that these first urban settlements held little attraction for the native Irish inhabitants. In recent years early Irish historians have questioned these assumptions and have begun to recognise that not only did some of the large monastic settlements of early Christian Ireland possess some of the characteristics of incipient urban communities but also that early Irish kings were concerned to acquire political and economic control of Hiberno-Norse towns like Dublin and Waterford. It is to be regretted that this exciting research has not yet reached a stage where publication is possible and consequently, the first paper presented here deals with urban life in post-Norman Ireland. The implications of the earlier research for the later period should not, however, be overlooked.

Prominent among the reasons for the neglect of Irish urban history in the medieval period is, of course, the absence of adequate source material. As Professor MacNiocaill points out, we do not possess for Ireland records like the medieval tax books which enable the social and economic structure of many German towns to be analysed. Nevertheless, as Professor MacNiocaill's own research and publications testify, the surviving documentation for Irish medieval towns may be meagre but much still remains to be learnt from it. In the paper published here, Professor MacNiocaill examines the position of the ruling families who controlled some of the large Irish borough towns in the medieval period and asks whether they constituted an oligarchy in the sense of being a small, exclusive ruling class. His

1

exploration of this problem raises many interesting questions such as the effect of the population crisis in the later medieval period on the recruitment of members to the governing bodies in the towns, and the nature and extent of the wealth possessed by individual burgesses in towns like Dublin and Waterford. Professor MacNiocaill stresses the tentative nature of his conclusions but his work does suggest new lines of approach and indicates the sort of information which can be gleaned from the extant material.

Obviously, any comprehensive account of urban life in medieval Ireland will require clarification of what exactly we mean by the term 'town' in terms of size, population, government and commercial life. Professor G. H. Martin makes a contribution to this discussion by elaborating the work of Dr R. Glasscock and Dr B. J. Graham in listing all the Irish medieval boroughs for which he could find printed documentary evidence. The list, which reveals the wide variety of post-Norman settlements which were granted the status of a borough, will need to be examined with care. As Professor Martin points out, each entry does not represent a flourishing urban community. Enfranchisement was offered as a bait to attract Norman tenants and, consequently, many of the places described as boroughs may never have got beyond the paper plans of the government. Like Professor MacNiocaill's paper, Professor Martin's work indicates the need for more research, particularly at a local level which would eventually make possible a more refined classification of the different categories of medieval towns which existed in Ireland.

The incorporation of towns could be undertaken for a variety of reasons. Professor Martin points to the economic and social appeal which it had in the Norman period. In the early modern period political considerations became more important and so towns, or in many cases small villages, were incorporated for the political purpose of ensuring a Protestant majority in parliament. Thus, James I created forty new boroughs before the summoning of the parliament of 1613–15. As with the boroughs created by the Normans, not all the new Stuart nominations developed into towns. Some did, however, and prominent among these were the towns organised under the terms of the Ulster plantation which are the subject of Mr R. J. Hunter's paper. Mr Hunter here examines the relative size of the towns in terms of their population, buildings, the services they provided and the nature of the trade which was conducted in them. His analysis reveals the small scale of many of the plantation towns. As Mr Hunter indicates, by English contemporary standards, most of them were no bigger than the average English village. Yet, as he points out, and as archaeologists are also beginning to realise, it is perhaps fairer and more fruitful to compare urban growth in the Ulster plantation with its counterpart in colonial Virginia and Maryland rather than with English towns which had, after all, centuries of growth behind them. In such a colonial comparison the Ulster towns emerge in a more favourable light.

The value of Mr Hunter's research lies not only in the information which he gleans from the sources but also in his ability to discover and make use of much hitherto unknown or obscure documentation. His work demonstrates how, despite the destruction of much material, many repositories still contain potentially useful and informative documents, if historians are prepared to ask the right questions of them. One such document for a later period is the 1770 census of the population in Armagh which Dr Clarkson located in Armagh Public Library. Dr Clarkson's analysis of the information in the census enables him to examine the extent to which the inhabitants of eighteenth-century Armagh possessed a sense of community, regardless of or despite their religious divisions. Dr Clarkson's work is not only valuable for the conclusions which it draws but also for the methods which he uses to analyse the census material. His methodology shows how much historians can learn from considering the techniques of other disciplines such as economics and social science. As Dr Clarkson notes, this is the type of approach which is now being applied with profit to the study of pre-industrial towns in England.

The problems facing the historian in Ireland after the Act of Union differ substantially from those confronting scholars analysing the earlier period. The wealth of source material which exists for nineteenth- and twentieth-century Ireland allows more complex issues to be examined and enables historians to investigate in detail the growth of individual towns and cities. Dr Peter Jupp here sets the scene for the essays which follow on political, economic and social developments in Cork, Belfast and Dublin in the nineteenth and early twentieth centuries. Dr Jupp examines the impact of the Act of Union upon Irish politics, and their conduct up to 1831—a period during which in Ireland, as elsewhere in Europe, tension mounted between established landed control and ambitious middle class demands.

Emphasising the continuing importance of the Anglo-Irish ascendancy in urban affairs, especially in the twenty-eight towns and cities with a restricted corporation franchise, Dr Jupp also establishes the complex nature of local politics, and demonstrates the variety of methods by which oligarchies continued their self-perpetuation despite increasing disharmony between their interests and the economic and social interests of the communities which they managed: disharmony 'resolved' in 'typically English' fashion by proposals for reform that pleased no one. Throughout he goes beyond existing generalisations which here, as in so many areas, are shown to be inadequate when applied to particular cases.

In the first of four individual studies, Miss Maura Murphy expands upon one particular in her study of nineteenth-century Cork, concentrating on the basic structure of the city, its political complexion, social composition and diminishing economic fortunes. Her observations are backed by carefully culled evidence, expressed in tables and narrative, to show changing patterns, decade by decade, throughout the century. The relative decline of what had been Ireland's second city, its population, trade, social mobility and its local political response to national issues are all plotted to construct a profile of considerable interest when compared to the composite picture of Belfast built up by Dr Froggatt, Professor O'Leary and Mrs Gribbon. Miss Murphy shows how the growth of nationalism, the impact of local press and clergy, and above all the predominant role of the small master in the artisan class inhibited social radicalism in Cork as the nineteenth century progressed.

Turning to that city which was to replace Cork as Ireland's second city, the first aspect examined, from the perspective of the historian of community medicine, and covering the first half of the century, is the impact of increasing industrialisation and urbanisation upon the health of Belfast's citizens. With wit and illuminating example, Dr Froggatt's pioneering essay, rich in data, will have considerable comparative interest for those analysing an all too common, but neglected phenomenon, particularly as the field is strewn with obstacles of contemporary polemic. With a great textile complex, Belfast had a particular scourge in byssinosis, but its overwhelming crowding, sanitation, housing and medical provision problems were far from unique. The response of its city fathers, its medical practitioners and its concerned citizenry has more than local or merely Irish relevance.

It is the city fathers who occupy the centre of Professor O'Leary's stage: their management of that booming, expanding borough, from the Royal Commission of 1833 to the Local Government Act of 1898. Once again this essay has comparative value, fulfilling a basic purpose of this study of Irish towns: that the Irish experience be available to the urban historian of other lands. Professor O'Leary has much to say about property management, judicial duties, local government and the parliamentary franchise function of Belfast's corporation that is specific, but his references to the experience of British cities are frequent and concrete. The domination of the conservative interest in Belfast may have been against the trend in the United Kingdom, though Belfast's continued development, its taint of corruption, even its sectarian divisions, were more widely shared experiences than has been supposed. More remarkable was the conservative commitment to change and improvement and it is part of Professor O'Leary's purpose to point out that in this regard the Belfast record bares comparison with progressive English cities such as Liverpool, Birmingham and Manchester, rather than with cities in the rest of Ireland.

In making this comparison, Professor O'Leary cites a study of nineteenth-century Belfast by Sybil Gribbon and it is fascinating to follow this by reading her own appraisal of Belfast in the early twentieth century. Here she makes a sparkling case for considering the fundamentally Irish nature of Belfast, despite the economic orientation of its industries and the political focus of the majority of its inhabitants. Arguing both the Irish and the British aspects of Belfast as well as its specifically Ulster characteristics and its purpose above all as a port, she concludes nonetheless that the original plantation purpose of the city, expressed by Essex in 1575, still held good three-and-a-half centuries later.

It is fitting that final pride of place should be given to the capital, Dublin, having considered the provincial pretenders, Cork and Belfast. Dr Mary Daly's sweeping review of the city's economic, political and social aspects links admirably with the modern issues already raised, and shows how their interaction with one another and also with national politics rendered Dublin's problems well nigh insoluble by 1914. Along the way it illuminates, in particular, employment patterns, the spread of the suburbs and their relations with the city, corporation administration, public health, main drainage and tenement housing. Dr Daly provides a wealth of source reference for those anxious to take these issues further—a characteristic of her essay shown by so many of the others that it is surely one of the chief distinctions of this volume as a whole.

D.W.H. and M.O'D., Belfast, October, 1980

Socio-Economic Problems of the Late Medieval Irish Town

Gearóid MacNiocaill

Urban history has not been particularly prominent among the preoccupations of Irish historians in the last century or so, and such work as has been done has been biased in one of three directions: the antiquarian,[1] the topographical, in which geographers have been to the fore,[2] and the legal, in which the present author must plead a measure of guilt.[3] It will be admitted that the nature and extent of the available sources, certainly for the medieval period, in some measure excuses this, but no one familiar with the work done on the continent over the last two generations can be unaware that the social and economic history of the medieval Irish town has been sorely neglected. The object of this paper is not, single-handed, to remedy this, but rather to draw attention to some of the primary problems of the social structure of the Irish town in the late middle ages, and of its economic underpinnings, and suggest some working hypotheses.

We do not, of course, possess for any Irish city or town the equivalent of the tax books which enable the German historian to analyse in considerable detail the social structure of many of the towns of medieval Germany, but one obvious starting point for enquiry is the ruling body of the town. Cologne, Metz, Arras, all

[1] See the publications listed in P. Wolff (ed.), *Guide international d'histoire urbaine,* i (Paris, 1977), pp 403, 405, 425–7. This lists only books; if articles were listed, the bias would be yet more obvious.
[2] For example, R. A. Butlin (ed.), *The development of the Irish town* (London, 1977).
[3] G. MacNiocaill, *Na Buirgéisí, xii–xv aois* (2 vols, Dublin, 1964)—hereafter cited as Mac-Niocaill, *Na Buirgéisí*—of which part i is entirely devoted to the constitutional documents (charters and custumals) of the towns.

provide examples of what has been termed a patriciate which monopolized the ruling positions in these cities;[4] and it is natural to ask whether the Irish towns offer examples of similar structures. Some years ago the present author raised the question whether the ruling families of Dublin, Waterford, Kilkenny and so on constituted oligarchies, and on the basis of a perhaps too brief discussion reached a verdict of not proven.[5] It is, however, worthwhile examining the evidence in greater detail for the late medieval period at least, since the earlier period, shall we say the thirteenth to fourteenth centuries, provides relatively little evidence, although we have a fairly full list of mayors and bailiffs for Dublin,[6] and it is not uncommon for the same man to hold the office of mayor or bailiff more than once. For Dublin in the later fifteenth century, we have full details not only of the mayors and bailiffs but also the lesser officers of the city.[7] Certain names recur again and again: Thomas Newbery, later Sir Thomas Newbery, was mayor in 1448, 1451, 1452, 1457, 1460, 1463, 1464 and 1467, and died in harness in 1469; Sir Robert Burnell was mayor in 1450, 1454, 1458 and 1461; Thomas Savage was bailiff in 1448, 1455, 1457 and 1458, but unlike many other bailiffs seems never to have attained the mayoralty; William Crampe, bailiff in 1450 for (apparently) the only time, was mayor in his own right in 1466, and finished off Sir Thomas Newbery's term in 1469. Examples at this level are numerous, and can be paralleled in Waterford.[8] If we turn to Kilkenny, we find something similar: once elected to the council, a man was likely to continue in office for perhaps a quarter of a century: all previous sovereigns of Kilkenny were automatically, it seems, members of the council, thus excluding new recruits; and members of the same family crop up repeatedly—the Archers, for example, provided at least eight sovereigns in the fifteenth to early sixteenth centuries. Table I exemplifies this continuity and makes clear the cohesiveness of the group: it shows the sovereign and council that came into office at Michaelmas 1499,[9] those who were sovereigns, the earliest date of their appearance in municipal office, and their latest occurrence. The majority of them had been, or were to be, sovereigns

---

[4] E. Ennen, *Die europäische Stadt des Mittelalters* (Göttingen, 1975), pp 169–72.
[5] Op. cit., p. 345.
[6] H. F. Berry, 'Catalogue of the mayors, provosts and bailiffs of Dublin city, A.D. 1229 to 1447' in *R.I.A. Proc.*, xxviii, sect. C (1910), pp 47–61; for some corrections, see *Reg. St. John Dublin*, p. xx.
[7] *Anc. rec. Dublin*, i, 271 ff., passim.
[8] *H.M.C. rep 10*, app. v, 296–324, passim.
[9] *Liber primus Kilkenn.*, p. 110.

of Kilkenny, and equally the majority figured on the council for a full generation.

Table I

Name	Earliest Mention	Sovereign	Latest Mention
John Archer	1473	1499	1501–2
Walter Archer	1469	1469, 1490	1504
John Sherlock	1473	1486	1504
William son of Elias Archer	1467	1467	1515
William Ragged	1499		1515
John Knaresburgh	1472	1472	1515
Thomas Ley	1472		1515
Robert Leonard	1487	1487	1517
Nicholas Ragged	1472		1502
Denis Maldony	1487	1491	1524
John Mothill	1487		1528
Peter Archer	1494	1498, 1503	1535
John Savage	1472	1501	1501
Thomas Marshall	1487	1502	1516
John Courcy	1498		1502
Mothill	1473		1501

Is this however adequate evidence of an oligarchy in the sense of a small, exclusive, governing class? On this, some observations are in order. In the first place, the pool of potential candidates was limited. In Dublin, effectively, it amounted to two dozen *jurati,* in addition to the existing mayor and bailiff, which in turn, elected a second string of forty-eight *demijurati*: seventy-two in all. Waterford, which had borrowed its customs from Dublin, had a still smaller pool of twelve *jurati* who picked another dozen *demijurati*,[10] the same number as Kilkenny, which in the early fifteenth century described them as the chief twelve (*magna duodena*) and the secondary twelve (*secunda duodena*). In 1383–4 Kilkenny seems to have had a total of 119 burgesses,[11] and the sovereign, provosts and council would work out at slightly over a fifth of the total eligible population, which does not appear particularly exclusive. Secondly, before jumping too hastily to conclusions, a little reflection on one's own experience of committees will remind one that anyone who shows the slightest interest in, or capacity for, the work of a committee is liable to be elected or co-opted time and again, not counting those to whom this kind of activity is a kind of alcoholism. In the available pool these are normally balanced by those who for reasons of temperament or profit would prefer to steer clear of them, and there is sufficient

10 MacNiocaill, *Na Buirgéisí,* pp 354–5.
11 *Liber primus Kilkenn.,* pp 68–70.

9

evidence in Dublin, Waterford and Kilkenny to suggest that there was also a fair number of these. Waterford, in 1461, laid down that anyone eligible to be mayor who stayed away from the election meeting should be fined 100s, and those eligible to be bailiffs 50s; outright refusal to accept the post, if elected, would cost the reluctant mayor 9 marks (£5.6.8) and the bailiff 4 marks (£2.13.4).[12] Dublin in the same period was legislating for precisely the same problem: by an ordinance of 1483, the reluctant bailiff who declined the office, or evaded it by failing to take the oath during the three-day period assigned for taking it, was liable to a fine of £10, and deprivation of his rights as a freeman.[13] In 1485 the assembly laid down that any *jurate* who absented himself from the assembly on the feast of the exaltation of the cross (14 September) without reasonable cause should be fined 40s: the date was significant, since it was then that the *jurati* named one of themselves as mayor for the coming year, to be elected on Michaelmas day, and apparently it was not acceptable to nominate an absent *jurate*. For the reluctant mayor the next resort was to absent himself on Michaelmas day, but here again absence would cost him £40, of which half would be paid to the person willing to stand in for him for the following year. The carrot attached to this formidable stick was a guarantee of immunity from re-election against his will for the next three years.[14] A little further bait was attached in Dublin in 1504 by providing that the stand-in for would-be evaders would be entitled to half the fine.[15]

It was of course possible to obtain royal letters of immunity, and we have a few examples of these,[16] but any citizen of Waterford who sought these after 1465 could expect to lose his citizenship;[17] and a safer means to the same end was to buy one's immunity from the city itself: Thomas Kilbery bought immunity from Kilkenny, significantly *in forma consueta,* in 1351–2, as Philip Tonker had done in 1337 and as William Bacon was to do in 1359.[18] What this was worth to them is not recorded, but in 1472 it was worth 100s to Walter Courcy, a member of the council and later recorder of Kilkenny, to be exonerated from holding the office of sovereign in that year.[19] And Kilkenny also provides us with an example of a substitute, recorded

[12] *H.M.C. rep. 10,* app. v, 300 § xviii.
[13] *Anc. rec. Dublin,* i, 367–8, 363–4.
[14] Ibid., pp 367–8.
[15] Ibid., p. 392.
[16] MacNiocaill, *Na Buirgéisí,* p. 346.
[17] *H.M.C. rep. 10,* app. v, 302 § lvi.
[18] *Liber primus Kilkenn.,* pp 24, 27, 21.
[19] Ibid., p. 102.

TII 2

in the *Liber Primus* apparently as a precedent, from 1460, when Elias Archer, elected superior, after some dispute was allowed to pay Thomas Sherlock to carry out the duties of the office.[20]

If then exclusiveness be the mark of an oligarchy, then it seems reasonably clear that by the late middle ages the problem of the ruling group in the Irish town was not that of maintaining a closed group, but rather that of recruiting fresh members. The rule in Dublin, that nobody should be a *juratus* who had not already been a bailiff, was annulled in 1457,[21] since it was liable to restrict unduly recruitment into the ranks of the *jurati*. This obviously raises questions about mortality and replacement rates in Dublin in this period which cannot yet be answered; however, a list of the *jurati*[22] of the year 1500 shows them to be a little below their full theoretical strength, with twenty-two instead of twenty-four, as were the *demijurati* from whom the *jurati* were drawn, with forty-five instead of forty-eight. In 1483 the Dublin council had appointed a commission of four to pick suitable persons to bring the *demijurati* up to strength,[23] but a city ordinance of 1504 seems to express some doubt as to the feasibility of getting together the twenty-four *jurati* and the forty-eight *demijurati* to elect a replacement for the recorder.[24]

It seems that these difficulties experienced in Dublin in recruiting councillors are reflected also in Kilkenny. For the entire fifteenth century, in so far as we have evidence for it, the earlier system of a council composed of two groups of twelve remained in force; and while the records of its membership are fragmentary, nonetheless sufficient survives to indicate that the level of continuity of membership was almost as high towards the end of the century, even over a fair period of years. Of the 1410 *magna duodena*, for example, seven were already on the council in 1403;[25] of the 1417 council, six were already on it in 1410.[26] By the end of the fifteenth century however the terms *magna duodena* and *secunda duodena* are beginning to be dropped in favour of the flat term *consilium,* although the older *magna duodena* still surfaces in certain years;[27] and the numbers fluctuate: in 1498 the *magna duodena* numbered sixteen, in 1499 the *consilium* numbered fifteen, and eighteen in 1515, settling down by the third decade of the sixteenth century to an average of twelve, give

[20] Ibid., p. 60.
[21] *Anc. rec. Dublin,* i, 293–4.
[22] Ibid., pp 385–6.
[23] Ibid., p. 364.
[24] Ibid., p. 392.
[25] *Liber primus Kilkenn.,* pp 43, 53.
[26] Ibid., pp 53, 67.
[27] From 1525 to 1529, and 1535–7.

or take one.[28] Here again the *de facto* reduction in the size of the council seems to reflect difficulties in recruitment rather than any policy of exclusion.

If this analyis is correct, then the question which arises is why there were these difficulties in recruitment. In the case of the primary offices—mayor and bailiffs, sovereign and provosts—there were obviously disadvantages attached which in contemporary eyes outweighed the advantages. The pomp of office, with a gilded sword borne before the mayor, and a silver mace before the bailiff, as well as the standing accorded to both officials and council, which made offences against them more costly than against others,[29] no doubt had their attractions; but the theoretically harsh penalties laid down for insult or injury seem often in practice to have been mitigated or suspended.[30] Privileges such as that granted to the mayor of Waterford in 1467 of twice as many votes in elections as a bailiff or councillor[31] naturally appealed only to those already committed to this kind of activity. Active service in the city government might indeed carry not only fees (£10 yearly for the mayor of Dublin, 10 marks for the mayor of Waterford) but also perquisites in the form of favourable terms in leases from the city: William Grampe, merchant, 'for his gode service, the wich he have done unto the citte' was granted an abatement of 2s for life on the rent of 4s yearly he owed for a garden in St Francis Street in Dublin,[32] Thomas Newbery was similarly granted a fifty per cent abatement of his rent from a house by the quay, in 1459, for a term of 60 years.[33] Examples are to be found scattered in the municipal records of Dublin and Kilkenny of leases of city lands to members of the council,[34] whether on particularly favourable terms or not we have usually no means of telling; but from 1456, mayors and bailiffs of Dublin were forbidden to hold leases of city lands during their term of office.[35] As against this, the mayor and bailiffs were expected to suspend trade during their years of office, and there are cases of officials violating this rule and indeed obtaining exemption from it by royal authority.[36] To some

[28] Op. cit. pp 110–52, passim.
[29] MacNiocaill, *Na Buirgéisí*, pp 343, 352.
[30] E.g. *Liber primus Kilkenn.*, pp 67–8: two cases of suspended sentences.
[31] *H.M.C. rep. 10*, app. v., 304 § lxv.
[32] *Anc. rec. Dublin*, i, 310 (1461).
[33] Ibid., p. 303.
[34] Ibid., pp 331, 333, 338, 347, 374, 384 (it should be noted that what sometimes appear to be favourable terms are balanced by the obligation for the tenant to repair or rebuild); *Liber primus Kilkenn.*, pp 70, 82, 83, 85, 87, 88, 89, 100, 104 (rentals of city lands in which the tenants are often identifiable as members of the council).
[35] *Anc. rec. Dublin*, i, 292.
[36] MacNiocaill, *Na Buirgéisí*, pp 349–50.

potential candidates election would have meant forfeiting a substantial part of a year's income, and to this extent the higher offices were of necessity restricted to the men of substantial property. If we analyse the lists of officials of Dublin in this period, it rapidly becomes apparent that there are two classes within them; those who have sufficient property to be distrainable for any liabilities they might incur, and those who would have to find pledges for the adequate performance of their duties. The first monopolise the offices of mayor, bailiff, auditor, and so on, and are also found acting as pledges for the humbler second group, keeper of the crane, city gaoler and so on, who are drawn not from the council but from the commons.

Nevertheless, the argument for the imbalance of advantage and disadvantage does not seem to be sufficient to account for the narrowness of membership of the council. A second limitation must be considered: the available pool of men of property on the one hand, and their proportion within the total pool on the other. Property in this sense means primarily property in land, and the land-holdings of the citizens of the Irish towns have hardly been studied yet. Here again one misses documents such as the tax books of the German towns, which show the extent to which the landed element in the town was very much in a minority. In Ireland, the closest we come to such texts is the incomplete landgable roll of Cork of the mid-fifteenth century, which sets out a little less than 180 holdings, mainly houses, in Cork, and their assessment for the landgable,[37] and it is noteworthy that there is a high proportion of multiple holdings listed in it: Geoffrey Galway had thirteen, John Skiddy had ten, as had Margaret Candebek and John Wynchedon; Richard Ston had nine, William Gowllis had six, Thomas Milok had five, John Miagh had four, Edmund White had three, these nine persons between them accounting for some forty per cent of the recorded holdings; if we had the full text of the roll, the percentage might be higher, and obviously the text leaves out of account the land-holdings outside Cork itself. The Dublin assembly in 1485 laid down that persons appointed to the mayoralty and living outside Dublin should, during their term of office, reside in Dublin,[38]

---

[37] This document, now B.L., Add. Charter 8671, has the distinction of having been printed no less than three times: by F. H. Tuckey, *The County and City of Cork Remembrancer* (Cork, 1837), pp 279–82, a book now very rare; by myself, in total ignorance of Tuckey's text, in MacNiocaill, *Na Buirgéisí*, pp 589–95; and lastly by E. Bolster, in ignorance of my text, in *Collect. Hib.*, no 13 (1970), pp 7–20. I dated the text to the mid-15th century, whereas E. Bolster prefers a date circa 1400.

[38] *Anc. rec. Dublin*, i, 368.

implying that those eligible might be as involved in agriculture as in more narrowly urban activities; and Waterford legislation, imposing residence in the city on all citizens, in 1394 and again in 1480, may also have been aimed at this group.[39] For our scant information on such persons, however, we are dependent on the chance survival of wills. John Gogh, citizen of Dublin, as far as one can trace, held no official position, at least in the last twenty years of his life when the general likelihood of this was highest: but his will, in 1472, refers to unspecified but apparently extensive holdings in land in Waterford and County Kilkenny.[40] Thomas Kilbery of Kilkenny, in 1463, had lands not only in England but also in Waterford, Kilkenny and New Ross.[41] Peter Higely, citizen of Dublin, and father of a canon of Holy Trinity, in 1476 possessed nine acres of wheat and barley, nine cows, three oxen, thirteen calves, seven pigs, fifty sheep and various agricultural implements and necessities as well as forty acres of land at term from the baron of Skreen, outside Dublin; and within Dublin a number of messuages and tenements in Patrick Street and New Street.[42] Cases of this kind are found, although scattered, in most cities: John Wynchedon, of Cork, who died in 1306, is apparently the most extreme example, with two houses and two holdings in Cork and in Dungarvan, plus 87 acres of wheat, 100 acres of oats, 10 of barley and peas, 739 sheep of various kinds, 38 oxen and a dozen cows, and so on.[43] As for Waterford, attention has been drawn elsewhere to the evidence for the concentration of property in the hands of a few in Waterford, supplied by their generosity to the chantry of St Saviour's in Waterford: James Rice gave it six messuages, three shops, two gardens and a quarter, rents to the value of 33s 4d and other tenements of unspecified value; William Lyncoll gave it four shops, two messuages and a lime-kiln: all productive of rent.[44] Since then, Kenneth Nicholls has discovered fresh evidence, in a rental of the cathedral of Waterford in 1483, of which he has very generously given the present author a transcript. Obviously, in its own right the cathedral was a ground-landlord on a large scale in Waterford, in much the same way as the two cathedrals in Dublin; but equally significant for our purposes is the light

[39] *H.M.C. rep. 10*, app. v, 393 § vii, 315–6 § ciii.
[40] H. F. Berry (ed.), *Register of wills and inventories of the diocese of Dublin . . . 1457–83*, (Dublin, 1898), pp 38–41.
[41] Text in MacNiocaill, *Na Buirgéisí*, pp 485–6 n.
[42] Berry, op. cit., pp 128–33.
[43] D. O'Sullivan, 'The testament of John de Wynchedon of Cork, anno 1306' in *Cork Hist. Soc. Jn.*, lxi (1956), pp 76–83. Cf. also the list of warranties in B.L., Add. Charter 8667, printed in MacNiocaill, *Na Buirgéisí*, p. 483 n.
[44] MacNiocaill, *Na Buirgéisí*, p. 484.

it throws on multiple holdings both by those who contributed to the chantry (William Lyncoll figures several times as a tenant of the cathedral) and by others: Peter Hunt who held six shops and a messuage, and the late Cecilia Stevens, of whose property something over seven shops, three gardens, a messuage, a hall and two tenements passed into the possession of the cathedral.

Stray fragments of evidence of this kind are sufficient to persuade us of the existence of a group who held a plurality of stakes in the city, without giving sufficient information on the size of this group or the extent to which it coincided with the pool from which officials and councillors were drawn. It seems likely, from the case of John Gogh, that if the overlap was large it was by no means complete. And to such cases might be added that of the shoemaker John Hamound, who in 1388 seems to have held no land worth speaking of in Dublin, but held nonetheless elsewhere, seemingly in Luttrellstown, land for the lease of which he was owed £46.13.4, and also had twenty acres of wheat, eight acres of barley, and thirty-three acres of oats.[45] Persons of this kind, with one foot in the city and the other in the country, were perhaps more common than our evidence records. Certainly, the accounts of monastic property at the dissolution throw up a number of persons in Dublin who had invested directly or indirectly in land outside. Nicholas Bennet, mayor in 1539, had the tithes of two townlands by indenture, three watermills, and three townlands at farm; of his colleagues, Robert Tailor, William Queytrot, Arland Usher, Thomas Barby, John Shilton, Thomas Stevens, and Robert Shillingford had invested in tithes, singly or jointly with others.[46] Robert Roth, sovereign of Kilkenny in 1537-8, along with Richard Roth, a member of his council in the same year, held the tithes of two rectories belonging to the Hospitallers;[47] and undoubtedly a systematic comparison of the membership of the various town councils with the confiscation documentation of the same period will turn up other examples. The important point, however, is that the apparently close correlation between wealth and municipal office of the most important kind; and the concentration of wealth in the hands of a relative few, which has yet to be fully established, would in part at least explain the difficulties of recruitment.

There is, however, an alternative, or at least a supplementary, explanation. Among the fortunate survivals of the late fifteen

---

[45] *Anc. rec. Dublin,* i, 127-9.
[46] Cf. ibid., p. 405 and *Extents Ir. mon. possessions,* pp 13, 35, 56, 58, 86, 105, 115, 161, 289.
[47] Ibid., p. 99.

century must be counted the franchise roll of Dublin for the years 1468 to 1485, although neither the first year nor the last is complete for the full calendar year.[48] From this it is possible to construct a picture of the admissions over a period of sixteen years, omitting the first and the last, and from it some interesting points emerge.

Table II

Year	Special Grace	Apprenticeship	As Son	As Daughter	By Marriage	Year's Total
1469	39 (8)	17 (2)	4	—	4	64(10)
1470	18 (3)	18 (3)	4	(3)	2	45(9)
1471	17 (1)	9 (2)	7	—	2	35(3)
1472	10 (1)	11	6	—	2	29(1)
1473	7 (1)	19 (3)	2	—	—	28(4)
1474	17 (2)	15 (3)	4	(2)	—	40(7)
1475	9 (2)	14 (2)	4	(2)	4	33(6)
1476	9 (1)	13 (2)	1	—	1	24(3)
1477	4 (1)	18 (2)	1	(2)	3	26(5)
1478	8	3 (1)	3	(2)	3	20(3)
1479	22 (5)	17 (2)	2	(1)	—	42(8)
1480	10 (2)	15 (5)	1	(2)	2	30(9)
1481	16 (2)	13 (3)	2	(2)	1	34(7)
1482	14 (3)	29 (5)	1	—	4	48(8)
1483	15 (3)	23 (4)	2	(1)	3	44(8)
1484	14 (6)	25 (4)	2	—	3	44(10)
Totals	229 (41)	259 (43)	46	(17)	32	586 (101)

The first is the relatively low proportion of those who acquired citizenship, or franchise, by inheritance: no more than eleven per cent of the total, and in no year exceeding seven. If we add to this those who acquired the franchise by marriage to women who possessed the franchise, we raise it to a little over sixteen per cent; this means, however, that only one in six of the new citizens was previously connected with the city by blood or by marriage; and this in turn implies that the new citizens were drawn either from outside the city altogether, by immigration from the surrounding country-side—many of those admitted by special grace—or were drawn from the lower, unenfranchised levels, primarily by the device of apprenticeship, or a mixture of both. It is not possible to distinguish their origins more precisely than this, but there is a clear implication either that the replacement rate of the body of citizens themselves was inadequate to maintain their own numbers, or alternatively that the population of Dublin was rising very rapidly. For reasons that will be returned to below, the second explanation seems unlikely.

[48] *Anc. rec. Dublin*, i, 330–68 passim.

One of the limitations on population expansion in this period, of course, was the prohibition on the native Irish: the conditions of citizenship excluded them, under legislation of 1448, and in 1454 the city took steps to exclude

all maner of men of Iryshe blode and women, that is to sayn Iryssh nonnys, Irish clerkys, and Irysh jornaymen, Iryshe prentesys, Iryssh servantes, and Iryssh begeris, men, women and children, also all maner of Irysh house holderis, excepte al the that hath bene xii. yer dwellynge within the said cite, that they and every of them avoyde by this day iiii. wekys

and to forbid the acceptance of Irish apprentices or servants henceforward.[49] In the late thirteenth century, in an era of expansion and self-confidence, the city could accept a guild of Irish merchants;[50] in the fifteenth century, with both city and colony on the defensive, it was regarded as a hazard; and we find legislation in Waterford in 1465 to regulate the possible admission of Irish who had married the widows or daughters of citizens.[51]

If then we accept the hypothesis of an inadequate replacement rate, a number of problems present themselves: that which was noted earlier, of the mortality in Dublin in this period, either perinatal mortality, or at a later age. A similar failure in replacement has been noted in some Hanseatic towns,[52] and if this interpretation is correct, it is likely that similar causes are in operation: lack of hygiene, and consequent disease, particularly in the early years of life. The ordinances of Dublin, and to a lesser extent Waterford, refer frequently to the problems raised by cowdung and other less attractive droppings in the streets; pigs roaming the streets were a constant problem, both in themselves and in fouling the water supply.[53] And if this is correct, then it is likely that mortality was as high, if not higher, in the lower levels of the population as among the more prosperous who were already in the ranks of citizens, and hence that the topping up of the citizenry came rather from outside the city than within. When one analyzes in more detail the crafts and skills offered by the new arrivals, this impression is reinforced. Of those who became citizens by apprenticeship a substantial number has no craft specified for them, the normal thing with women admitted on these grounds; but of the rest, while some are relatively

[49] Ibid., pp 272, 280-81; cf. also p. 331 (1469).
[50] MacNiocaill, *Na Buirgéisí,* p. 473.
[51] *H.M.C. rep. 10,* app. v, 303 § lxiii.
[52] Cf. Heinrich Reincke, 'Bevölkerungsprobleme der Hansestädte', in C. Hasse, *Die Stadt des Mittelalters,* iii (Darmstadt, 1973), pp 265 ff.
[53] MacNiocaill, *Na Buirgéisí,* pp 285-6.

Socio-Economic Problems of the Medieval Irish Town

skilled craftsmen—smiths, glovers, tailors, shoemakers, carpenters, tanners, weavers—a remarkably high number are merchants, adding up to some thirty-eight per cent of the total admitted; indeed, they also constitute almost thirty-five per cent of those admitted because their fathers had been franchised before them. The craft guilds seem to be relative latecomers in Dublin: the earliest—glovers and tanners —seem to be of the late thirteenth century, the candlemakers of the fourteenth, and the barbers, bakers and shoemakers of the middle to late fifteenth century,[54] which may imply that their numbers until then were none too significant. This clearly gives us very little information on the craftsmen and artisans, who nonetheless constituted part of the body of citizens; on the evidence of the number of admissions either by special grace, apprenticeship or parentage— a little over one new smith per year, less than one new shoemaker— the market for their wares must have been fairly limited, or their productivity high. John Hamound, at his death in 1388, had in stock 232 shoes, as well as several hides and skins, and was owed money for shoes and boots by twenty-two different persons, one for as many as thirty pairs of shoes, another for fourteen dozen;[55] whether these represent arrears over a period of years is not specified, but the impression certainly emerges that one shoemaker could keep a substantial portion of the population of Dublin shod. The thorny question of the population of Dublin in the later fifteenth century will be side-stepped here since there seems to be no basis for estimation, any more than for the population as a whole. The estimates of Josiah Cox Russell for the late thirteenth century and the theories on which they are based are well known,[56] and the criticisms made by Hollingsworth are equally familiar.[57] It is not proposed to add to them: it suffices to say that although Russell's figures have been quoted as an authoritative estimate, there is no sound historical basis for them. One might, indeed, as Hollingsworth does, venture an estimate on the basis of the average number of admissions to franchise, coming up with a figure for 1246 of about 20,000; by a similar calculation, the population of Dublin about 1476 would be about 6,000. But this is the merest guesswork, since Hollingsworth's

[54] These are the dates assigned in the *First report of the commissioners appointed to inquire into the municipal corporations in Ireland,* H.C. 1835 (27) xxvii, p. 276. The smiths and weavers claimed origins under Henry II.
[55] See note 45 above.
[56] In 'Late thirteenth-century Ireland as a region', in *Demography,* iii (1966), pp 500–12, and the version of this, shorn of its documentation, in *Medieval regions and their duties* (Newton Abbot, 1972), pp 130–45. The claim that Galway's 'wealthy hinterland' must have supplied it with commerce raises some question of Professor Russell's familiarity with the area.
[57] T. H. Hollingsworth, *Historical demography* (London, 1969), pp 268–70.

18

Gearóid MacNiocaill

estimate depends on applying multipliers of assumed family size — of which we know nothing, except that it was unlikely to be uniform[58]—to an estimate of the numbers of guild members, with the degree of plausibility and probability dropping sharply at each step. Another approach to the problem is possible, through an assessment of the potentialities of the Dublin area to support a given population. If we take the area within a radius of 40 kilometres or 25 miles from Dublin, about a day's journey and approximately the distance from Dublin to Wicklow, the tithe figures supplied by the monastic extents of 1540–41 indicate a level of productivity which would suggest, by a simple and crude calculation, allowing one quarter of grain per person per year (the conventional figure), that the area could support approximately 9000 persons.[59] This would of course cover both city and country, and some deduction, perhaps ten per cent, would have to be made, giving a potential figure for Dublin itself of 8000 inhabitants around 1540. It is a method which has been applied, with plausible results, to the population of England before the Black Death; but in an Irish context, a number of caveats must be entered. In the first place, it is not clear to what extent the valuations of the tithes, in couples of acres of grain, are conventional, and while in one case it is explicitly stated that they were taken on a three-year average, which may be true for most, it is as well to bear in mind that in England, at least, the years around the 1540s were years of above average harvest.[60] If the population of Dublin around 1280, as Hollingsworth suggests, was really about 25,000 then the productivity of the city's hinterland must have dropped drastically between the thirteenth and the fifteenth century; there is indeed some evidence for a decline in the early fourteenth century, but we are in no position to pronounce on the later fifteenth century.

That the city fathers were much concerned about the city's grain supply is clear from the ordinances of the fifteenth century, from at least 1452 on. Prohibitions on 'hagardmen' within the city selling grain to strangers in the city, or selling it out of the city after the price had passed 8p a peck, rendered the offender liable to loss of franchise, if he possessed it, and a fine of £10 in any case. The corn

[58] Cf. the literature cited by Hollingsworth himself, pp 118–20.
[59] I use the rectories of Santry, Holmpatrick, Portrane, Waspalston, Ballymadun, Chapelizod, Ballyfermot, Palmerston in the barony of Balrothery West, and Clontarf (*Extents Ir. mon possessions,* pp 8, 51, 75, 86, 88, 89) and assume an average yield of three to one, with a third being set aside for seed; the conventional assumption is that one person requires one quarter of grain per year (cf. Hollingsworth, op. cit., pp 264–5).
[60] Cf. W. G. Hoskins, *The age of plunder: the England of Henry VIII 1500–47* (London, 1976), p. 87.

19

would be forfeit to the city, and searchers were appointed to check on the hagards within the city. In 1457 the previous legislation was reinforced by penalties for overseers who took bribes to allow corn to be laden out of the city, and in 1461 legislation tightened up the conditions under which corn could be brought—house-holders only, by licence from the bailiffs, with fines for hoarding it—and the legislation is specific that there was in fact a dearth of corn. The same kind of prohibition was repeated in 1465, in 1469 and in 1471, when a more explicit analysis of the situation in Dublin was offered: the blame was laid on those who exported corn to England, Scotland and Wales, with the implication that prices were higher there, and it was asserted that this brought dearth and famine to the king's lieges, forcing them to emigrate from the country and from Dublin.[61] How far this analysis is accurate, particularly in the scape-goats chosen, is unverifiable, nor is it clear how far it was general-ising from a few instances of emigration. The problems of Dublin are not, of course, necessarily those of Cork, Waterford, Limerick or Galway: in the late fourteenth century it had been frequently necessary to bring corn by sea to Cork, Youghal, and Waterford, and most of this seems to have come from the Dublin-Meath-Louth area. But for the later fifteenth century, if the repeated Dublin legislation is any guide, this was no longer feasible or desirable, and it makes it clear that a problem of supply was believed to exist. In this context the involvement of some at least of the more prosperous burgesses in argriculture is understandable. Indeed, one aspect of the admissions to franchise between 1468 and 1485 may also be connected with this problem: the remarkably high number of husbandmen and yeomen admitted to citizenship, almost all of them by special grace (71 out of 82) and constituting thirty per cent of all those so admitted. Is it too hazardous to suggest that admission to citizenship thus gave the city some measure of control over a group by definition heavily involved in agriculture?

If the argument may be summarised at this point, what is being suggested is that towards the end of the middle ages, the Irish town was suffering from a population crisis, not necessarily in the form of falling population at this period, but perhaps stagnation after a fall at an earlier period, which rendered difficult the recruitment of a governing class within the town; that this difficulty was compounded by the con-centration of wealth in the hands of a relative few within the towns, thus reducing the number of those who were in a position to answer

[61] *Anc. rec. Dublin*, i, 172–3, 275, 278, 284–5, 287, 293, 300, 308, 310–11, 320, 336, 337, 343, 346–7.

for the faithful discharge of their duties and secure the mayor and commons against all claims, as one text puts it; and that at the same time the town in general suffered from difficulties of supply which in turn hindered recovery. Put thus baldly, it will be clear how hazardous it is, and how badly needed are studies in other areas to test it. An obvious criticism, and a valid one, is that it is based, for the most part, on the municipal records of Dublin, supplemented to some extent by those of Waterford and of Kilkenny: where lies Cork, Limerick, Galway? The problem of these, with hinterlands largely outside the control of the government to which Dublin more or less gave allegiance, were not necessarily the same, nor for that matter those of Drogheda. Secondly, the impression of a concentration of wealth requires documenting by the compilation of dossiers on as many as possible of the burgesses at least of these three cities, and some attempt made to trace the origins of the wealth which some of them accumulated: thus something of the kind is possible with the Blakes of Galway,[62] with the Dowdalls of Dundalk,[63] and the will of Thomas Kilbery of Kilkenny gives details on the origins of some of the lands he acquired. And thirdly, the problem of supply brings us into the problems of agricultural progression or regression in the late medieval period, which so far have been even less attractive to historians than the relatively prosperous period of the later thirteenth century. It is suggested that these lines of approach, although not realisable in the same fullness as in England, France or Germany, do offer some prospect of getting behind the somewhat constitutionalist bias which studies of Irish urban history have laboured under, at the same time as they have profited by it.

[62] MacNiocaill, *Na Buirgéisí,* pp 493–503.
[63] Cf. *Dowdall Deeds.*

Plantation Boroughs in Medieval Ireland, with a Handlist of Boroughs to c.1500

Geoffrey Martin

Whether or not there were towns in Ireland before the Norman invasion, there certainly were thereafter. It may be that they were not wholly and exclusively an alien growth. It is arguable that even without the intrusion of Norman lords and Anglo-Norman clerks and merchants, medieval Irish society would in its own time have produced urban settlements and institutions. There were the large and intricately-ordered monastic communities, there was a pressing curiosity amongst the clergy about the reform and developments current in the western church, which would have brought social innovation with them, and there were the mercantile settlements of the Norsemen, which grow more complex and interesting as we learn about them.[1]

That towns would eventually have appeared under those and other influences seems likely enough. Something similar began to happen in Wales in the thirteenth century, on the eve of the Edwardian conquest, when the last of the Welsh princes was feeling his way towards a manorial organisation of his estates with support from licensed settlements of craftsmen and merchants. Llewellyn's principality was more straitened than the swirling medley of the twelfth-century Irish kingdoms, and it was open to strong pressure and example from England and the March. However, if Ireland had resisted the violent importunities of her neighbours effectively it

---

[1] See Liam de Paor, 'The Viking towns of Ireland' in Bo Almqvist and D. Greene (eds), *Proc. Seventh Viking Congress, 1973* (Dublin, 1976), pp 29–37 and D. Ó Corráin, 'Nationality and kingship in pre-Norman Ireland' in T. W. Moody (ed.), *Nationality and the pursuit of national independence* (Belfast, 1978), especially p. 32 and n. 134.

would probably have been by, or at the price of, some such transformation of her society as the new settlements produced. The question is academic, and it may yet find a suitably academic answer. In the meantime the invaders came; they made towns of what they found at Dublin, Waterford, and elsewhere, and they planted others for themselves.

It was natural enough that the new settlements should suffer casualties in the process. They were all in some sense experimental, and they were cruelly exposed. Some flourished more readily than others, which they eclipsed and outlived. We should expect competition, economic change, and the scouring of war to have reduced the numbers of towns in Ireland, and therefore to find a substantial tally of failed enterprises to set against the familiar names of the cities and boroughs which have survived, and which we recognize as historic. Even so, it is surprising to find how large a tally it was.

The origin of the present list lies in a continuation of Charles Gross's *Bibliography of British municipal history* (London, 1897). In his day, Gross surveyed the towns of the United Kingdom as a whole, and produced a critical and most valuable conspectus of their historical literature. To extend the chronological usefulness of his work, it seemed sensible to continue its terms of reference, and acknowledge the common experience of Irish and other British towns before partition, as well as the characteristic development of municipal institutions in the Republic. The new bibliography therefore treats Britain and Ireland together, and covers the municipal government of the British Isles, with a common alphabetical gazetteer of British and Irish towns.[2]

The criteria for the inclusion of a town in both Gross's work and the continuation are deceptively simple: that the place should at some time have been a borough, and that it should have been the subject of published work. Either definition may occasion discussion, and each works to some extent upon the other. Gross's own list, the subsequent studies of charters by Ballard, Tait, and Martin Weinbaum, and the continuing tradition of local studies ensured that within the United Kingdom boroughs with royal charters, parliamentary boroughs, and other places effectively enfranchised were well-enough known.[3] Not all enfranchisements, however, were

---

[2] Gross, *Bibliog. Brit. mun. hist.*; G. H. Martin and S. C. McIntyre, *Bibliography of British and Irish municipal history, vol. 1, general works* (Leicester, 1972).

[3] A. Ballard (ed.), *British borough charters, 1042–1216* (Cambridge, 1913); A. Ballard and J. Tait (eds), *British borough charters, 1216–1307* (Cambridge, 1923); M. Weinbaum (ed.), *British borough charters, 1307–1660* (Cambridge, 1943).

effective: many were speculative, some were merely sanguine. In 1951 H. P. R. Finberg published a handlist of medieval boroughs in Devon which enumerated 67 of them.[4] It showed that there were many more manorial boroughs, at least in that large county, than had been commonly noticed. Down to the early fourteenth century the expanding European economy called an extensive network of market towns into being, and kings and magnates responded to the opportunities and the fashion of the time, successfully or ineffectively, like other men with resources to exploit. Medieval boroughs, though some may have been no more than boroughs in name, were at least as numerous as urban districts in modern England.

Professor Beresford subsequently reviewed that wide spread of plantation towns in medieval England, Wales, and Gascony, identifying some sites from topographical rather than from explicit documentary evidence.[5] What Maitland called 'little towns, or rather villages, which long ago received a few chartered privileges from a . . . baron, and therefore were allowed a precarious place on the roll of English boroughs'[6] may never have been candidates for incorporation, but as posthumous candidates for historical studies and bibliographies they had extended the roll. In 1972 Beresford and Finberg's joint *Handlist* of medieval English boroughs distinguished 609 founded in England before 1500, against Gross's total of 409 medieval and modern cities and boroughs for the United Kingdom as a whole.[7]

Although Wales was excluded from that list, Professor Beresford's work on new towns, added to the discussion in E. A. Lewis's *Medieval boroughs of Snowdonia* (London, 1912), seemed to have provided a reasonable coverage. Scotland was in a class of its own, given the documentation of G. S. Pryde's admirable work, *The burghs of Scotland: a critical list* (London, 1965). The very large additions that those works had made to the number of boroughs treated by Gross suggested, however, that Ireland would present a substantial problem. The major towns were as well provided for as those of England. The municipal corporations commission in 1835–6 listed 60 boroughs that functioned before 1603. Ballard, Tait, Martin Weinbaum, and most recently Professor MacNiocaill have studied

---

[4] H. P. R. Finberg, 'The boroughs of Devon' in *Devon and Cornwall Notes and Queries*, xxiv (1950–51), pp 203–9; xxvii (1956–8), pp 54–5.
[5] M. W. Beresford, *New towns of the middle ages* (London, 1967).
[6] F. W. Maitland, *Township and borough* (Cambridge, 1898), pp 16–17.
[7] M. W. Beresford and H. P. R. Finberg, *English medieval boroughs: a handlist* (Newton Abbot, 1972).

and annotated the medieval charters of some 40 of them.[8] Those were, however, either communities still in existence, or at least towns that flourished long enough to be recognised. They include the principal cities, and the oldest of the county and assize towns. How many unsuccessful or merely nominal boroughs there may have been remained an open question, and a successful search for their historical literature depended in some measure upon a preliminary identification of the places themselves.

For the purposes of this study let us accept Gross's implicit criterion that a borough is a place called a borough, or a place in which there were once burgesses, or tenants in burgage. Even in the middle ages the connection between such a *burgus* as Ipswich and, say, Newton Arlosh, was a tenuous one. Yet the name is the same, and the connection lies in a degree of autonomy marked by the status of the inhabitants. At one end that status might be simply a matter of paying rent instead of rendering services; at the other it could extend to a separate commission of the peace, and even to the administration of a county. In both instances there was some sense of community, distinctive but only as powerful, in a political sense, as local circumstances and the effluxion of time could make it. Indeed, at the lower end we might be dealing with an opportunity to pay rent, an opportunity that was in fact never realised, whereupon the connection is stretched into abstraction. If we are to proceed to distinctions of that sort, however, we need at the outset to take notice of all *burgi,* wherever the search may lead. When we have, if not all, a convincing assemblage, we can take further stock of them, and bibliography will have served a wider purpose.

The interest in the history of towns, and especially in their economic and social development, which has absorbed much scholarly energy elsewhere since the second world war was relatively slow to make its mark on Irish studies. J. C. Russell's *British medieval population* included a schedule of 41 Irish boroughs for which some demographic material survived, and pointed out that 'there were probably other and small boroughs of which little trace was left . . . Furthermore, . . . some of the places represented have not been identified'.[9] Professor A. J. Otway-Ruthven discussed boroughs and burgesses in both regional and general terms in a number of works, notably 'The medieval county of Kildare', and

[8] *First report of the commissioners appointed to inquire into the municipal corporations in Ireland* H. C. 1835 (23–25, 27–28), xxvii–xxviii; 1836 (2, 6, 29), xxiv. Gearóid Mac Niocaill, *Na buirgéisí, xii–xv aois* (vols, Dublin, 1964).
[9] J. C. Russell, *British medieval population* (Albuquerque, 1948), p. 354.

'The character of Norman settlement in Ireland',[10] and in 1964 Professor Gearóid MacNiocaill's *Na buirgéisí* examined the established communities in detail. In the meantime archaeologists and historical geographers were pursuing the topography and morphology of settlement, and in 1970 and 1971 Dr R. E. Glasscock published two valuable essays: the first, 'Moated sites and deserted boroughs and villages: two neglected aspects of Anglo-Norman settlement in Ireland', and the second 'The study of deserted medieval settlements in Ireland (to 1968)'.[11] In them he took particular notice of what appeared to be depopulated towns. He referred to such ill-starred communities as 'rural boroughs' in order to distinguish them clearly from true chartered towns and from other villages.[12] 'In fact,' he added, 'perhaps it would be better to speak of them as sites in which the tenants cannot be shown to have proceeded beyond formal enfranchisement'.[13] Or, presumably, to have been there long in any guise. Dr Glasscock's useful and suggestive second paper, which contained some timely recommendations for the scheduling and excavation of sites, has recently been followed by a volume of essays edited by Dr R. A. Butlin, *The development of the Irish town,* to which Dr B. J. Graham contributed a chapter on 'The towns of medieval Ireland'. Dr Graham's survey ends with an appendix of boroughs, arranged by counties, which names 174, almost all identified by grid references.[14]

A list of that size, had it appeared sooner, would certainly have served the purposes of a municipal bibliography, and rather more. Like Gross, I take account only of explicit published works, and there is no doubt that a substantial proportion of the 174 lay unremarked between their first brief efflorescence and their exhumation by modern students of settlement. However, searches are apt to become ends in themselves and, more usefully, to raise questions that ought not to be left unconsidered. Accepting all Dr Graham's identifications, and including one or two of Dr Glasscock's that he seems to have rejected, such as Kiltinan, the present list adds some 50 boroughs to his list, an increase of the order of 30%. There are another 30 places which seem worth further consideration, al-

[10] *I.H.S.,* xi (Mar. 1959), pp 181–99; *Hist. Studies,* v (1965), pp 75–84.
[11] *Ir. geog. studies,* pp 162–77; M. W. Beresford and J. G. Hurst (eds), *Deserted medieval villages: studies* (London, 1971), pp 279–301.
[12] Ibid., p. 288.
[13] Ibid., p. 289.
[14] R. A. Butlin (ed.), *The development of the Irish town* (London, 1977), pp 52–55. Dr Graham has subsequently discussed some aspects of the early growth of towns in 'The evolution of urbanisation in medieval Ireland' in *Journal of Historical Geography,* v (1979), pp 111–25.

though there is as yet no reference to burgesses or burgage tenure there: some of them have been noted by Dr Graham, amongst many other sites, as the subjects of market charters. The present total of boroughs can therefore be taken as around 225, and might rise above 250.

It would be absurd to read very much in the way of institutions into those figures as they stand. They certainly do not represent such numbers of effective urban communities engaged in trade, paying rents and taxes, and managing their own affairs. Some may have been only token settlements, and many were probably settlements which enjoyed only a token enfranchisement. Of those which functioned long enough to deserve consideration as distinctive communities it would often be difficult to speak so precisely as to relate them effectively one to another. In particular it would seem that any attempt to draw detailed conclusions from their physical distribution ought to wait on some further investigation of their endurance. At the same time, if we are tempted to dismiss them simply because they were evanescent and primitive, we must remember that the history of towns in general is much complicated by our knowledge of what they have lately become. Medieval Irish settlements, large and small, have to be seen against the very modest realities of English and many other towns in the same period. The use of expressions such as 'incorporated towns' in the older literature, and of 'urban' in more recent works is not consistently helpful. What distinguished town-life at this time was not the complex of economic functions and social catastrophe that are today's urban stigmata, but status. Our own first concern may be with that status, and perhaps with its potential, but beyond those matters there are questions of men's motives, intentions, and assumptions that are certainly as interesting as events and financial transactions.

The plantation boroughs of medieval Ireland were numerous. They represent a substantial endeavour; an imposing outlay of energy, whether it was misapplied or not. Their founders' objectives were probably complex, and we ought not lightly to assume that the functions served by the settlements were much more simple. The business of colonization, the settlement of the land, was no doubt fundamental, and it is certain that enfranchisement was used as a bait for tenants.[15] At the same time, the burgesses' liberties were directed to an economic end. Specialised work in any society needs economic support: that support was provided in Irish society in traditional forms, with conventions that are strange to us. The

---

[15] Otway-Ruthven, 'Character of Norman settlement', p. 79.

invaders enjoyed the services of manufacturers, merchants, and markets in a manner that is more broadly familiar, although in its intricacies it is no easier to understand than the usages of tribal society and the clan. What seems the surest ground may the more readily lead us astray. We assume, as a matter of common sense, that craftsmen and markets needed the protection of castles, and clustered about them for shelter. The plantation boroughs in Ireland were duly associated with castles, and most of them demonstrably would have benefited from more protection than they received. Their numbers, however, might make us think that the relationship was not simply a passive one. Any castle that was more than a marching camp might in turn depend upon the crafts and market of a borough: it looks as though most of them did.

The list that follows is an annotated catalogue of boroughs extant in Ireland before 1500: the annotation is sparing, its object being to provide a documentary reference sufficient to justify each entry. The most substantial early lists in print were the schedules in the report of the royal commission (1835–6), and the principal additions made subsequently came from the inquisitions *post mortem*. Russell made some reference to the inquisitions, as he wished to recover numbers of tenants and tenements, but they have been used more extensively for the reconstruction of lordships. In the present list, however, many further references come from the Ormond deeds, as calendared by Edmund Curtis, a source which emphasizes the density of settlement in County Tipperary and County Kilkenny, and the neighbouring lands, but which in this instance may not distort the general picture as much as is sometimes supposed.[16] In all the minor places cited, there is evidence of a charter, of burgage tenure, or of a community of such tenants. It is notable that Samuel Lewis's *Topographical dictionary of Ireland,* (1st ed., London, 1837) pays particular and accurate attention to traditions of early charters, burgage lands, and the physical features of decayed towns, and the places noted in the Appendix (pp 33–53, below) as probable sites of boroughs have mainly been drawn from general indications in Lewis. Lewis provided a comprehensive and interesting picture of developments in the early nineteenth century in all parts of Britain. The antiquarian and early historical material in the Irish *Dictionary* is presumably drawn from work done for the Ordnance Survey. Its accuracy where it can be checked against documentary sources is

---

[16] *Ormond deeds, 1172–1603* (6 vols). Whatever losses there may have been, it seems reasonable to suppose that the survival of documents broadly reflects the patterns of early settlement.

encouraging, and suggests that serious attention should be paid to it when it stands alone. The features taken as significant in the present study include the existence of early castles, communal defences, friaries and certain other religious houses, and traditions of an enfranchised community.

The planting of several hundred ordered settlements could be expected to have left marks on the records that survive, fragmentary though they often are. The licensing of markets was kept as firmly in the king's hand in Ireland as it was in England, but a prohibition of 1200 implies that markets were nevertheless appearing in some places without the blessing of a royal charter. There is a reference in the same year to the business of colonization in a license to Hamo de Valoignes to lead his men to colonise his lands. The accompanying reservation of the king's demesne and 'the assize of the barons of Ireland touching their villeins' does nothing to define the district or the nature of the enterprise, but some such provision must lie behind all the places noted here.[17] The process was full of danger, as we are vividly reminded by an inquest of 1300 into the slaughter of 27 English men and women travelling between Moylinny and Twescard.[18] In that area and at that date they are most unlikely to have been settlers on their way to a borough, and they were murdered by Irishmen at the instigation of Sir Hugh de Mandeville, bailiff of Twescard, so there was more than racial antagonism at work, but the story is a reminder, more haunting than narratives of campaigns, of some of the realities of the settlement. There is a token of accomplishment in Walter de Lacey's grant to St Mary's, Mount Cresswell, confirmed by Henry III in 1231, of a burgage with the ninth sheaf in all his boroughs, besides corn from his demesne lands.[19] Even so, the accomplishment is a modest one: *summa rusticitas.*

It is even more difficult to assess the internal organization and progress of those smaller boroughs which functioned for a time but left no more than casual traces. If the name *burgus* meant anything at all, beyond an aspiration, we should expect some degree of freedom for the inhabitants, a measure of independence in the management of their day-to-day affairs. The only organisation by which they could have maintained their status, however precarious, was a court, though such an organisation almost certainly had another, a guild, behind it. There seem to be no traces of guilds

[17] *Cal. doc. Ire., 1171–1251,* p. 52 (markets); ibid., p. 18 (de Valoignes).
[18] *Calendar of inquisitions (miscellaneous),* i (London, 1916), p. 136.
[19] *Cal. doc. Ire., 1171–1251,* p. 284.

amongst the scattered and fragmentary references to the plantation boroughs, but it was the universal means of applying private energies to public ends in the society of which the settlements were part, just as the borough court was not purely a legal tribunal, but performed administrative business in a judicial form.[20] The Tipperary boroughs appear with a brief formality in the fourteenth- and fifteenth-century records of the steward's court of the liberty, when the reeve and community of such places as Athassel present themselves, or make fine for non-attendance. Their formal acknowledgment of the service that they owed demonstrated a corporate identity, which they presumably expressed in some other forms on their own ground. A further glimpse of the borough of Lisronagh, however, reveals that in 1465 its community, although it claimed to have a seal of its own, *ignotum pluribus,* preferred to use the common seal of Clonmel to authenticate a charter.[21]

At that level of corporate existence there is unlikely to be much documentary evidence of institutions of work. If the courts kept court rolls, none seems to have survived. The administrative arrangements were probably of the the simplest kind, and their archives often oral. Even the better-found communities are thinly documented, and it is only a fortunate accident, in the survival of some items amongst the Dowdall deeds, that enables us to distinguish the common clerks of Dundalk by name in the early fourteenth century.[22] Economic functions are even more difficult to explore: they leave lighter marks in the records, and they may have weakened early in places in which some token of administrative independence was preserved. Rents of pepper and cummin at Knockgraffon are at least indications of inland trade, but few of our passing references offer such detail.[23] On the other hand the very large numbers of fairs which survived in Ireland, to be noted by Lewis almost on every page, are a reminder that some forms of business are as tenacious as they are unobtrusive. Annual and seasonal cattle trysts are a feature of the traditional economy that could easily be adapted to the invaders' patterns of towns and markets. They seem so to have been.

To sum up, then, we might suppose that, at least within the period of invasion, first conquests, and expansive settlement there would

[20] G. H. Martin, 'The English borough in the thirteenth century' in *R. Hist. Soc. Trans.,* 5th ser., xiii (1963), pp 126–7.
[21] See below, p. 34 (Athassel), p. 45 (Lisronagh).
[22] *Dowdall deeds.*
[23] See below, p. 44. A coiner held by the sheriff of Kilkenny, c. 1240, affords an early example of enterprise, though not of pure commerce, in Thomastown (*Cal. just. rolls Ire., 1295–1303,* p. 395).

have been a substantial number of enfranchised communities in Anglo-Norman Ireland, modelled variously upon the royal and seignorial boroughs of England and Wales. Their role would have been to support and serve the garrisons of castles, to stabilise the rural settlement, and to gather and apply its wealth. Such communities, large and small, successful and unsuccessful, but all called by the name of borough, do indeed appear, and they number some hundreds.

They were subject from the beginning not only to the ordinary wastage of economic and political change and development, but to the stresses of continuous war. They were not all still-born or short-lived, but the number of lesser towns that could thrive depended on the greater, themselves few, and upon an effective civil government, which could not be long achieved.

The survivors were then exposed to the abrasive rigours of the Tudor and Stuart re-settlement and the tragedy of the seventeenth-century wars. It is surprising not that many of the smaller towns disappeared, but that their traditions survived at all. At the least what we can discover about them will tell us something of the incomers, and their economy and society. Beyond that, it may be that here as in other respects the invaders left marks in Irish society itself, and that just as Irish chieftains built castles and retained soldiers, so they may have retained tenants for other services whom in other societies we might equate with burgesses. It would not be strange if they did so, and not all the forms of the traditional society would be inimical to such an innovation. It seems, at least, that the *betagh* had some claim to a corporate identity: it remains to be demonstrated that the rural burgesses enjoyed so much.[24]

The destruction of the public records of Ireland, at a time by which photography might have made their contents safe, was a great misfortune, but it concentrates our attention marvellously upon what we have left to us. Title deeds are a hardy and long-lived species, and their uses are abundant. The references to the Ormond deeds in the following list tell their own story, and Professor MacNiocaill has shown again what can be done with fragmentary evidence, and a fresh eye.[25] There is still a great deal to be discovered about the towns of Ireland, and their significance goes even beyond the wide range of what is now called urban history. If the historian wishes to pursue the subject, he will not need to look far for his quarry in Ireland, wherever he may be.

[24] G. J. Hand, *English law in Ireland, 1290–1324* (Cambridge, 1967).
[25] See below, pp 7–21.

APPENDIX I

AN ANNOTATED HANDLIST OF IRISH BOROUGHS TO c.1500

Boroughs listed by Dr R. E. Glasscock and Dr B. J. Graham are indentified here by the Grid references cited in their respective papers. A Grid reference and an annotation therefore merely confirms an entry in their lists. The absence of a Grid reference distinguishes the present additions, and is not meant as a slur upon any extant community. References to *Cal. inquis. post mortem* are to page not item numbers.

ADARE, County Limerick (17 R 463460)
Murage granted to the bailiffs and worthy men of Adare and of Cromoth, 1310 (*Chart. privil. immun.*, p. 42); burgage tenements there in 1331 (*Red Bk Kildare*, p. 124).

AGHNIRLE, County Kilkenny
40s 3d rent due from the burgesses, 1356 (*Ormond Deeds, 1350–1413*, p. 27).

ANTRIM, County Antrim
80 burgesses paying a rent of 2d each, and accounts of tolls charged in town, 1358–9 (P.R.O., SC6/1239/32–33; information from Dr T. E. McNeill).

ANY see KNOCKANY

APANE see KNOCKTOPHER

ARD see MALLOW

ARDAGH, County Limerick (17 R 280377)
Paid a subsidy of 40s to the crown, with other boroughs, 1300 (*Cal. justic. rolls Ire., 1295–1303*, p. 305).

ARDEE, County Louth
Murage granted to the reeves and commonalty, 1376 (*Chart. privil. immun.*, p. 73); the portreeves to be J.P.s *ex officio*, and clerks of the market, 1455 (*Proc. king's council Ire., 1392–3*, p. lxii).

ARDFERT, County Kerry (21 Q 784208)
Pleas heard before the provost, 1295 (*Cal. justic. rolls Ire., 1295–1303*, p. 21); burgess of, 1297 (ibid., p. 128).

ARDFINNAN, County Tipperary
The burgesses's liberties as granted by James, 4th earl of Ormond, exemplified for the bishop of Waterford, 1558 (*Ormond Deeds, 1547–84*, pp 108–9).

ARDGLASS, County Down
Burgages, 1442 (*Stat. Ire., Henry VI*, p. 199); named as a customs port with Carrickfergus and Dundalk, 1467-8 (*Stat. Ire., 1-12 Edw. IV*, p. 569). See also Kilclief.

ARDMAYLE see CASTLE ARDMAYLE

ARDRAHAN, County Galway (14 M 461122)
Burgages, 1289 (*Red Bk Kildare*, p. 56). See also Kilcolgan.

ARDREE, County Kildare (16 S 687925)
2 burgages (*Reg. St Thomas, Dublin*, p. 162).

ARDSCULL, County Kildare (16 S 726977)
160 burgages worth £8 in Arscol, 1282 (*Cal. inquis. post mortem*, ii, 251).

ARKLOW, County Wicklow (19 T 250730)
Covenants between the burgesses and Thomas, 10th earl of Ormond, to procure a new charter for the borough, 1571 (*Ormond Deeds, 1547-84*, pp 211-12).

ATHASSEL, County Tipperary (18 S 011365)
Paid a subsidy of 5m to the crown with other boroughs, 1300 (*Cal. justic. rolls Ire., 1295-1303*, p. 304); reeve and community fined 40d on the assize of bread and ale, 1359 (*Ormond Deeds, 1350-1413*, pp 38, 42); reeve and community cited to the seneschal's court, 1432 (*Ormond Deeds, 1413-1509*, p. 95).

ATHBOY, County Meath (13 N 713638)
Charters of 1407 and 1446 quoted by Lewis (*Topog. dict. Ire.*, i, 82); exempted with other boroughs from act of resumption, 1460 (*Stat. Ire., Henry VI*, p. 731).

ATHENRY, County Galway
Grant of murage like that to Adare, 1310 (*Chart. privil. immun.*, p. 43); Lewis refers to M.P.s from Richard II's reign (*Topog. dict. Ire.*, i, 83).

ATHLONE, County Westmeath and County Roscommon (12 N 040415)
Burgage by the castle ditch granted to St Mary's, Dublin (*Chartul. St Mary's, Dublin*, i, 239).

ATHMETUM, County Waterford
Paid subsidy of 100s with other boroughs, 1300 (*Cal. justic. rolls Ire., 1295-1303* i, p. 304).

ATHY, County Kildare (16 S 685940)
10 burgesses paying 23s 0½d, 1331 (*Red Bk Kildare*, p. 112).

BALACHE, County Cork
Burgesses held 7 carucates in free burgage for 7m 40d, 1250 (*Cal. inquis. post mortem*, i, 65).

BALIGERAN see GOWRAN

BALIOPANE see KNOCKTOPHER

BALLINACLOGH, County Wicklow (16 T 278920)
Formerly Weyperous; burgesses noted by Otway-Ruthven (*Hist. Stud.,* v (1965), p. 84n.); site identified by Glasscock (Beresford and Hurst, *Deserted medieval villages,* p. 295).

BALLINCLOCH, County Tipperary
Listed by Graham as a borough (Butlin, *Development Irish town,* p. 54).

BALLINROBE, County Mayo
Listed by Curtis with Athenry, Dunmore, and Galway (*Med. Ire.,* p. 149).

BALLINTOBBER, County Roscommon (12 M 729744)
Listed by Graham as a borough (Butlin, *Development Irish town,* p. 54).

BALLYHAGHILL, County Tipperary (18 S 063598)
The burgesses used to render 8m, but now only 20s in time of peace, and nothing in time of war because of the Irish, 1338 (*Cal. inquis. post mortem,* viii, 118).

BALLYINNYVIR, County Tipperary
Messuages, lands, and tenements in the burgage of Ballyinnyvir, 1521 (*Ormond Deeds, 1509-47,* pp 71, 77).

BALLYMASCALLUR, County Wexford
Burgesses rendered 60s rent, 1385 (*Cal. inquis. post mortem,* xvi, 21).

BALLYMORE EUSTACE, County Kildare (16 N 927102)
Burgesses with the laws of Breteuil, 1256-66 (*Alen's Reg.,* p. 120).

BALLYRAGGET, County Kilkenny
200 acres of burgage land in Ballyraghtane, 1589 (*Ormond Deeds, 1584-1603,* p. 121).

BANNOW, County Wexford (23 S 823072)
Named as a town with privileges in Bigod's charter to New Ross; later references to burgage rents (Lewis, *Topog. dict. Ire.,* i, 183).

BAPTIST GRANGE, County Tipperary (18 S 21030)
Noted by Glasscock (Beresford and Hurst, *Deserted medieval villages,* p. 296) as a nucleated settlement; a parcel of land (¼ acre) in the burgesy or franchises of the Graunge, 1598 (*Ormond Deeds, 1584-1603,* p. 108).

BELFAST, County Antrim
Le Ford: a manor, castle, and a borough town totally burned and destroyed, 1333 (*Cal. Inquis. post mortem,* vii, 374).

BELLONAR, County Cork
Burgesses rendering £7 6s from 10 carucates, 1250 (*Cal. inquis. post mortem,* i, 65).

BLATHEWYC see DUNDONALD

BORRISLEIGH or TWO-MILE BURRIS, County Tipperary
100 acres in the borough (? burgage) of Boreishlee (*Ormond Deeds, 1509-47,* p. 65).

BOULEK, County Tipperary
Reeve and community fined 20d for the assize of bread and ale, 1359 (*Ormond Deeds, 1350–1413*, p. 38); messuage and lands in the borough of Boulek, 1372 (ibid., pp 126–7); seneschal's court held there, 1389 (ibid., pp 132–6).

BRAY, County Wicklow and County Dublin (16 O 270190)
Burgesses, 1311 (*Red Bk Ormond*, p. 25).

BUNRATTY, County Clare (17 R 453608)
226 burgages, 1228 (*Cal. inquis. post mortem*, ii, 432).

BURGAGE, County Wicklow
The men of Donahemeloke (Burgage) had the same liberties as those of Ballymore Eustace, 1256–66 (*Alen's Reg.*, p. 120); Lewis identifies Burgage with Blessington, itself incorporated in 1669 (*Topog. dict. Ire.*, i, 213).

BURRISCARRA, County Mayo
Noted by Curtis (*Med. Ire.*, 2nd ed., p. 134) as the site of a borough.

BURRISHOOLE, County Mayo
Noted by Curtis (*Med. Ire.*, p. 214) as the site of a borough.

BUSHMILLS, County Antrim (2 C 940406)
Burgesses of Porchaman in Twescard, 1272 (*Cal. inquis. misc.*, i, 136).

BUTTEVANT, County Cork (21 R 541090)
Community allowed £105, to be applied to walling the town, 1317 (*Chart. privil. immun.*, p. 48).

CAHERCONLISH, County Limerick (18 R 680493)
Burgage tenements, 1300 (*Red Bk Ormond*, p. 156).

CALLAN, County Kilkenny (18 S 413437)
Writ for the exemption of merchants of Callan and Kilkenny from toll, 1380 (*Chart. privil. immun.*, p. 78); rental of the borough, 1401 (*Ormond Deeds, 1350–1413*, pp 55–6).

CARBRY, County Kildare (16 N 690344)
Listed as a borough by Graham (Butlin, *Development Irish town*, p. 53).

CARLINGFORD, County Louth
'A borough of very great antiquity, probably by prescription'; grants of murage from 1326 (Lewis, *Topog., dict. Ire.*, i, 254).

CARLOW, County Carlow (19 S 722768)
Chartered by William Marshal, earl of Pembroke, 1223 (A. Ballard and J. Tait (eds), *British borough charters, 1216–1307*, pp xxxv, cii); granted £50 towards cost of walling the town by Lionel, earl of Ulster, 1362 (*Chartul. St Mary's, Dublin*, ii, 396).

CARNMONEY, County Antrim
Le Coul, or Le Coly: a borough town, 1333 (*Cal. inquis. post mortem*, vii, 374).

Geoffrey Martin

CARRICK-BEG, County Waterford
A settlement south of the Suir, joined to Carrick-on-Suir by a bridge, but formerly a borough (Lewis, *Topog. dict. Ire.*, i, 268–9). See Carrick-on-Suir.

CARRICKFERGUS, County Antrim (5 J 415875)
Mayor and commonalty, 1273 (*Cal. Doc. Ire., 1252–84*, pp 165–6); a borough town, 1333 (*Cal. inquis. post mortem*, vii, 374).

CARRICK McGRIFFIN see CARRICK-ON-SUIR

CARRICK-ON-SLANEY, County Wexford (23 T 016235)
Listed as a borough by Graham (Butlin, *Development Irish town*, p. 55).

CARRICK-ON-SUIR, County Tipperary (22 S 398215)
Usually identified with Carrick McGriffin; charter of 1366, from James (II), earl of Ormond (*Ormond Deeds, 1350–1413*, pp 95–6); there are other references in the volume. Lewis distinguishes it from Carrick-Beg, however, and attributes the name Carrick McGriffin to the suburb: see above.

CASHEL, County Tipperary (18 S 077405)
Charter from Archbishop Mairin to the reeve and 12 burgesses, 1250 (*Chart. privil. immun.*, p. 21).

CASTLE ARDMAYLE, County Tipperary (18 S 058457)
8 carucates held by the burgesses, 1338 (*Cal. inquis. post mortem*, viii, 119); reeve and community made fine for assize of bread and ale, 1359 (*Ormond Deeds, 1350–1413*, p. 38).

CASTLE DERMOT, County Kildare (16 S 782852)
Tristeldermot: burgesses paid 46s 6d for a moiety of the burgage, and owed suit of court, 1311 (*Red Bk Ormond*, p. 13).

CASTLEDOIGH, County Kilkenny (? Castletown, 18 S 421273)
Burgagery of Casteldoigh, c. 1410 (*Ormond Deeds, 1350–1413*, pp 353, and see p. 361).

CASTLEFRANK, County Louth (9 H 955036)
Listed by Graham (Butlin, *Development Irish town*, p. 54).

CASTLEMORA, County Cork (21 W 566931)
Listed by Graham (Butlin, *Development Irish town*, p. 52).

CASTLEROE, see NEWCASTLE, County Limerick

CASTLETON, County Laois (15 S 341920)
Burgesses paid 30s 1d, 1354 (*Cal. Inquis. post mortem*, ix, 128. The index places Castleton in Killaban).

CASTLETOWN, County Kilkenny, see CASTLEDOIGH

CASTLETOWN, County Louth (9 J 031084)
Listed by Graham (Butlin, *Development Irish town*, p. 54).

CATHIRDOUESKE (? County Tipperary)
Reeve and community fined for non-appearance at the seneschal's court, 1359 (*Ormond Deeds, 1350–1413*, p. 42).

37

CLANE, County Kildare (16 N 877278)
Grant of tolls (specified) to bailiffs and community to rebuild the bridge, 1389 (*Chart. privil. immun.*, p. 87).

CLONBUN see NEWTOWN TRIM

CLONCURRY, County Kildare (16 N 803411)
The burgesses had the assize of ale (*Red Bk Ormond*, p. 28; see also p. 31, for land held in burgage).

CLONDALKIN, County Dublin (16 O 070313)
32 burgages and 2 parts, and 33 messuages with 2 carucates, paying £17 8s 0½d, c. 1260; burgesses' labour is worth 5s *per annum (Alen's Reg.*, p. 187).

CLONMEL, County Tipperary (22 S 200226)
Extent of the borough, 1243 (*Cal. inquis. post mortem*, i, 6); writ maintaining Otto de Grandison's court in the borough, 1299 (*Chart. privil. immun.*, p. 38). See also Lisronagh.

CLONMINES, County Wexford (23 S 843129)
A borough, with burgage tenure (Lewis, *Topog. dict. Ire.*, i, 372); merchant of the town, 1521 (*Ormond Deeds, 1509-47*, pp 71-3).

CLOYNE, County Cork (25 W 918678)
Charter from Bishop Daniel, 1251 (Mac Niocaill, *Na buirgéisí*, i, 151-2).

COLLAGHMORE, County Kilkenny (18 S 421389)
Coillagh, or Sumertone near Callan: charter of Gilbert Marshal, 4th earl of Pembroke, 1234-41, confirmed 1362 (*Ormond Deeds, 1350-1413*, pp 73-80). (For 'Messuages and tenements in the borough of Kylamery, Co. Kilkenny' see *Ormond Deeds, 1413-1509*, p. 21).

COLLON, County Louth (13 N 998822)
'On the frontier of the marches of Uriel, and ... the key to that part of the country': (?) given a murage grant, 1472 (Curtis, *Med. Ire.*, p. 382).

COLP, County Meath (13 O 126744)
Listed by Graham (Butlin, *Development Irish town*, p. 54).

CORK, County Cork (22 W 6070)
Charters, 1189-1330 (Mac Niocaill, *Na buirgéisí*, i, 158-72).

CORKMOY, County Limerick
Burgesses in 'Corkmoid' paid £4 2s in rents, 1321 (*Cal. inquis. post mortem*, vi, 160).

COUL see CARNMONEY

COULBALYSIWARD, County Limerick
2 carucates held by burgesses, 1315 (*Cal. inquis. post mortem*, v, 287).

COYKETTLE, County Kilkenny
53 burgages, 1283 (*Cal. inquis. post mortem*, ii, 268).

CROMOTH see CROOM

CROOM, County Limerick (17 R 513411)
Grant of murage to Cromoth and Adare, 1310 (*Chart. privil. immun.*, p. 42); burgesses of Cromych paid 11s 9½d for two parts of their borough, 1331 (*Red Bk Kildare*, p. 111).

CURTUN, County Wexford
Listed by Graham; site unknown (Butlin, *Development Irish town*, p. 55).

DALKEY, County Dublin (16 O 265274)
Provost and bailiffs, 1358 (Lewis, *Topog. dict. Ire.*, i, 147).

DINGLE, County Kerry
Noted by Curtis as a town, with Tralee (*Med. Ire.*, p. 259).

DONAGHMORE, County Wicklow (16 S 923941)
3 carucates that were the burgesses' land, 1303 (*Red Bk Ormond*, pp 19–20).

DONAHEMELOKE see BURGAGE

DONKERYN, County Offaly
12 carucates held by the burgesses for £6 13s 4d (*Red Bk Ormond*, p. 151).

DORBARD'S ISLAND see GREAT ISLAND

DOUGLAS, County Cork (25 W 710692)
£8 9s 10d paid for 7½ carucates in free burgage, 1252 (*Cal. inquis. post mortem*, i, p. 65).

DOURLESS see THURLES

DOWN, County Down (9 J 487446)
A borough town, 1333 (*Cal. inquis. post mortem*, vii, 374).

DROGHEDA, County Louth (13 O 090752) and County Meath (13 O 090750)
Charters, 1194–1331 (Meath), 1213–1364 (Louth), and to the conjoint community, 1412 (Mac Niocaill, *Na buirgéisí*, i, 172–210).

DRUMCONDRA (13 N 886898)
£3 rent from burgage tenements, 1371 (*Cal. inquis. post mortem*, xiii, 64).

DUBLIN, County of the City of Dublin (16 O 1030)
Charters, 1171–1485 (Mac Niocaill, *Na buirgéisí*, i, 75–106); the city's records are calendared in *Anc. Rec. Dublin* (19 vols, 1889–1944).
See also Ostmantown.

DULEEK, County Meath (13 O 046687)
77 acres and 3 carucates held by the burgesses, 1361 (*Cal. inquis. post mortem*, x, 470).

DUNAMASE, County Laois (16 S 530980)
Dummas burgus, £104 19s 1d (*Chartul. St Mary's, Dublin*, ii, 403);

Glasscock (Beresford and Hurst, *Deserted medieval villages,* p. 296) suggests that Dunamase was the New Town of Leix (Leys).

DUNBOYNE, County Meath
Provost and community ordered to Trim with all their power, 1423 (Lewis, *Topog. dict. Ire.,* i, 568).

DUNDALK, County Louth (9 J 031084)
Recital and confirmation of liberties by Richard II, 1377–99 (Mac Niocaill, *Na buirgéisí,* i, 210–14).

DUNDONALD, County Down
Blathewyc, New Town of Dundannald: burgages in the New Town, 1333 (*Cal. inquis. post mortem,* vii, 375).

DUNFIERTH, County Kildare
£24 9s 4½d, 1273 (*Cal. inquis. post mortem,* ii, 253); granted the liberties of the Honour of Clare and the city of Bristol by act of 1463 (Weinbaum, *British Borough Charters,* p. 209).

DUNLAVIN, County Wicklow (16 N 871013)
Burgagers of the vill hold 4 carucates and 13½ acres for £5 12s 5½d, c. 1260 (*Alen's Reg.,* p. 190).

DUNLECH, County Carlow
Burgage in Dunleckny, c. 1215 (*Chartul. St Mary's, Dublin,* i, 112, 118).

DUNLOST, County Kildare
6 acres in the tenement of the burgesses, c. 1320 (*Ormond Deeds, 1172–1350,* pp 226–7).

DUNMALYS, County Antrim (5 Dc 400025)
Le Grenelowe in Larne parish; a borough town, worth little on account of the war, 1333 (*Cal. inquis. post mortem,* vii, 374).

DUNMANOGUE see MOUNMOHENNOK

DUNMORE, County Galway (11 M 509634)
Noted by Curtis as a borough with Athenry and Galway (*Med. Ire.,* p. 149).

DUNNAMAGGAN, County Kilkenny
A half-burgage, paying 6d a year, 1293 (*Ormond Deeds, 1172–1350,* p. 125); grant by Henry Walsch 'formerly burgess of Downomegan', 1483 (*Ormond Deeds, 1413–1509,* p. 256).

DUNOURE, County Dublin
A burgage in Dunour, 1228 (*Alen's Reg.,* p. 62)

DUNSHAUGHLIN, County Meath
'Formerly an incorporated town'; reeve and commonalty summoned to Trim with their power, 1423 (Lewis, *Topog. dict. Ire.,* i, 589).

EDERMINE, County Wexford (23 S 978245)
Burgesses render only 60s (formerly £9 10s) because of war, 1324 (*Cal. inquis. post mortem,* vi, 324).

EMLY, County Tipperary (18 R 764348)
Grant of murage, with tolls specified, 1303 (*Chart. privil. immun.*, p. 41).

ERNIA see NORNY

FAYTH, County Cork (25 Wo 660700)
Listed by Graham as a borough (Butlin, *Development Irish town*, p. 52).

FEATHARD, County Tipperary (18 S 207350)
Grant of murage specifying tolls, 1375 (*Chart. privil. immun.*, p. 71).

FERNS, County Wexford (19 T 020498)
A castle, with 160 burgages in the town, a watermill, and 160 carucates, now totally wasted, 1324 (*Cal. inquis. post mortem*, vi, 326).

FETHARD, County Wexford (23 S 792050)
'Some of its earlier lords (before its acquisition by St Thomas's, Dublin) procured for it a charter of incorporation' (Lewis, *Topog. dict. Ire.*, i, 627).

FETMOTHAN, County Tipperary
Burgesses paid 2m 22d in time of peace, 1338 (*Cal. inquis. post mortem*, viii, 118); Graham (Butler, *Development Irish town*, p. 54).

FORD see BELFAST

FORE see ST FÉICHÍN OF FORE

FORTH, County Carlow
Burgages against the town of Fothered, beside the Slane (*Reg. St Thomas, Dublin*, p. 120); burgage rents and tolls specified, 1307 (*Cal. inquis. post mortem*, iv, 305).

FYDOUNE (? County Kilkenny)
The burgagery of Fydoune, c. 1410 (*Ormond Deeds, 1350–1413*, p. 359; see also pp 300, 345).

GALWAY, County of the Town of Galway (14 M 298250)
Grant of a staple, 1375 (*Chart. privil. immun.*, p. 69); charter granting the burgesses the liberties of Drogheda, 1396 (Mac Niocaill, *Na buirgéisí*, i, 225).

GLASSELY, County Kildare (16 S 756982)
Identified as a borough by A. J. Otway-Ruthven (See map in *I.H.S.*, xi (Mar. 1959)).

GLENOGRA, County Limerick (17 R 595149)
Listed by Graham as a borough (Butlin, *Development Irish town*, p. 54); Lewis refers to a large abbey church, and to what 'are supposed to be the ruins of an ancient city' (*Topog. dict. Ire.*, i, 662–3).

GOWRAN, County Kilkenny (19 S 630535)
Extent of manor, with burgages (*Red Bk Ormond*, pp 34–41); rental (ibid., pp 41–5); enfeoffment of an heir by the constable and portreeve, 'according to the laudable customs of that town', 1532 (*Ormond Deeds, 1509–47*, pp 59–9).

GRANGE see BAPTIST GRANGE

GREAT ISLAND, County Wexford (23 S 687163)
3 carucates held by the burgesses (*Cal. inquis. post mortem,* iv, 307); 'Dorbardes Iland *alias* the Great Iland' (*Ormond Deeds, 1547–1584,* p. 199).

GREENCASTLE, County Down (9 J 247117)
Noted as a borough by Glasscock (Beresford and Hurst, *Deserted medieval villages,* p. 294); valued at £2 in 1326, nothing in 1333 (G. H. Orpen, 'The earldom of Ulster' in *R.S.A.I.Jn.,* xliv (1914), p. 60).

GREN, County Limerick (18 R 758437)
Listed as a borough by Graham (Butlin, *Development Irish town,* p. 54).

GRENAN see THOMASTOWN

GRENELOWE see DUNMALYS

GREENOGUE, County Meath (13 O 096500)
A burgage in Grenoe (*Chartul. St Mary's, Dublin,* i, 71).

HACHENYRHYN (? County Wexford)
In or by Cradokeston (? County Wexford): 'the land of the tenement of the new burgesses of Hachenyrhyn, 1343' (*Ormond Deeds, 1172–1350,* pp 323–4).

HERNIE see NORNY

HOLLYWOOD, County Wicklow
Burgesses have the free customs of Breteuil, 1255 x 1266 (*Alen's Reg.,* p. 122).

HOLYWOOD, County Down
A borough valued at 26s 8d in 1326, and 13s 4d in 1333 (G. H. Orpen, 'The earldom of Ulster' in *R.S.A.I.Jn.,* xliv (1914), p. 64).

IMMAL, County Wicklow
Burgage tenements abandoned by 1300 (*Red Bk Ormond,* pp 19–20).

IMELAGH see EMLY

INCHCOYN (? County Cork)
The burgesses of Inchcoyn distinguished from the burgesses of Youghal, 1288 (*Cal. Doc. Ire., 1171–1251,* p. 203); 3 carucates of land in borough tenure at New Town of Inchcoyn (M. Hemmeon, *Burgage tenure in medieval England* (Cambridge, Mass., 1914), p. 58 and n.) See also Kinsalebeg.

INISTIOGE, County Kilkenny (19 S 634378)
Charter to the burgesses from Alured, prior of Inistioge (P. Gale, *An inquiry into the ancient corporate system of Ireland* (London, 1834), appendix 4, pp xi–xiii).

IRISHTOWN see KILKENNY

JERPOINT see NEW TOWN OF JERPOINT

KARKEUL, County Tipperary
Burgesses, 1338 (*Cal. inquis. post mortem*, viii, 120); Graham (Butlin, *Development Irish town*, p. 54) says the site is unknown.

KELLS, County Kilkenny (18 S 493432)
Charter from William fitz Geoffrey, 1211 x 1216 (*Chart. privil. immun.*, pp 16–17).

KELLS, County Meath (13 N 741758)
Grant of the laws of Breteuil by Walter de Lacey, c. 1200, and grant of liberties including murage by act, 1472 (Mac Niocaill, *Na buirgéisí*, i, 124–6).

KILBIXY, County Westmeath (12 N 32615)
Burgages against the canons' ditch, 1200 & 1244 (*Reg. Tristernagh*, p. 5). See also Killucan.

KILCLIEF, County Down
The bishop of Down granted the right to make a borough by John de Courcy (*Cal. patent rolls, 1340–43*, p. 509); the community was a signatory to the Savage petition, c. 1410 (Curtis, *Med. Ire.*, p. 323). See also Ardglass.

KILCOLGAN, County Galway (14 M 421178)
Burgages, 1289 (*Red Bk Kildare*, p. 56); the burgesses paid £7 6s 8d, against £4 1s from Ardrahan (H. T. Knox, 'Occupation of the county of Galway by the Anglo-Normans after 1237' in *R.S.A.I.Jn.*, xxxi (1902), pp 366–7).

KILLCULLEN, County Kildare
Fortified with walls and gates before 1319; later displaced by Kilcullen Bridge (Lewis, *Topog. dict. Ire.*, ii, 76).

KILDARE, County Kildare (16 N 727127)
A parliament held in Kildare in 1309 (Lewis, *Topog. dict. Ire.*, ii, 85).

KILKEA, County Kildare (16 S 744890)
Burgesses and cottagers paid 13s 6d for half the borough (*Red Bk Ormond*, p. 13).

KILKENNY, County of the City of Kilkenny
Charters, 1207–23, and customs, 1383 (Mac Niocaill, *Na buirgéisí*, i, 135–49). See also Callan and Rosbergen.

IRISHTOWN, or ST CANICE, KILKENNY
Writ of 1363 maintaining immunity of Irishtown from the sovereign of Kilkenny (*Chart. privil. immun.*, p. 62).

KILLABAN see CASTLETOWN, County Laois

KILLALOE, County Limerick
Grant to Ranulf Glanville and Theobald Walter, including 'the burgh of Kildalowe, with a half of the cantred in which [it] is situate', 1185 (*Ormond Deeds, 1350–1413*, p. 321).

KILLENAUL, County Tipperary
Reeve and community summoned to the seneschal's court, 1432
(*Ormond Deeds, 1413–1509*, p. 95); lands in the burgage of Killenaul,
1544 (*Ormond Deeds, 1509–1547*, p. 276).

KILLUCAN, County Westmeath
Named with Kilbixy as a town burned by MacGeoghegan, 1450 (Curtis,
Med. Ire., p. 365).

KILLURE, County Kilkenny
'35 acres of arable land in possession of divers burgesses, 1594' (*Ormond
Deeds, 1584–1603*, p. 127).

KILMACBERNE, County Wicklow
Listed as a borough by Graham (Butlin, *Development Irish town*, p. 55);
site unknown.

KILMACLENNAN, County Cork (21 R 505062)
Charter granting the laws of Breteuil, 1251 (*Rotulus pipae Clonensis ...*,
ed. R. Caulfield (Cork, 1859), pp 15–22).

KILMALLOCK, County Limerick (17 R 610276)
Grant of murage, 1374 (*Chart. privil. immun.*, p. 68).

KILMANAGH, County Kilkenny (18 S 391522)
Burgesses, 1307 (*Cal. inquis. post mortem*, iv, 327).

KILMEADAN, County Waterford (23 S 513108)
Granted the customs of Breteuil, 1216 × 1272 (M. Bateson, 'The Laws
of Breteuil, part 2, the English evidence' in *E.H.R.*, xv (1900), p. 515).

KILSHEELIN, County Tipperary
Reeve and community made fine of 40d for assize of bread and ale, 1359
(*Ormond Deeds, 1350–1413*, p. 38); summoned to the seneschal's court,
1432 (ibid., *1413–1509*, p. 95).

KILTINAN, County Tipperary
The burgesses held their burgages by service of 6m 3d, 1308–9 (*Ormond
Deeds, 1172–1350*, p. 164).

KILWORTH, County Cork
8m rent from the borough, 1341 (*Cal. inq. post mortem*, x, 153).

KINSALE, County Cork (25 W 637505)
Grant of murage, 1381 (*Chart. privil. immun.*, p. 79).

KINSALEBEG, County Waterford
24 burgesses rendering 34s 4d to the lord of the manor of Inchcoyn, 1348
(*Cal. inquis. post mortem*, ix, 131).

KNOCKANY, County Limerick (18 R 682359)
Burgesses, 1287 (*Cal. inquis. post mortem*, ii, 430–31).

KNOCKGRAFFON, County Tipperary (18 S 053298)
Rental of the burgages, 1274 (*Ormond Deeds, 1172–1350*, p. 78; see also

p. 164); burgesses render 119m, 1 lb of pepper, and 1 lb of cummin (*Red Bk Ormond*, p. 146).

KNOCKTOPHER, County Kilkenny (19 S 530376)
The burgage of Baliopane, *alias* Knockoffre (*Ormond Deeds, 1413–1509*, p. 166); seal of Knocktopher (ibid., p. 169).

KYLBLENYN (? County Kilkenny)
The burgesses render 25s a year and suit of court (*Ormond Deeds, 1350–1413*, p. 340).

KYLDENALL, County Tipperary
'The borough of Kyldenall in Founteston'; 7 burgesses named 1441 (*Ormond Deeds, 1413–1509*, p. 131); site unknown (Graham, (Butlin, *Development Irish town*, p. 55)).

LEA, County Laois
'A small burgh with market and fairs, destroyed in 1315' (Lewis, *Topog. dict. Ire.*, ii, 247).

LEIGHLIN, County Carlow (19 S 860655)
Grant of murage, 1310 (*Chart. privil. immun.*, pp 43–4).

LEIXLIP, County Kildare (16 O 033354)
A burgage, with 3 acres (*Chartul. St Mary's, Dublin*, i, 236).

LIMERICK, County of the City of Limerick (17 R 575565)
Charters, 1197 and later (Mac Niocaill, *Na buirgéisí*, i, 236–46).

LISRONAGH, County Tipperary (18 S 201295)
Burgesses, 1331 (*Ormond Deeds, 1172–1350*, p. 236) a grant by the community under the common seal of Clonmel (*Ormond Deeds, 1413–1509*, p. 203).

LOCHSWEDY, County Westmeath (12 N 210490)
A burgage in the town (*Chartul. St Mary's, Dublin*, i, 229).

LOUGHMORE WEST, County Tipperary
Reeve and community made fine for assize of bread and ale, 1359; summoned to seneschal's court, 1432 (*Ormond Deeds, 1350–1413*, p. 38; *1413–1509*, p. 95).

LOUGHREA, County Galway (14 M 620166)
'A town . . . of so much importance that it was fortified' Lewis, *Topog. dict. Ire.*, ii, 316).

LOUTH, County Louth (9 H 057011)
Grant to the bailiff and commons by Henry IV, 1406 (Lewis, *Topog. dict. Ire.*, ii, 320) ; a charter shown in the court there, for security (*Chartul. St Mary's, Dublin*, i, 62).

LUCAN, County Dublin (16 O 032350)
Burgesses' suit to watermill, 1315 (*Ormond Deeds, 1172–1350*, pp 200–01); a burgage there, 1316 (ibid., p. 210).

LUSK, County Dublin (13 O 214546)
A burgage there, 1276 (*Cal. inquis. post mortem*, ii, 127).

LYNNANE, County Tipperary (18 Rc 940400)
New Town Lennan: 38s from the burgesses (*Red Bk Ormond*, p. 121); reeve and community summoned to seneschal's court, 1432 (*Ormond Deeds, 1413–1509*, p. 95).

MACUNKERDE (? County Meath? near Cloncurry, County Kildare)
A moiety of the town of Macunkerde, with all the burgages (*Reg. St Thomas, Dublin*, p. 79).

MAGHERA, County Down
The bishop of Down granted the right to make a borough (*Cal. Patent rolls, 1340–43*, p. 509).

MALLOW, County Cork (21 W 561983)
A grant of specified tolls in Mallow and Ard, 1286 (*Cal. doc. Ire., 1285–1292*, p. 107).

MARINERSTOWN, County Meath (13 O 133760)
A burgage, 1235 (*Cal. doc. Ire., 1171–1251*, p. 341).

MAYGLASS, County Wexford (23 T 015112)
Listed by Graham as a borough (Butlin, *Development Irish town*, p. 55).

MEELICK, County Galway
The borough of Milok, destroyed, 1333 (*Cal. inquis. post mortem*, vii, 377).

MOLING see ST MULLINS

MOONE, County Kildare (16 S 797923)
Charter, c. 1223 (Mac Niocaill, *Na buirgéisí*, i, 246–50); a burgage of 10 acres (*Reg. St Thomas, Dublin*, p. 161).

MOUNMOHENNOK, County Kildare (19 S 730832)
Later Dunmanogue; burgesses (Otway-Ruthven, *I.H.S.*, xi (Mar. 1959), p. 182).

MOURNE, County Cork
'An ancient corporate and walled town, destroyed in the reign of Edward IV' (Lewis, *Topog. dict. Ire.*, ii, 397).

MOYALIFF, County Tipperary
60 burgesses held 200 acres for £4 16d, 'nothing can be levied in time of war', 1338 (*Cal. inquis. post mortem*, vii, 120).

MULLINGAR, County Meath
Provost and bailiffs of the town amerced for not appearing before the justiciar, 1297 (*Cal. Justiciary rolls, 1295–1303*, p. 79).

MUNGRET, County Limerick (17 R 544538)
Granted the customs of Breteuil by Bishop Robert, 1251 x 1272 (Curtis, *Med. Ire.*, p. 214).

NAAS, County Kildare (16 N 892192)
A weekly market granted in the borough to William fitzMaurice, c. 1185 (*Chart. privil. immun.*, p. 5).

NARRAGH, County Kildare (16 S 780989)
Listed by Graham as a borough (Butlin, *Development Irish town*, p. 53).

NAVAN, County Meath
Charters, 1469 and 1494 (*First report of the commissioners appointed to inquire into the municipal corporations in Ireland*, pp 9–10, H.C. 1835 (27), xxvii, 15–16)

NENAGH, County Tipperary (18 R 867791)
Reeve and community summoned to seneschal's court, 1432 (*Ormond Deeds, 1413–1509*, p. 95).

NEW ROSS, County Wexford (23 S 720275)
Charters, 1283 & 1286, 1389 (Mac Niocaill, *Na buirgéisí*, i, 300–19). See also Bannow.

NEW TOWN, County Limerick
Listed by Graham (Butlin, *Development Irish town*, p. 54); site unknown.

NEW TOWN OF DUNDALK see DUNDALK

NEW TOWN OF DUNDONALD see DUNDONALD

NEW TOWN OF INCHCOYN see INCHCOYN

NEW TOWN OF JERPOINT, County Kilkenny (19 S 570403)
A borough, established c. 1200 (W. J. Pilsworth, 'Newtown Jerpoint' in *Old Kilkenny Review*, x (1958), pp 31–5).

NEW TOWN OF LEYS see DUNAMASE

NEW TOWN TRIM, County Meath (13 N 814569)
Listed by Graham as a borough (Butlin, *Development Irish town*, p. 54); Lewis, *Topog. dict. Ire.*, ii, 645 refers only to the ruins of religious houses at 'Newtown Clonbun'.

NEWCASTLE, County Limerick
Anciently Castle-Roe, a fortified and chartered town (Lewis, *Topog. dict. Ire.*, ii, 425–6).

NEWCASTLE, County Tipperary
Reeve and community summoned to the seneschal's court, 1432 (*Ormond Deeds, 1413–1509*, p. 95).

NEWCASTLE MACKINEGAN, County Wicklow (16 O 298042)
12 burgages (*Chartul. St Mary's, Dublin*, i, 240).

NEWTOWN LENNAN see LYNNANE

NEWTOWN OF RONAN, County Kilkenny
'A borough (? burgage) in the Newtown of Ronan' (*Ormond Deeds, 1547–84*, p. 78).

NOBBER, County Meath (13 N 824864)
Three burgages in Nobber, 1290 (*Cal. doc. Ire., 1285–92*, p. 341).

NORNY, County Kildare
Variously Nurny, Hernie, Ernia: a burgage at Hernie (*Reg. St Thomas, Dublin*, pp 142–3).

ODOGH, County Kilkenny (18 S 457623)
Listed by Graham as a borough (Butlin, *Development Irish town*, p. 53).

OLD LEIGHLIN see LEIGHLIN

OLD ROSS, County Wexford (23 S 799273)
Listed by Graham as a borough (Butlin, *Development Irish town*, p. 55).

OLOMOR, County Kerry
1 messuage and 10 acres of arable in the burgage of Olomor, 1361 (*Ormond Deeds, 1252-84*, p. 66).

OPANE see KNOCKTOPHER

OSTMANSTOWN, Dublin
Something of a Norse community seems to have survived for a century or so after the conquest: its members' liberties were personal rather than territorial, but their vill was recognizable (Curtis, *Med. Ire.*, pp 195, 198; *Chartul. St Mary's, Dublin*, i, 248).

OUGHTERARD, County Kildare (16 N 958263)
Listed by Graham as a borough (Butlin, *Development Irish town*, p. 53).

OWENSTOWN, County Kilkenny
A burgess of Woweynstoun and a messuage in the borough in the barony of Arley, 1487 (*Ormond Deeds, 1413-1509*, pp 259-60); the burgagery of Owenstown, 1524 (*Ormond Deeds, 1509-1547*, p. 84).

PASSAGE WEST, County Cork
Seal of the sovereign of Passage, 1572 (*Ormond Deeds, 1547-84*, p. 327).

PORCHAMAN see BUSHMILLS

PORTRUSH, County Antrim (2 C 859406)
Burgesses of Porcros, 1272 (*Cal. inquisitions (misc.)*, i, 136); Lewis speaks of 'the remains of an ancient town' exposed under drifted sand by a storm in 1827 (*Topog. dict. Ire.*, ii, 468).

PORTUMNA, County Galway (15 M 853047)
Listed by Graham as a borough (Butlin, *Development Irish town*, p. 53).

RATHANGAN, County Kildare (16 N 675192)
£6 3s 2d rent from the borough, 1331 (*Red Bk Kildare*, p. 102).

RATHCOOL, County Dublin (16 O 020270)
Charter 1228 & 1255 (Mac Niocaill, *Na buirgéisí*, i, 293-4); the burgesses shared 'pasture and turbary in the mountain of Slescol' with the men of Newcastle-juxta-Lyons, 1240 (Lewis, *Topog. dict. Ire.*, ii, 492).

RATHFERNAN, County Roscommon
Listed by Graham as a borough; 'site unknown' (Butlin, *Development Irish town*, p. 54).

RATHKEALE, County Limerick
A corporation 'disfranchised by Cromwell' (Lewis, *Topog. dict. Ire.*, ii, 499); the community granted 40s to the crown in 1300 (*Cal. Justic. rolls Ire., 1295-1303*, p. 304).

RATHMORE, County Kildare (16 N 960195)
Charter, c. 1220, granting the liberties of Breteuil (Mac Niocaill, *Na buirgéisí*, i, 294–5).

RATOATH, County Meath (13 O 020519)
'Classed among the borough towns of Meath', *temp.* Henry VI, and returning M.P.s until the Union (Lewis, *Topog. dict. Ire.*, ii, 509).

RATTOO, County Kerry
Anciently Rathtoy, 'said to have had seven churches', ground called burgess lands in the vicinity (Lewis, *Topog. dict. Ire.*, ii, 510).

RINDOWN, County Roscommon (12 N 004541)
Said to be the site of a town fortified in 1351 (Glasscock (Beresford and Hurst, *Deserted medieval villages*, p. 293)).

ROCHE, County Louth (9 N 990118)
Listed by Graham (Butlin, *Development Irish town*, p. 54).

RONAN see NEWTOWN OF RONAN

ROO (? County Londonderry)
The castle of Roo, and the burgh there, 1296 (*Ormond Deeds, 1350–1413*, p. 328).

ROSBERGEN, County Kilkenny (23 S 713277)
Charter, 1289 × 1295, granting the burgesses the liberties of Kilkenny (Mac Niocaill, *Na buirgéisí*, i, 296–9).

ROSCOMMON, County Roscommon (12 M 876644)
Confirmation of unspecified liberties, 1310 (*Chart. privil. immun.*, p. 43).

ROSCREA, County Tipperary (15 S 135893)
Reeve and community amerced with representatives of other boroughs, 1399–1400 (*Ormond Deeds, 1350–1413*, p. 244).

ROSSCARBERY, County Cork
A charter granted by John at the instance of the bishop (Lewis, *Topog. dict. Ire.*, ii, 534).

ROSS see NEW ROSS and OLD ROSS

ROTHEBA (? County Galway)
Borough of Rotheba mentioned in an inquest at Adrahan, Co. Galway, 1341 (*Cal. inquis. post mortem*, vi, 161).

SAGGART, County Dublin (16 O 038267)
Listed by Graham as a borough (Butlin, *Development Irish town*, p. 52).

ST CANICE see KILKENNY: IRISHTOWN

ST FÉICHÍN OF FORE, or FOWRE, County Westmeath
'Formerly a borough', two of the town gates were standing in 1837 (Lewis, *Topog. dict. Ire.*, i, 616); 'Fowre' in a statute of 1462 (P. Gale, *Inquiry into the ancient corporate system of Ire.*, p. 121).

ST MULLINS, County Carlow
Tech Mulin or Moling: a burgage *super magnam aquam* (*Chartul. St Mary's, Dublin*, i, 112–13).

SALMONLEAP see LEIXLIP

SHANDON, County Cork
A burgage in Shandon excepted from an exchange of lands (*Reg. St Thomas, Dublin*, p. 186).

SHANKILL, County Dublin (16 O 235270)
Listed by Graham (Butlin, *Development Irish town*, p. 52).

SIDDAN, County Meath (13 N 893848)
Granted the liberties of Breteuil c. 1250; confirmed with a grant of murage, 1475 (Curtis, *Med. Ire.*, p. 382).

SKREEN, County Meath (13 N 952604)
A burgage in Scrin with 3 acres of land, held at a burgage rent of 12d (*Chartul. St Mary's, Dublin*, i, p. 236).

SLANE, County Meath (13 N 961742)
24 burgage tenements, 1371 (*Cal. inquis. post mortem*, xiii, 64).

SLIGO, County Sligo (7 G 693359)
180 burgages in 3 *villate* of land, paying £9 *per annum*, 1289 (*Red Bk Kildare*, p. 113).

STRADBALLY COLGYN, County Waterford (22 X 370978)
30s 9d rent from the burgesses, rendered by Martin Poer, reeve of the town, 1338 (*Ormond Deeds, 1172–1350*, p. 304).

STRAFFAN, County Kildare (16 N 909302)
Listed by Graham as a borough (Butlin, *Development Irish town*, p. 53).

SUMERTONE see COLLAGHMORE

SWORDS, County Dublin
Charter, c. 1200 (Mac Niocaill, *Na buirgéisí*, i, 321).

TAGHMON, County Wexford (23 S 916198)
5 carucates of the burgesses, 1296 (*Cal. inquis. post mortem*, iv, 244); 48 burgages, 1324 (ibid., vi, 325).

TALLAGHT County Dublin (16 O 093277)
Burgages there, 1326 (*Reg. Alen.*, p. 177). See Tamlaght.

TAMLAGHT (? Tallaght)
Grant of the murage to the bailiffs and good men, 1311 (*Chart. privil. immun.*, p. 44).

TECH MULIN see ST MULLINS

TERMONFECKIN, County Louth (13 O 142805)
A burgage in the vill, 1321 (*Dowdall Deeds*, pp 27–8).

THOMASTOWN, County Kilkenny (19 S 585419)
Otherwise Grenan; grant of pontage to reeve, bailiffs, and worthy men,

1346 (*Chart. privil. immun.*, p. 58); murage, with tolls specified, 1374 (ibid., p. 68).

THURLES, County Tipperary (18 S 131588)
Two knights' fees held as burgage by the burgesses in their burgages for £22 17s 2d, 1336 (*Cal. inquis. post mortem*, viii, 118); reeve and community summoned to the seneschal's court, 1432 (*Ormond Deeds, 1413–1509*, p. 95).

TIPPER, County Kildare (16 N 918185)
A burgage settlement (Glasscock, (Beresford and Hurst, *Deserted medieval villages*, p. 295)).

TIPPERARY, County Tipperary (18 R 890358)
Grant of murage, 1310 (*Chart. privil. immun.*, p. 43).

TRALEE, County Kerry (21 O 834146)
A grant of specified tolls in the town, 1286 (*Cal. doc. Ire., 1285–1292*, p. 107).

TRIM, County Meath (13 N 800568)
Granted the liberties of Breteuil, 1189 x 1241 (*Chart. privil. immun.*, p. 10). See also Dunboyne and Dunshaughlin.

TRISTELDERMOT see CASTLE DERMOT

TULLOPHELIM or TULLOW, County Carlow
Tyllagh Offelmeth; rents of one-third of the burgagery valued at 61s, 1345 (*Ormond Deeds, 1172–1350*, p. 329); grant of murage, 1343 (*Chart. privil. immun.*, p. 57).

TWO-MILE BURRIS see BORRISLEIGH

WATERFORD, County Waterford (23 S 605120)
Charters, 1232–1462 (Mac Niocaill, *Na buirgéisí*, i, 251–93); the vill of the Ostmen by Waterford paid a rent to Tomas an Apa (Curtis, *Med. Ire.*, p. 169).

WEXFORD, County Wexford (23 T 050215)
Charter, 1317 (*Chart. privil. immun.*, p. 47).

WEYPEROUS see BALLINACLOGH

WICKLOW, County Wicklow (16 O 315940)
Burgages confirmed by John to St Mary's abbey, *ante* 1199 (*Chartul. St Mary's, Dublin*, i, 85).

WOWEYNSTOUN see OWENSTOWN

YOUGHAL, County Cork
Charters, 1462–85 (Mac Niocaill, *Na buirgéisí*, i, 215–25). See also Inchcoyn.

APPENDIX II

SOME PROBABLE SITES OF BOROUGHS

The following list contains the names of places which seem, from indications in Lewis, *Topog. dict. Ire.,* or from the references cited, to have had some of the characteristics of boroughs. Those marked (M) are the subject of market-charters noted by Graham, (Butlin, *Development Irish town,* pp 56–7). The full tale of such charters, whether speculative or effective, to hold markets in Ireland, remains still to be reckoned, but as Dr Graham remarks, burgage tenure would be a natural accompaniment to them.

BALLINASKELLIGS, County Kerry

BALLINGARRY, County Limerick

BALLYNAHINCH, County Tipperary
Noted by Glasscock (Beresford and Hurst, *Deserted medieval villages,* p. 296) as a potential borough-site.

BANAGHER, County Offaly

BLACKCASTLE OF BURRIES, County Tipperary
A *burris* place-name (*Ormond Deeds, 1584–1603,* p. 172).

CAVAN, County Cavan

CLONARD, County Meath

CLONES, County Fermanagh and County Monaghan

CONG, County Mayo

CROARGH, County Limerick

DERVER, County Louth

EARLSTOWN, County Kilkenny

ENNIS, County Clare

ENNISCORTHY, County Wexford (M)

GLANWORTH, County Cork (M)

GRANARDKILLE, County Longford

INNISHANNON, County Cork (M)

KILLYBEGS, County Donegal

LIXNAW, County Kerry

MALAHIDE, County Dublin

NEWCASTLE LYONS, County Kildare
See Rathcool (p. 48 above).

PIPERSTOWN, County Tipperary
  A settlement noted by Glasscock (op. cit., p. 297).

POWERSCOURT, County Wicklow

RATHVILLY, County Carlow

TREVET, County Meath

Ulster Plantation Towns 1609–41

R. J. Hunter

Although there were urban aspects to various colonising schemes in Ireland in the second half of the sixteenth century, the plantation in Ulster in the six escheated counties of Cavan, Fermanagh, Donegal, Derry, Tyrone and Armagh was the first with formal urban proposals. The plan in 1609 stated that twenty-five incorporated towns should be established, to the corporations of which quantities of land should be assigned, townsmen of unspecified number to be recruited by 'levy or press' in England. Most of the locations proposed were places of longstanding political importance where in many instances castles had recently been occupied or small fortifications established. Many of these were also monastic centres. A smaller group, Armagh, Raphoe and Clogher, were based on surrounding areas of episcopal land. The significance of a further three, indicated by their names, Mountjoy, Mountnorris and Charlemont, derived from the forts recently established there. Indeed entirely new foundations were to be few—essentially two, a town midway between Kells and Cavan to provide an extra link with Dublin and one midway between Lisgoole and Ballyshannon, presumably to take advantage of the Erne.[1]

The choice of predominantly traditional sites, not surprisingly in view of their changed circumstances, was, however, to present

[1] R. J. Hunter, 'Towns in the Ulster plantation' in *Studia Hib.*, no. 11 (1971), pp 40–79 (hereafter cited as Hunter, 'Towns'); 'Ulster plantation papers, 1608–13', ed. T. W. Moody, in *Anal. Hib.*, no. 8 (1938), pp 286–96; James Buckley (ed.), 'Report of Sir Josias Bodley on some Ulster fortresses in 1608' in *U.J.A.*, 2nd series, xvi, nos 1 and 2 (Feb. and May 1910), pp 61–4; *Anal. Hib.*, no. 3 (1931), pp 151–218. For a list of the proposed towns see Table I.

problems. Many were based on small contiguous areas of monastic, termon and erenagh or episcopal land, all land which did not form part of the forfeited temporal land, and which was coming into the hands of local army officers independently of the plantation conditions or which was to be granted to the bishops simultaneously with the plantation.[2] In addition, a few of these and the newly established forts had already had areas of land allocated to them in support of the forts.[3] It would only be if additional land were granted (and it was not) or if these new owners were bought out that urbanising arrangements could be made, and it was really only at Derry, based on ecclesiastical land that had come into the hands of Sir Henry Docwra, military governor of Lough Foyle and incorporated in 1604 as a place 'fit to be made both a town of war and a town of merchandize', that new English urban beginnings of any scale had been made.[4]

The compensation of prior interests was an essential implication of the arrangement made with the city of London by the English privy council for the colonisation of the entire county of Londonderry in January 1610. Accordingly, the city was granted a notional 4,000 acres at Derry and 3,000 at Coleraine and was required to build at the former place 200 houses and leave space for a further 300 with corresponding figures of 100 and 200 for Coleraine.[5] But these were special arrangements made some months before final plans for the plantation as a whole were concluded. More interesting from the point of view of the plantation in the remaining five counties, which was to be based on grants of land to individuals, was the last minute arrangement made in July, when it had already been decided that tradesmen would not be 'pressed out of England to inhabit the towns',[6] for building and settling the town of Belturbet in the English undertakers' barony of Loughtee in County Cavan.[7] This, although the details cannot be precisely recovered

[2] This sentence derives from the cartographic identification of land grants.
[3] Hunter, 'Towns', p. 46.
[4] Moody, *Londonderry plantation*, pp 55, 58; T. W. Moody and J. G. Simms (ed.), *The bishopric of Derry and the Irish Society of London* (I.M.C., Dublin, 1968), i, 27–8, 29–31, 40–2; *Cal. pat. rolls Ire., Jas I,* pp 10, 15, 65, 113; R.I.A., charters of Irish towns, 7, charter of Derry, 11 July 1604.
[5] Moody, *Londonderry plantation*, p. 78; *Cal. Carew MSS, 1603–24,* p. 36.
[6] *Cal. S. P. Ire., 1608–10,* pp 415–6.
[7] The essential framework of the plantation, as far as settler landowners was concerned, was one whereby groups of baronies or precincts were allocated to undertakers, English and Scottish, whose estates should be settled with a British population only and servitors, military officers whose estates were in the same precincts as lands restored to some Irish grantees, who might have Irish tenants. For a map and discussion see T. W. Moody, F. X. Martin and F. J. Byrne (ed.), *A new history of Ireland* (Oxford, 1976), iii, 198–9.

owing to the destruction of the relevant London privy council records, was an attempt to forge a device for joint operations by the individual landowners in that barony. Essentially, the town land was granted to a neighbouring undertaker, Stephen Butler, but the other undertakers were to build and live there, or procure freeholders, on sites to be allocated, presumably, by Butler. They should also build a church. Related to this was a privy council order whereby Sir Francis Rushe and his wife should be compensated for their rights in the castle of Belturbet and lands and fishings.[8] This imaginative effort to insert a co-operative element into a colony based on individual planters may have been intended as a model but there is no evidence of its being attempted with any other group of undertakers, English or Scots. Instead London's instructions to Dublin on 1 August merely transferred responsibility: the lord deputy and council should arrange for 'peopling' the towns 'so far as the means of the country will yield' and when forty houses and families were attained they should be incorporated.[9]

Thereafter matters proceeded more slowly. The lord deputy and plantation commissioners distributed the forfeited land to its grantees in an Ulster tour in August and September, but land was allocated to only one town, Cavan, a small established Irish town incorporated in November and the only town corporation to actually receive the town lands.[10] Indeed some corporation land was silently allotted to other owners—notably in Fermanagh where endowments for three proposed towns were reduced to sufficient for only one—or allocated in inconvenient places.[11] However by the end of the year the Dublin government had come up with an expedient (already tentatively adopted in a lease made in October of the town lands for Lifford to the local military commander, Sir Richard Hansard, on condition that he should assign plots for houses to sixty people[12]) agreed to by London in the spring of 1611: the lands intended for the corporations should be granted to a local undertaker or servitor with conditions for urban development.[13] Later in

[8] Hill, *Plantation,* pp 282-2, 465–6; *Hastings MSS,* iv, 163; P.R.O.I., Lodge MSS, vi, 169; B.L., Add. MS 11, 402, f. 159; *Anal. Hib.,* no. 8 (1938), pp 237, 246–7.

[9] *Cal. Carew MSS, 1603–24,* pp 56–7. It seems very likely, however, that when the patron of nearby Enniskillen, Capt. William Cole nominated six County Fermanagh landowners to be burgesses of the town in 1612 he was himself seeking to imitate the Belturbet arrangement (R. J. Hunter, 'Sir William Cole and plantation Enniskillen, 1607–41' in *Clogher Record,* ix, no. 3 (1978), pp 344–5 (hereafter cited as Hunter, 'Enniskillen').

[10] R.I.A., Charters of Irish towns, 4, 130–52; Hunter, 'Towns', pp 42, 69.

[11] Hunter, 'Enniskillen', p. 339. The town lands for Augher were located close to the town of Clogher.

[12] *Cal. pat. rolls Ire.,, Jas I,* p. 182.

[13] Lambeth, Carew MS 629, ff 68–72; *Cal. Carew MSS, 1603–24,* pp 141–2; *Cal. S.P. Ire., 1611–14,* pp 36–7.

1611 the number of proposed incorporations was reduced to eighteen.[14]

Land grants to patrons or superintendents were ultimately made, mainly in 1612, for only eight places—Dungannon and Augher in Tyrone, Lifford, Donegal, Rathmullan and Killybegs in Donegal, Enniskillen in Fermanagh and Virginia in Cavan.[15] Thus only in these places, along with Derry, Coleraine and Belturbet, were formal urbanising conditions laid down. The minimum size of settlement now prescribed in these grants was also a reduced one: the grantee should procure within four years twenty persons 'English and Scotch and chiefly artificers and mechanics' who should be burgesses of the town when incorporated, though 'cottagers and other inferior inhabitants' were also envisaged.[16] The town should be built 'in streets and squares, in such manner and form as shall best suit with [its] site and situation, and for the defence and decency of the said town'.[17] He should 'build or cause to be built . . . twenty burgages or houses of stone or framed timber according to the form of building usual in England',[18] and allocate two acres each to ten of these and one acre each to the remainder in an area to be known as the 'burgage field', houses and lands to be held forever in fee farm. If the houses were built by the landlord he should charge rent at the rate of 10% of the sum expended; if built by the tenant (this option was available) then the ten with two acres should pay 5s, the others 2s 6d per annum.[19] Normally he should allocate sites for a church and churchyard, a market place and a public school and, occasionally, for a gaol or prison. The amount of land to be employed to the uses of the town, its site, the burgesses acres and a common, did not generally exceed one-quarter or one-third of the notional acreage allocated to the patron.

[14] Hunter, 'Towns', p. 45. See Table 1.

[15] *Cal. pat. rolls Ire., Jas I,* pp 206–7, 217, 219–20, 224–5, 232, 236, 256, 300.

[16] These extracts are taken from an uncalendared translation of the patent made to Capt. William Cole for Enniskillen (*Cal. pat. rolls Ire., Jas I,* p. 232) published in W. C. Trimble, *History of Enniskillen* (Enniskillen, 1919), i, 165–70.

[17] Very similar language was used in the Virginia Council's orders in 1609 to Sir Thomas Gates, governor of Virginia, who was told that in building his towns he should 'prepare for ornament and safety at once' (S. M. Bemiss (ed.), *The three charters of the Virginia company of London with seven related documents, 1606–1621* (Williamsburg, Virginia, 1957), p. 61).

[18] It may be noted that in London at this time the use of timber in constructing the outer walls of houses was forbidden by proclamation as a fire precaution and to conserve timber (J. F. Larkin and P. L. Hughes (ed.), *Stuart royal proclamations, i: royal proclamations of King James I, 1603–1625* (Oxford, 1973), nos 51, 78, 87, 120, 175, 186).

[19] These stipulations as to rent and otherwise are referred to and embodied in a surviving building lease for the town of Augher of 1 Apr. 1615 (P.R.O.I., D 4859). It required that the house be built of 'stone, brick or timber with chimneys'.

58

The process of incorporation followed speedily, so that by 1613 fourteen places, excluding two, Virginia and Rathmullan, for which land grants had been made and including Strabane, not originally proposed for incorporation, had received charters, later to be extended, with Killybegs and Clogher, to sixteen. However these incorporations were part of a wider move to create forty 'new boroughs', whose charters should follow regulations sent from London in September 1612, hence urban planning in plantation Ulster was merged with a scheme of borough-making throughout Ireland which was in part a tactic of parliamentary management. The corporations were generally made up of thirteen members, were empowered to fill their own vacancies and had a limited income since they did not receive grants of the town lands.[20]

Any attempt to view the corporate towns as a whole in this period is severely restricted by problems of sources. Municipal records (apart from a few deeds) and subsidy rolls do not survive; landlord's accounts are scant. Furthermore the superficial completeness of the principal sources used for the study of the plantation as a whole, the series of government surveys between 1611 and 1622 and the muster of 1630, is in fact deceptive. The depositions of 1641, while they offer little on towns which did not surrender in 1641 such as Derry and Enniskillen, are not sufficiently numerous to provide more than valuable supplementary material on other towns. In the absence of standard sources a number of oblique (and somewhat discontinuous) approaches have been adopted.

The upper limits of urbanisation can be seen in the four towns of Derry, Coleraine, Strabane and Armagh. At Derry within the walls some 215 stone and slated houses (though considered inadequate in size) had, by 1616, been built by the Irish Society, the body appointed by the city of London to manage its Ulster affairs, about 25 more being built by private individuals.[21] A rental in 1628 indicates 265 houses apart from suburban growth outside the walls which was already underway by 1616[22] The location of this and an indication that its scale was not inconsiderable emerges from

[20] Hunter, 'Towns', pp 48–54; transcripts of many of the charters are to be found in R.I.A., Charters of Irish towns, 1, 4, 5, 7 and in P.R.O.I., R.C. 3/2, 4, 5, 7, 8. For a detailed discussion of the charters of Londonderry and Coleraine see Moody, *Londonderry plantation,* pp 122–42.

[21] Moody, *Londonderry plantation,* pp 81–3, 274–6; Corporation of London Records Office (hereafter C.L.R.O.), Jor. 30, f. 136v.

[22] R. G. S. King (ed.), *A particular of the howses and famylyes in Londonderry, May 15, 1628* (Londonderry, 1936), pp 6–23; C.L.R.O., Jor. 30, f. 138; Moody, *Londonderry plantation,* pp 243–4.

partially surviving agreements for leases in 1639.[23] At Coleraine 116 houses had been built by the Irish Society by 1616. However some were built of timber, others of 'loam and lime' and were decaying 'by reason of the bleakness of the weather' so that already remedial slating was necessary. By 1622 80 additional privately built houses had been erected, some in response to a premium of £20 per house and favourable rents offered by the Londoners.[24] At Strabane, on a site somewhat removed from Turlogh Luineach O'Neill's former castle, the town built by 1619 'about' the castle of its Scottish undertaker landlord, James, Earl of Abercorn, consisted of some 80 houses, 'a great many of them . . . of lime and stone' others of timber and had 'above' 100 by 1622. It seems almost certain that at least some 30 of these houses, held by freeholders, had been built by the earl.[25] This descending scale is reflected in the muster returns of adult male residents in 1630, some 500, 300 and 208 respectively.[26] Two factors would seem to account for the growth of these larger settlements—energetic landlord sponsorship especially in house building and favourable geographical location for sea-borne trade. In sharp distinction to these three towns Armagh, like Cavan but perhaps twice as large and having an English corporation and episcopal landlord, initially retained its essential Irish character. Of 123 houses held from the archbishop in 1618, four fifths, described in 1622 as 'cottages . . . let yearly to the natives' were in Irish occupation. An elaborate building lease scheme initiated by the archbishop in 1615 for the 'replanting and re-edifying of the decayed city' whereby the tenant would undertake to erect a two-storeyed house, of specified dimensions, to be built of brick or stone and timber 'according to the form of English houses and buildings' did not generate wide interest. Yet here, as also in Cavan, a settler element grew which could muster ninety males for the town and surrounds in 1630.[27]

Urban growth at the other places rarely exceeded some thirty to forty houses, while in a few cases it did not reach the minimum of twenty stipulated in the patronage grants. Lifford, at the upper end of this scale, developed around a royal fort on land held by the English servitor Sir Richard Hansard, had at least 54 houses by 1622 (of which 21 had been built by Hansard as early as 1611) and so

[23] C.L.R.O., Irish Society MSS, Great Parchment Book, ff A1–A26.

[24] Moody, *Londonderry plantation,* pp 274–5; C.L.R.O., Jor. 30, f. 136v.

[25] Hill, *Plantation,* pp 527–8; B.L., Add. MS 4756, f. 110; County of Huntingdon and Peterborough Record Office, Kimbolton MSS, ddM70/35; A. A. Campbell, *Notes on the literary history of Strabane* (Omagh, 1902), pp 4–5.

[26] Moody, *Londonderry plantation,* p. 279; B.L., Add. MS 4770, ff 94v–8.

[27] For a more detailed discussion see Hunter, 'Towns', pp. 57–66 (Armagh), 68–73 (Cavan).

presumably a male population of about 100.[28] Enniskillen with
some 60 adult males in c. 1630 and where a careful town building
plan in relation to the royal fort had been worked out, may probably
be taken as the typical inland plantation town.[29] Town growth was
in fact vulnerable to the fortunes of the town patrons. This is
obvious at the lower end of the scale. Virginia underwent a number
of changes of ownership, eluded incorporation and only had about
19 male inhabitants by the 1630s.[30] The 'new town' of Killybegs had
only some 17 'British and Irish inhabitants' in 1622. Here the patron
Roger Jones was constable of Sligo, his right to the town lands was
disputed by the bishop of Raphoe and the town was later disposed
of to a local Scottish undertaker, the Earl of Annandale.[31] For the
most of the period the bishops did not live at Clogher.[32] It is
tempting to suggest that too many of the towns were granted to
servitors who did not have an immediate English or Scottish
background from which to draw settlers. Certainly, at some towns
set in servitors' areas (for example Virginia), where the landlords
generally were not required to introduce settlers, growth was smallest. This applies to some extent to Ballyshannon, a servitor town
(like Donegal) essentially of 'Irish houses' lived in by 'soldiers for the
most part and some few Irish' and set in an exceptional area of the
plantation, the barony of Tirhugh, where the settler colony achieved
was a sparse one.[33] An important consideration was whether the
landlord built houses or availed of the option of the building lease.
At Augher the latter took place and growth there was relatively
small.[34] Also, it would be wrong to suggest that the towns had
entirely stable populations: there seems to have been both movement out of the towns and between towns.[35]

Population figures cited so far refer only to British adult males.
Plantation regulation only expressly forbad the leasing of town land

[28] B. L., Add. MS 4756, f. 115v; *Cal. Carew MSS, 1603–24*, p. 221. Its size has been concealed
by the absence of a muster return in 1630.
[29] Hunter, 'Enniskillen', pp 340–9. However for a number of towns which were based on forts
without land grants to patrons and therefore technically outside of the formal plantation, e.g.
Charlemont, there is no adequate documentation.
[30] R. J. Hunter, 'An Ulster plantation town—Virginia', in *Breifne*, iv, no. 13 (1970), pp 43–51.
[31] B.L., Add. MS 4756, f. 114v; P.R.O.I., C.P., W/65; T.C.D., MS 550, pp 224–5; *Cal pat.
rolls Ire., Jas I*, p. 300.
[32] M. Perceval-Maxwell, *The Scottish migration to Ulster in the reign of James I* (London,
1973), p. 262.
[33] B.L., Add. MS 4756, f. 113v.
[34] P.R.O.I., D 4859; B.L., Add. MS 4756, f. 111v; Hill, *Plantation,* p. 540; Emanuel Ley's
certificate, 1622 (N.L.I., MS 8014/viii); notes by commissioners in 1622 on Clogher barony
(ibid.).
[35] Hunter, 'Enniskillen', p. 347.

to Irish, though a clause in a lease of a house in Enniskillen made in 1634 by the then provost, Gerald Wiggen, stipulating that the tenant should not 'alien set or let the aforesaid premises . . . unto any of the mere Irish nation' suggests that a wider exclusion was intended.[36] There was, however, a small Irish element in the population of many of the towns, not just in Armagh and Cavan where up to 1641 settlers were probably a minority. Irish residents in Dungannon were a significant minority; the name of Farrell O'Reilly, tobacco merchant, of Belturbet survives.[37] At Derry there were two priests in the *parish* in 1631 and the prior of the Dominicans there had a silver chalice made in 1640.[38] Not only were there some Irish householders within the walls, but the suburbs housed a settler and seemingly also an Irish population of considerable size. Roger Markham who was ironmaster to Sir Thomas Staples of Lissan, who had been lease-holder of the bishop's land in the immediate vicinity of the city, stated in his deposition in February 1642: 'It had been often desired by my master and others that they would put the Irish out of Derry which we heard they did, 300 men in one day and pulled down the suburbs'.[39]

Urban growth of this scale need not be surprising. The plantation plan had set a realistic target of some 5,000 adult males for the plantation as a whole.[40] This was in fact well surpassed and towns had grown proportionally. However the plan also militated against substantial concentrated urban growth by prescribing a settlement pattern to be based on landlord villages on each undertaker's estate. The kind of settlement pattern that did emerge was in fact a compromise varying from estate to estate between dispersed and village settlement. While many villages were smaller than ten houses, some, for example Lurgan, Lisnaskea, Letterkenny, Ramelton and Rathmullan, were of forty and above.[41] Only if the Belturbet arrangement had been somehow adapted, after the model agreed with the Londoners for Derry and Coleraine, perhaps to promote one town per county, might comparable systematic urban development have taken place in the other counties. Also the

[36] P.R.O.I., D 1040. Towns in undertakers' baronies were probably considered to be covered by the general exclusion of Irish intended in those areas.
[37] Certificate by provost of Dungannon and others, 1622 (N.L.I., MS 8014/viii); T.C.D., MS 832, ff 166, 166v, MS 833, f. 36.
[38] W. P. Burke (ed.), 'The diocese of Derry in 1631' in *Archiv. Hib.*, v (1916), p. 3; [W. Doherty], *Derry Columbkille, souvenir of the centenary celebrations . . . of St Columba in . . . Derry, 1897–9* (Dublin, 1899), pp 103–7.
[39] C.L.R.O., Irish Society MSS, Great Parchment Book, f. A10; T.C.D., MS 839, f. 22.
[40] *Cal. S.P. Ire., 1615–25*, p. 224.
[41] Hill, *Plantation*, pp 477, 523, 524–5, 557; B.L., Add. MS 4756, f. 116v.

quantities of land granted to the town patrons (for example 730 statute acres to Capt. William Cole for Enniskillen, some 1,297 acres to Capt. John Ridgeway for Virginia) were minute in comparison to the amount of land (29,900 acres) held by the Irish Society in relation to Derry and Coleraine, and were in fact no larger than the allocations (for example 1,552 acres in County Armagh, 917 in Cavan) made available for the county schools.[42] The income from land of that quantity (some £60 per annum from the Augher lands)[43] was not sufficient to encourage a town patron to expend money in house building (twenty houses built by Sir Arthur Chichester at Dungannon may well have cost close to £100 each)[44] or in promoting immigration. Nevertheless, although the circumstances were very different, urban growth in the Ulster plantation compared favourably with its counterpart in colonial Virginia where what initial town growth there had been declined, and in the later colony of Maryland where by the 1670s the capital, St Mary's City, contained at most eighteen buildings.[45] The most fruitful comparison (religious matters aside) is probably between the two ports of Derry and Boston both with populations of between 1,000 and 2,000 by 1640 and some similarities in structure.[46] However, although the term town was applied to them by contemporaries, by English seventeenth-century standards most of the plantation towns were no larger than the average village with a population of less than 200. Comparison with the average English market town, with a population of about 1,000, should be restricted to the few

[42] Hunter, 'Enniskillen', p. 342; Moody, *Londonderry plantation,* p. 454; cartographic identification of land grants.
[43] T.C.D., MS 550, p. 175. In 1620 an arrangement was made whereby for five years £40 per annum out of the rents of the corporation lands should be expended on 'the building, enlarging and strengthening of Spur-Royal castle [the landlord's castle at Augher], and . . . building fit and necessary houses, edifices or buildings for and near or adjoining to the said castle' (P.R.O.I., D 4862).
[44] Certificate concerning manor of Dungannon, 1622 (N.L.I., MS 8014/ix). For house building costs in Derry see Moody, *Londonderry plantation,* pp 249, 254 and in Armagh Hunter, 'Towns', pp 59–60.
[45] W. E. Washburn, *Virginia under Charles I and Cromwell, 1625-60* (Williamsburg, Virginia, 1957), p. 2; L. G. Carr, 'The metropolis of Maryland: a comment on town development along the tobacco coast' in *Maryland Historical Magazine,* 69, no. 2 (Summer 1974), pp 124–45.
[46] For a valuable discussion of Boston at this time see D. B. Rutman, *Winthrop's Boston: portrait of a puritan town, 1630–49* (Chapel Hill, North Carolina, 1965). There may even have been some contemporary connections. Thus, Owen Roe of London, who exported tobacco to Derry (or possibly Coleraine) via Chester in 1634 (P.R.O., E190/1335/1, f. 53), can probably be identified with that Owen Roe of London who acquired a house and land in Boston in 1635 to which he dispatched servants and cattle and which he rented out as an absentee (Rutman, *Winthrop's Boston,* pp 83, 158).

larger towns. Even Derry must be regarded as 'micro-urban' in terms of one recent definition which would limit the term town in early modern England and Wales to settlements of 5,000 and above.[47]

The county towns fulfilled functions entirely independent of their size. After the plantation got underway, the assizes which had begun tentatively in Ulster a few years earlier, were held in the six county towns of Cavan, Enniskillen, Derry, Lifford, Dungannon and Armagh.[48] Also in Tyrone we have evidence that quarter sessions were held at Strabane (where a sessions house and prison, under the market cross, for the temporary custody of prisoners prior to their transfer to the king's gaol at Dungannon, had been erected), Augher and Dungannon; the arrangement which limited quarter sessions to Derry in the neighbouring county being probably exceptional.[49] Such county functions required public buildings. The allocation of sites for sessions houses and gaols was the responsibility of the town landlords, while their building was seen as a county responsibility. In August 1619 royal directions were issued for the erection of a sessions house and gaol in Armagh.[50] In moves not confined to Ulster counties the assize judges in 1619 and 1621 imposed fines on the county of Londonderry for failure to build a sessions house at Derry.[51] These pressures were not without effect. By 1622 £500 or £600 collected in Fermanagh and received by Sir William Cole had been expended in building a sessions house in Enniskillen and money had similarly been collected in County Cavan.[52] In Derry on the other hand a town hall costing at least £500 was erected by the Irish Society.[53] The sessions house in Dungannon erected between 1619 and 1622 at the charge of the county was of a crudely classical design. Timber-built, of 'extraordinary strong and curious cage work', supported by a 'rank of fair large turned pillars', it incorporated a market house on the ground floor. The gaol was a separate building, made of stone, battlemented and with 'strong

[47] Peter Clark and Paul Slack, *English towns in transition, 1500-1700* (Oxford, 1976), p. 19; Penelope Corfield, 'Urban development in England and Wales in the sixteenth and seventeenth centuries' in D. C. Coleman and A. H. John (ed.), *Trade, government and economy in pre-industrial England* (London, 1872), p. 62.

[48] J. F. Ferguson (ed.), 'Ulster roll of gaol delivery, 1613-18' in *U.J.A.*, 1st series, i (1853), pp 260-70, ii (1854), pp 25-8.

[49] P.R.O.N.I., T808/15090/1, 8, 16 (I am engaged on an edition of this document); Moody, *Londonderry plantation,* pp 114-5, 209.

[50] Hunter, 'Towns', p. 65.

[51] P.R.O.I., Ferguson MSS, ix, 198; Moody, *Londonderry plantation,* p. 285.

[52] Rich journal notes, 1 July 1622 (N.L.I., MS 8014/v).

[53] Moody, *Londonderry plantation,* pp 249, 254, 272.

vaults'—though not escape-proof—while the sessions house and gaol in Armagh were both in the same building.[54] Such building within the towns were the visual representation of fundamental political change in the six escheated counties. But there were limits to institutional building. No Ulster plantation town had a privately endowed almshouse or a county sponsored house of correction such as were, at least, receiving active consideration in County Cork, at Bandon and Mallow respectively, in 1634.[55]

The most common ancillary building operations were of bridges, churches and mills. Thus the ford of 1613 at Belturbet had been replaced by the bridge of 1641. Cole built two bridges at Enniskillen prior to 1613, demolished, incidentally, by him in 1641. The building of a new bridge at Charlemont was, after debate in the privy council in 1627, made an inter-county responsibility; it had been erected by 1634.[56] But here too there were limits to achievement. Thus at the Tyrone assizes in 1636 Sir Arthur Leigh of Omagh was fined £15 because at the previous assizes he had been paid for building a bridge at Omagh which he had not done.[57] Although there was a bridge beside the mill at Strabane, river crossings at Lifford, Derry and Coleraine were served by ferries.[58] Road maintenance between the towns fell to the appropriate parishes, whose inhabitants were often fined for their remissness.[59] Church building, or rebuilding, proceeded, often slowly 'as in all works of that nature' by means which included landlord building (conspicuous at Derry where the crown provided bells) and the application of the recusants' fines.[60] The principal constraint on public

[54] Certificate concerning manor of Dungannon, 1622 (N.L.I., MS 8014/ix); P.R.O.N.I., T808/15090/11; T.C.D., MS 836, ff 119–9v, 121, 133v.

[55] N.L.I., MS 13237/17–20. Licences to collect charitable contributions, issued by patent, appear as a means to deal with disasters, urban and individual, e.g. those to a Derryman and for the 'poor inhabitants' of Enniskillen 'which town has suffered much by fire', both in 1616 (*Cal. pat. rolls Ire., Jas I*, pp 304, 308). A system of parish alms was functioning in Derry by at least 1670 (R. Hayes (ed.), *The register of Derry cathedral (St Columb's), parish of Templemore, Londonderry, 1642–1703* (Parish Register Society of Dublin, Exeter and London, 1910), p. 206, also pp 207–9). An example of private benevolence to the poor at Derry, prior to 1637 (Moody and Simms (ed.), *Bishopric of Derry and Irish Society*, i, 219) many be taken along with one at Belfast, after 1623, 'being the first money left in that kind' (R. M. Young (ed.), *The town book of the corporation of Belfast, 1613–1816* (Belfast, 1892), p. 233).

[56] *Hastings MSS*, iv, 163, 167; T.C.D., MS 833, ff 265–6v, MS 835, ff 131–2; C. R. Elrington (ed.), *Works of Ussher* (Dublin, 1864), xv, 373–4; P.R.O.N.I., T808/15090/19.

[57] P.R.O.N.I., T808/15090/21.

[58] B. L., Add. MS 4576, f. 110; *Cal. pat. rolls Ire., Jas I*, pp 107, 182; Moody, *Londonderry plantation*, pp 148, 247–8, 250, 345.

[59] P.R.O.N.I., T808/15090/17, 18, 19, 22.

[60] Hunter, 'Enniskillen', p. 347; Moody, *Londonderry plantation*, pp 276–7; *Cal. pat. rolls Ire., Jas I*, p. 484.

works was inadequate urban income. Apart from Cavan, the corporations had not received grants of land by charter and such income as they had, for example from fairs and markets (themselves important but ill-documented urban functions), could not provide finance in any way appropriate to major operations. Thus when it was proposed to build a new quay at Derry in 1639, the building lease was the devise adopted. A consortium of leading townsmen undertook to expend £300 on the project.[61] Hence also only Derry and Coleraine were walled and so the defensive value of the towns was limited. Attempts were made to rectify this in later plantations, for example in Wexford where landholders were to pay by annual levy or cotization for the walling of Newborough (Gorey).[62] Nevertheless, the government, for reasons of economy, disposed of the inland forts in Ulster (and Connacht) around which a number of the towns were based, to the resident commanders, though under conditions of maintenance, in the early 1620s.[63]

Although it may be true of some of the smaller incorporated settlements that no 'course of corporation [was] observed' as Bishop Spottiswood, a hostile witness, asserted in the case of Augher, there is evidence, in the absence of all corporation books, that many of the town corporations did function with some continuity.[64] Thus what can be assembled of the succession of provosts of Strabane indicates that the members of the first nominated corporation of 1613 held the chief office in rotation amongst themselves as a closely-knit body.[65] The corporations of Enniskillen and Belturbet obtained privy council orders in their favour in disputes with the town patrons, and Belturbet had a silver mace.[66] Sir Richard Hansard made financial provision for the corporation of Lifford by will.[67] The provosts, like those of Strabane, were normally justices of the peace and can sometimes be found like Sir John Vaughan, mayor of Derry, in 1627, engaged in routine matters of legal administration.[68]

[61] C.L.R.O., Great Parchment Book, ff A24–4v; B. L., Harl. MS 2138, f. 188. It may be noted that the 'annual revenue' of Kilkenny as recorded in 1628 was £231.17.11 (Charles Vallancey (ed.), *Collectanea de rebus Hibernicis* (Dublin, 1781), ii, 398–412). For the property of the corporation of Kilkenny in 1639 see P.R.O.I., Lodge MSS, vi, 278–81.
[62] Hunter, 'Towns', p. 56.
[63] *Cal. pat. rolls Ire., Jas I*, pp 484–5. In 1622 the more important fortifications, where ordnance was located, were Ballyshannon, Derry, Charlemont, Mountjoy, Enniskillen and Mountnorris (List of 'brass' and iron ordnance in 1622 (N.L.I., MS 8013/vii)).
[64] T.C.D., MS 550, p. 175; see the lists of mayors of Derry and Coleraine in Moody, *Londonderry plantation*, pp 448–50.
[65] Bodl., Carte MS 62, f. 195; P.R.O.I., R.C. 3/8, pp 54–65; P.R.O.N.I., T808/15090.
[66] Hunter, 'Enniskillen', pp 345–6; B.L., Add. MS 4756, f. 102v; T.C.D., MS 833, ff 80–80v.
[67] B.L., Add. MS 19,841, f. 9v.
[68] P.R.O.N.I., T808/15090; B.L., Add. MS 19,841, ff 94–5.

Yet when in 1629 Bishop Downham of Derry wished the provost of
Strabane to take action likely to be unpopular with the landlord of
the town he wrote also to the landlord ordering him not to obstruct
the provost.[69] Internal order seems to have been the function of the
constable—Letterkenny, for example, had a constable and stocks.[70]
Townsmen were also subject to the control of the clerk of the
market, an official concerned with the regulation of prices, weights
and measures and standards, whose functions were given a new
impetus in Ireland, as in England, at this time.[71] A record survives of
fines inflicted by the deputy clerk of the market for County Tyrone
at his sessions held at Stewartstown, Augher, Clogher and Omagh
in January and February 1618.[72]

As centres for professional services—doctors, schoolmasters and
lawyers—many of the towns played important roles. Medical
practitioners can be found at least in Derry and Strabane and
possibly in Coleraine and Charlemont. In Derry two can be
identified, a 'chirurgeon' and, almost certainly, a physician as
householders in 1628. Four occur in the 1630s, three of them
surgeons or 'barber chirurgeons'.[73] A prominent Chester apothecary, Robert Blease, appears as supplier: he despatched 'drugs', five
boxes and one trunk of them, to Derry in January 1632.[74] By far the
most distinguished of these Derry doctors was the physician Paul de
Laune. Born in London, graduate of Cambridge, doctor of
medicine in Padua in 1614, and Fellow of the College of Physicians
in London in 1618, he was later in the 1640s professor of physic at
Gresham College and appears to have died acting as physician
general to the Cromwellian fleet at the taking of Jamaica in 1654.[75]
De Laune's period in Derry may have been relatively short, but
James Miller, chirurgeon, died in Derry in 1655 which suggests he
had practised there for some twenty years.[76] If some of these Derry
practitioners may have come there as army surgeons—one of them,

[69] P.R.O., S.P. 63/250, ff 69–77v; *Cal. S.P. Ire., 1625–32*, pp 509–13.
[70] B.L., Sloane MS 3827, ff 62–3v.
[71] *Cal. pat. rolls Ire., Jas I*, pp 565, 571. For the functions of the clerk of the market in England see Joan Thirsk (ed.), *The agrarian history of England and Wales* (Cambridge, 1967), iv, 578–9.
[72] P.R.O.N.I., T808/15090/2a.
[73] R. G. S. King (ed.), *A particular of the howses and famylyes in London Derry, May 15, 1628* (Derry, 1936), nos 85–6, 163; St Columb's Cathedral Chapter House, Tenison Groves MSS; C.L.R.O., Great Parchment Book, ff A8, A8v.
[74] P.R.O., E190/1334/14, f. 16; Cheshire Record Office, Chester, W.S. 1633. For further supplies of drugs from Chester in 1634 see P.R.O., E190/1335/1, ff 18, 53.
[75] William Munk, *The roll of the royal college of physicians of London* (London, 1878), i, 170–2.
[76] R. Hayes (ed.), *Register of Derry Cathedral*, p. 110.

William Walter, re-appears in that capacity in 1642[77]—Strabane was ungarrisoned, yet in 1629 it had its physician, Dr Berkeley, 'an apostate from the true religon', in the words of Bishop Downham 'having masses and meetings of priests in his house . . . [and] seeking to pervert whom he can especially on their deathbeds'.[78] As early as July 1614 William Wiggs, 'chirurgion', travelled with 'apothecary drugs and waters for his use' on a ship bound for Coleraine from Chester.[79] Dr Hodges, conscripted, unsuccessfully, to make gunpowder at Charlemont by Sir Philim O'Neill after the outbreak of the 1641 rising, must also have been a medical doctor.[80] A succession of schoolmasters served the county grammar schools located mainly in the county towns, each, except that in Derry, endowed with land as part of the plantation scheme, and there is evidence that buildings had been erected for these schools in at least a few towns. There is also evidence that schooling was not restricted to these centres. A schoolmaster at Stewartstown is recorded in 1622 and plans, at any rate, were being made to establish schools elsewhere, notably at Clogher and Lifford.[81] Lawyers may have been sparser: recorders (and a chamberlain) in Derry, Coleraine and Cavan are most conspicuous. However they carried out more functions than those purely of their office and may well have acted for litigants in the courts. Thus, Robert Goodwin, chamberlain of Derry, was also clerk of the peace for the county. Stephen Allen, king's attorney in Ulster, who lived in Cavan abbey, was not only recorder of the town and sovereign in 1641 but was also seneschal of thirteen manors in Counties Cavan, Fermanagh and Armagh.[82]

When we seek to examine the hinterlands and trade of the towns as a whole, an element of guarded speculation must intrude. The hinterland of Derry as a port can be shown, from identifiable destinations of imports, to have extended as far into Tyrone as Dungannon and to north-west Fermanagh. Strabane and presumably Lifford traded through it and there is ample evidence linking it with much of north Donegal. Its links in County Londonderry included Limavady and Desertmartin, yet the trade of Coleraine and its outports was also considerable.[83] Armagh (some-

---

[77] P.R.O., S.P. 28/120, f. 742v.
[78] P.R.O., S.P. 63/250, f. 77.
[79] P.R.O., E190/1330/11, f. 24v. It also unloaded at Derry.
[80] T.C.D., MS 836, f. 115v.
[81] For some discussion see my 'The Ulster plantation in the counties of Armagh and Cavan' (M. Litt thesis, University of Dublin, 1968), pp 629–38.
[82] Moody, *Londonderry plantation,* pp 448–50; Hunter 'Towns', p. 70; T.C.D., MS 832, ff 176–8.
[83] P.R.O., E190/1330/14, f. 21; E190/1332/1, *passim*; Derry port books, 1612–15 (Leeds City

what like Strabane in relation to Derry) was considered to be linked with Newry through Mountnorris and significantly some Drogheda merchants were amongst the first to build houses there.[84] Killybegs (and the west Donegal ports) had a seaborne trade of small proportions but was not a wide distributing centre. Thus while trade statistics in 1626 attribute some 12% of Irish herring exports to Killybegs, its share in land-based exports, butter and tallow, was negligible.[85] Furthermore such traces of this off-shore fishing industry as have been located in English port books reveal no participation of local vessels, English or Scottish shipping being involved. Many of the cargoes are noted as having been 'taken and killed' with the master's 'own nets and boats at his own proper costs'. Imports from England were minute.[86] Statistics for the 1630s and 1640–41 reveal very small exports of hogshead staves and pipe staves, hides and linen yarn.[87] Customs returns, for what they are worth, were, in the 1630s, amongst the smallest for the country as a whole, about ¼–½% of total returns.[88] Yet one local ship, the *Arthur* of Ballyshannon, which carried wine from Bordeaux in 1614–15 for Sir Henry Foliot, has come to light.[89] The three towns of Enniskillen, Belturbet and Cavan were, arguably, considerable centres of inland trade with boats in use at Enniskillen and Belturbet to avail of the navigational potential of the Erne.[90] Not only was there a carrying trade from County Cavan to Dublin and cattle were driven there from south Fermanagh,[91] but there is an accumulation of small pieces of evidence to link the trade of these three towns to Dublin also. Thus, for example, as early as 1612 a Belturbet merchant can be found importing goods from Liverpool through Dublin and the names of two Belturbet carriers in 1641 are recorded.[92] David Greer, one of a known group of Enniskillen

Council Libraries, Archives Dept., TN/P07/1/4a–d). As customary, for economy in foot-noting, detailed references within these port books are not cited. (I am engaged on an edition of the Ulster port books at Leeds.)

[84] Lambeth, Carew MS 630, f. 60v; T.C.D., MS 550, pp 1–2; Hunter 'Towns', p. 60.

[85] P.R.O., C.O. 388/85/A15 (I am grateful to Dr D. Dickson for this reference).

[86] P.R.O., E190/1329/9, ff 2, 2v; E190/1334/14, ff 2v–4 (fish shipments to Chester 1607 and 1634); E190/870/8, f. 8 (to Poole, 1611). For some Scottish connections, a visit by an East India Co. vessel and a pirate see B.L., Harl. MS 2138, ff 185v–6; Charles Conaghan, *History and antiquities of Killybegs* (Ballyshannon, 1974), pp 65–9.

[87] P.R.O., S.P. 63/259, ff 215v–25v (I am grateful to Professor M. Perceval-Maxwell for this reference).

[88] Leeds City Council Libraries, Archives Department, TN/P07/1/16–18.

[89] H. F. Kearney, 'The Irish wine trade' in *I.H.S.*, ix, no. 36 (Sept. 1955), p. 418.

[90] *Hastings MSS*, iv, 163; T.C.D., MS 832, f. 167; P.R.O.N.I., D1702/1/27/1; Hunter, 'Enniskillen', p. 348.

[91] T.C.D., MS 833, f. 144; MS 835, f. 48v.

[92] P.R.O., E190/1330/1, sub 22 July 1612; T.C.D., MS 833, ff 75, 256–6v.

merchants, exported yarn from Dublin to Liverpool in 1618.[93] In the 1630s a Dublin merchant and freeman of Cavan, John Gibson, became a major property owner in Cavan.[94] This attempt to set the towns in a regional context must, however, remain somewhat tentative.

The materials for occupational analysis are extremely restricted. The plantation surveys, when they reported on towns at all, referred only occasionally to occupations and then in very general terms. Scarcely more helpful is the pejorative description of the townsmen of Dungannon as 'shoemakers, saddlers and rascals' attributed to Patrick moder O'Donnelly in 1641.[95] Deeds and depositions provide occupations for only a minority of townsmen. In the case of Lurgan, a large village on an English estate in Armagh, however, a uniquely complete list of 47 householders in 1622 (holding 59 houses) with their occupations, can be analysed. Apart from a large agricultural group of 27, 4 gentlemen, 14 yeomen and 9 husbandmen, representing 57.4% of the names, 12 occupations are recorded, with coopers, joiners, turners and shoemakers represented more than once. Building trades, 1 carpenter and 1 mason, occupied only 4.3%; the largest group, 16 or 34%, being engaged in a number of simple manufacturing processes. Here 3 coopers, 4 joiners and 3 turners worked with wood, 2 shoemakers and 1 tanner with leather and in leather making, 1 weaver and 1 tailor in textiles, and there was one smith but no baker. Merchants and shopkeepers were represented by only 1 butcher (2.1%); there was only 1 labourer (2.1%), though perhaps more were sub-tenants. A miller can be inferred. The townsmen include two Irish names, a yeoman and a cooper. The tradesmen held areas of land also and were engaged in agriculture as well as providing services for the neighbourhood.[96] Other lists (surviving for Armagh and Tyrone) are less complete and concern smaller settlements. Of 30 leaseholders, 'indwellers of my town and certain land annexed to it dwelling about the church', listed by a Scot, Lord Ochiltree, also in 1622, for Stewartstown, 3 were gentlemen, 3 appear without occupation and 8 simply as tradesmen. Of the remaining 10 occupations, there were 3 butchers and 3 tailors, 2 weavers and 2 carpenters and 1 each of shoemakers, maltmakers, smiths, ditchers and quarriers as well as a school-

[93] P.R.O., E190/1331/8, sub April 1618. He and another Enniskillen merchant also had a connection with Drogheda (Hunter, 'Enniskillen', pp 347–8).
[94] Hunter, 'Towns', p. 72.
[95] J. J. Marshall, *History of Dungannon* (Dungannon, 1929), p. 119.
[96] Formerly P.R.O., Manchester Papers, 30/15/2/183 (location now unknown: N.L.I., Microfilm, Positive 6034).

master.[97] A petition in 1622 'of the poor tradesmen' of Clogher for relief from payment of 'trades money' to the dean originated from 9 individuals, probably the leading townsmen: 2 merchants, a cordwainer, a weaver, a tailor, a cooper, a carpenter, a sadler and a butcher.[98] Trades at Benburb included a pointmaker and a clothmaker.[99] Such a range of occupations is likely to represent the common core of pursuits in most of the small inland towns. Some more specialist crafts emerge by 1641, mainly from depositions: metal-workers (a brazier in Virginia, a gunsmith in Belturbet, a snapmaker in Strabane),[100] and others such as a feltmaker, a buttonmaker and a heel maker.[101] Such occupations may well have been more common. Innkeepers appear not only in county towns such as Armagh and Cavan, but also elsewhere.[102] Keepers of alehouses and winetaverns ('tap-houses' in Derry) were widespread.[103] While it is obvious that considerable allowance must be made for deficiency of sources, the wide range of manufactured goods which was imported tends to support the view that most towns must have had a fairly simple occupational structure.

The formation of a settler merchant and shopkeeping element in many of the towns, some of whom also held land on neighbouring estates, was a development of especial significance. Although merchants are not specifically mentioned in the landlord villages already examined, these were probably served, apart from pedlars and stalls at fairs and markets, by out-shops kept by merchants, such as that of John Gowrly, merchant of Armagh, at Loughgall.[104] The treatment which follows of the merchant class in Belturbet and Strabane, the one English the other Scottish, and of that in the port town of Derry, throws some light on the minimum size of the merchant community in three towns of average, large and largest population. It is not suggested that these provincial merchants had

[97] Certificate to commissioners in 1622 (N.L.I., MS 8014/viii); M. Perceval-Maxwell, *Scottish migration,* p. 277.
[98] N.L.I., MS 8014/viii.
[99] N.L.I., MS 8014/ix.
[100] R. J. Hunter, 'An Ulster plantation town—Virginia' in *Breifne,* iv, no. 13 (1970), p. 49; T.C.D., MS 833, ff 265-6v; Gertrude Thrift (ed.), *Indexes to Irish wills* (London, 1920), v, 148. Snapmaker, a maker of dental instruments (O.E.D.), but perhaps a snaphance maker.
[101] These examples come from Belturbet and the village of Farnham, Co. Cavan (T.C.D., MS 832, f. 129; MS 833, ff 148, 295-6v).
[102] T.C.D., MS 833, f. 268 (Cavan); MS 836, ff 100 (Armagh), 112 (Markethill): MS 833, ff 6-7v (Belturbet, here the innkeeper also operated a tanhouse). The dual occupation of butcher and innkeeper is found in Newtownbutler (MS 835, f. 158).
[103] D. A. Chart (ed.), *Londonderry and the London companies, 1609-29* (Belfast, 1928), p. 105; *Cal. pat. rolls Ire., Jas I,* pp 261, 267, 343, 431.
[104] B.L., Harl. MS 2138, ff 180, 182, 186; P.R.O.I., C.P., U/66; T.C.D., MS 836, ff 57-7v.

an exclusive control of trade—landowners sometimes traded in their own right; English and Scottish merchants operated through the ports; the role of merchants from the ports of Drogheda and Dundalk, while obscure, must have been considerable; old Irish merchants were important in Cavan and Armagh—but their presence represents a significant change in post-plantation society.

In Belturbet at the time of its occupation in 1641 there were, on the evidence of a deposition of Februrary 1643-4, four principal merchants specified by name whose 'houses, shops and goods' were, it was alleged, after a division of 'all the merchants shops there' occupied by individual members of the O'Reilly leadership including Phillip McHugh, 'the rest of the shops (being all very rich)' having been shared amongst his followers.[105] The depositions of four Belturbet merchants (two from the suggested more substantial group and two others) taken earlier, on separate dates in 1642 offer some corroboration: the larger merchants claimed losses in 'wares' much higher than the others. Also one of the smaller merchants specified the commodities: 'wares in the shop vizt broadcloth, kersies, frizes, hops, iron, steel, stockings, tobacco'—goods similar though perhaps more limited in range to those being imported by other Ulster merchants of this period—which he valued at £300. The degree of exaggeration in claims is hard to determine—two of the larger merchants claimed for £500 and £900, but in the latter case his son-in-law gave a figure of £700. In all, the names of eight merchants from a town with thirty-four houses in 1622 but probably larger by 1641 have been recovered from these sources.[106]

At Strabane evidence of a different kind throws light on a larger group of merchants, Scottish in origin. Here seven of the twelve first burgesses of the town are also to be found trading in the surviving port books of Derry for 1612-15, along with at least one other Strabane townsman, David Morrison.[107] The names of four more Strabane merchants of this period, though nothing of their trading context, can also be recovered.[108] The commodities imported demonstrate that the merchants dealt in a wide range of goods, domestic, agricultural and industrial. Thus, for example, David Morrison imported on the *John* of Dumbarton in January 1615 goods as varied as soap, fat madder (used for dyeing), iron and wrought iron, brass pans, iron pots, lead, woollen and course linen

[105] T.C.D., MS 833, ff 265-6v.
[106] T.C.D., MS 832, ff 223, 227; MS 833, ff 98-9v, 114-6, 189-9v.
[107] Leeds City Council Libraries, Archives Dept., TN/P07/1/4a-d; *Cal. pat. rolls Ire., Jas I,* p. 307.
[108] Ibid. p. 306.

cloth and aniseeds. Salt, including French salt (for the preparation of hides), was a significant import for industrial use; nets and ropes also appear 'for the fishings'. The activities in the year 1614–15 of William Hamilton, who became a freeholder in the town in 1616 and later held one townland on the earl of Abercorn's estate as well,[109] illustrate the nature of the export trade. His total exports, in three consignments, were made up of 13½ dickers (135) of hides, 3 barrels and 2 hogsheads (i.e. 7 barrels) of beef, 1½ cwt. of tallow, 6 barrels of oatmeal and 100 goat skins valued in total at £87.13.4. The destination of these goods, carried in Scottish ships, was Scotland, especially Glasgow and Renfrew. His imports were slighter: 3 half barrels of onions, 8 yards of grey cloth and ½ ton of salt. The career of Hugh Hamilton illustrates best that of the successful merchant with a considerable rural base. Born a third son in Lanarkshire, he was apprenticed in Edinburgh in 1603.[110] During the two years 3 October 1612 to 5 September 1614 he exported 'goods' valued at £215.10.0 to France and to Ayr in Scotland. His imports in the same period were made up of 79 tuns of French wines and 'goods' valued at £33.3.4. In 1615, when he was already living outside the town, he became a freeholder on the earl of Abercorn's estate, empowered to pay his rent (£6E per annum) either in money or merchandize—wine, pepper, loaf sugar and marmalade. He was also a freeholder on another estate in the Strabane barony. He was provost of Strabane in 1625.[111] By the time of his death in 1637 he had acquired interests in abbey land nearby, bequeathed, along with 'houses in Strabane', in his will.[112]

The investigation of the Strabane merchant community over a more extended period is hindered by intractable problems of sources. Some reconstruction can be made from English port books. Linen yarn was the principal commodity exported by two merchants, John Patterson and Hugh Kneeland, identified as Strabane townsmen in 1630,[113] to Chester in 1632.[114] The commodities imported in return illuminate the trade of the non-specialist merchant. Thus John Patterson's imports, in July, valued at over £40, included hardware (240 sickles and 12 lanthornes) and

[109] P.R.O.N.I., D.O.D., 623/7; Cal. pat. rolls Ire., Jas I, p. 306; County of Huntingdon and Peterborough Record Office, Kimbolton MSS, dd M70/35.
[110] G. Hamilton, A history of the house of Hamilton (Edinburgh, 1933), pp 716–7.
[111] P.R.O.N.I, D.O.D. 623/6; Perceval-Maxwell, Scottish migration, p. 275; Civil Survey, iii, 393; P.R.O.N.I., T808/15090/8.
[112] P.R.O.N.I, T808/6461; Civil Survey, iii, 401; Cal. pat. rolls Ire., Jas I, p. 183.
[113] B.L., Add. MS 4770, ff 94v, 97.
[114] P.R.O., E190/1334/14, f. 7v (also 100 calfskins).

drapery.[115] James Gibb, provost of Strabane in 1630, brother-in-law of Hugh Hamilton and one of the executors of his will,[116] emerges in the 1630s as a merchant trading with both Chester and Bristol. From Chester he imported commodities such as Sheffield knives and nails along with cloth of varied type—northern kersey, cottons, broad cloth and northern dozens singles—and kersey stockings. His imports from Bristol, to which he (probably) exported, in 1638, tallow, beef, wool, skins, butter, salt, hides and white herrings, were apparently more specialised: 'parcels of wares', i.e. pottery, appear in 1637, conveyed in a Derry ship, the *Margaret,* which traded regularly with Bristol.[117] Clearly no broad conclusions can be based on such minutiae; without them, in the absence of all other sources, a sizeable Strabane merchant community would remain entirely obscure.

Against this general background, the unique scale of development at Derry becomes readily apparent.[118] Here an allocation of land to the townsmen, carried out in 1616 by commissioners appointed by the city of London, contrasting sharply with the potential of the superintendancy grants elsewhere, forms an element in a coherent town plan. The householder normally received in leasehold, for thirty-one years, two distinct pieces of land: an area of perches 'for gardens and orchards' in the immediate surrounds of the town outside the walls, and, separated by episcopal land,[119] an area of acres, usually six to twelve, in the liberties to the north.[120] These allocations came to 45 and 1,142 acres in nominal Irish measure.[121] Earlier, by 1614, the corporation as a body had been assigned a notional 1,500 acres (some 3,482 statute) to the south-west of the city which was successfully claimed as episcopal by the bishop in the 1630s but continued to be held under him in lease by the corporation.[122] The remainder of the notional 4,000 acres held by the Irish Society in the Derry liberties was leased in larger areas, some to pre-plantation servitors such as Sir John Vaughan, or allocated to the keeper of Culmore fort.[123]

[115] Ibid., ff 29, 48v. Port books of this period are often unsatisfactory for the detail of consignments with a high proportion of the goods recorded as 'other wares'.
[116] B.L., Add. MS 4770, f. 94v; P.R.O.N.I., T808/6461.
[117] P.R.O., E190/1334/14, ff 28v, 48v; E190/1136/8, f. 14v, /10, f. 8.
[118] Moody, *Londonderry plantation,* passim.
[119] P.R.O.I., Q.R.O., Down Survey trace no. 98.
[120] C.L.R.O., Jor. 30, ff 135v, 138v, Great Parchment Book, ff A1–A26.
[121] Calculations based on 1628 rental (King (ed.), *Howses and famylyes*).
[122] Chart (ed.), *Londonderry and the London companies,* p. 45; Moody and Simms (ed.), *Bishopric of Derry and Irish Society,* i, 220; P.R.O.I., Lodge MSS, v, 470; Moody, *Londonderry plantation,* pp 392–3.
[123] C.L.R.O., Great Parchment Book, ff A1–A26; Moody, *Londonderry plantation,* p. 251.

This grander scale of urban organisation is reflected in the trade and occupational structure of the town. Although it had been disrupted by O'Doherty's rising in 1608, the Londoners not only inherited from Docwra's pre-plantation settlement a nucleus of townsmen including some who were to be amongst its most dynamic as merchants and shipmasters, but also its embryonic trade links with Scotland and with at least the English ports of Liverpool and Chester.[124] The port books of 1612 to 1615 reveal an established pattern of trade. It divides into three sections—Scottish, English and foreign European. In the year 1614–15 these three sectors appear to be represented by 44%, 31% and 25% respectively of exported goods valued in total at £9,935. The port books show a growth in the total volume of Derry's trade, itself double that of Coleraine, over these three years.[125] They also indicate the size and character of the town's merchant class. Out of more than 100 people (excluding shipmasters), mostly English and Scottish merchants but also some local landowners, trading, some twenty Derry merchants can be identified.[126] Amongst them were the three most active merchants, themselves representative of important strands in the town's population—Jesse Smith, probably freeman of Chester in 1585, a pre-plantation settler in Derry who was made a member of the town corporation in 1613 and was mayor in 1620;[127] George Hammond, of a family with London connections, who settled under the Londoners;[128] and John Power (or Poore) a Scot.[129] Smith and Hammond traded almost exclusively with Chester; Power added trade with Scotland to an extensive and largely export European trade with Bordeaux (whence he imported wine, sugar, whale bone and prunes), Dieppe, Bilbao and Rouen.[130] The merchant class in Derry was complemented by its ships and shipmasters, who usually traded in their own right. Seven ships (one a 'small boat of Lough Foyle') were already engaged actively in the trade of the town. In the

[124] P.R.O., E190/1329/9, E190/1328/11; information supplied by Mr J. D. Galbraith, Scottish Record Office.

[125] For a discussion of the Scottish trade see Perceval-Maxwell, *Scottish migration*, pp 290–303.

[126] English port books of this period were useful for identifications. The findings here are based on work in progress and are somewhat tentative.

[127] J. H. E. Bennett (ed.), *The rolls of the freemen of Chester* (The record society for the publication of original documents relating to Lancashire and Cheshire, 51, 1906), i, 60; Moody, *Londonderry plantation*, pp 132, 349, 448.

[128] Chart (ed.), *Londonderry and the London companies*, p. 114.

[129] *Cal. pat. rolls Ire., Jas I*, p. 307.

[130] His exports in the year 1614–15, all to Dieppe and Bilbao and valued at £1,212.19.8, were as follows: 93 tuns and 3 hogsheads salmon, 60 dicker hides, 57½ cwt. tallow, 1 cwt. 'yarnon' and 3 cwt. wool.

year 1614–15 Derry shipping (including also *The Gift of God* of Strabane and the *Jannet* of Mongavlin) carried 18.5% of total exports. The largest Derry vessel, the *Peter,* burthen 70 tons, of which the master, Wybrand Olpherts, a Dutchman, later became a Donegal landowner,[131] was mainly engaged in importing timber ('meiborough deal') from Norway.

Mounting criticism of the County Londonderry plantation as a whole culminated in the forfeiture of the Londoners patent and the appointment of commissioners in 1639 to make new leases on behalf of the crown.[132] Although severely damaged by fire, a substantial section of a book of entries of these agreements survives for Derry which, when taken in conjunction with other sources, indicates a much greater diversity of occupations than has been found elsewhere.[133] The following 25 trades, divided among 47 people, only some 10% of the settler population, are recorded: tailors (5), bakers (4), butchers,[134] smiths and vintners (3 each), sadlers, joiners, coopers, feltmakers, chandlers, shoemakers and weavers (2 each) and one each of buttonmakers, tanners, winecoopers, victuallers, masons, fellmongers, brewers, beerbrewers, cutlers, glovers, glasiers, pewterers and slaters.

A merchant element of some twenty members which also emerges may well represent not much more than half their total numbers.[135] Some of these merchants, along with other townsmen, also held land. Thus Henry Finch, mayor in 1640[136] and a wine importer from France, not only re-leased his house, 'near unto the market place', with other holdings in the town and liberties and acquired business interests which included a share in the operation of the ferry in 1639, but also held land on the Fishmongers estate near Ballykelly.[137] Luke Ashe, a merchant prominent in the trade with Chester and an alderman, also owned a small area of land in County Donegal.[138] Both, while leading Derry townsmen with appropriate territorial

---

[131] B.L., Add. MS 4756, f. 117; P.R.O.I., Lodge MSS, vi, 224.

[132] Moody, *Londonderry plantation,* pp 398–405.

[133] C.L.R.O., Great Parchment Book, ff A1–A26; St Columb's Cathedral Chapter House, Derry, Tenison Groves MSS, extracts from Bramhall's account as sequestrator, 1634–9; R. Hayes (ed.), *Register of Derry Cathedral;* Moody and Simms (ed.), *Bishopric of Derry and Irish Society,* i, 189–90; *Census Ire., 1659,* pp 123–4.

[134] Includes two Irish names.

[135] Many people appear only with titles such as alderman, also the document is extremely defective.

[136] Moody, *Londonderry plantation,* p. 450.

[137] Derry port book, 25 March–29 September 1644 (N.L.I., MS 2559, p. 215); C.L.R.O., Great Parchment Book, ff A16, A17, A24–25, F6.

[138] P.R.O., E190/1334/14; Moody and Simms (ed.), *Bishopric of Derry and Irish Society,* i, 226–7; C.L.R.O., Great Parchment Book, ff A3–3v, A17, A20v; *Civil Survey,* iii, 106.

ambitions, were representative figures in its trade. The existence in this period of a merchant fleet of at least eight ships, commonly of thirty tons burthen, has been established mainly from English port books.[139] These ships are likely to have employed some forty Derry seamen.[140] The trade of the town generated work for carmen, found in the 1630s, and labourers of various kinds, including porters who appear as mainly Irish in the parish register in the 1650s.[141] A tanhouse, held by Edward Rowley of Castle Roe, is the only specifically industrial premises to emerge in 1639.[142] Professional men included medical practitioners and civic officials, already noted, as well as clergy and a schoolmaster with whom may be linked a land surveyor (probably a by-employment) and various customs officials.[143] In sum, a wide range of some thirty-five occupations can be established. It is also worth noting that where evidence of literacy can be recovered sixty-four signed by name and twenty-three by mark in 1639.

In contrast to imports of extraordinary variety, the essential components in the export trade of Derry were basic agricultural products along with fish and, at least in the 1630s, timber.[144] Livestock products, hides, sheepskins, wool, beef and tallow; grain, especially oats and barley; linen yarn and salmon predominate in the early port books. With all port books before 1644 missing, trends in the nature and direction of the town's trade are difficult to establish. If Scottish trade declined until the late 1620s, all recorded exports (only three cargoes) in the period 25 March–29 September 1644 were to Scotland.[145] English port books suggest that the pattern established by 1615 in trade with England, principally with Chester, was sustained, and it also seems certain that the earlier European contacts were continued.[146] Imports in 1644 included, wine, vinegar and salt from France and timber (deal) from

[139] P.R.O., E190/1332/1, E190/1335/1, E190/1336/3, E190/1136/8, E190/949/1; N.L.I., MS 2559, p. 215.
[140] Similar Cheshire vessels carried crews of this magnitude (Donald Woodward, 'Ships, masters and shipowners of the Wirral 1550-1650' in *The Mariner's Mirror*, lxiii (1977), p. 235).
[141] Moody and Simms (ed.), *Bishopric of Derry and Irish Society*, i, 190; R. Hayes (ed.), *Register of Derry Cathedral*, pp 9-64, 70-101, 107-121.
[142] C.L.R.O., Great Parchment Book, f. A1.
[143] J. B. Leslie, *Derry clergy and parishes* (Enniskillen, 1937), pp 31-3; St Columb's Cathedral, Derry, Tenison Groves's extracts from Bramhall's account; Moody and Simms (ed.), *Bishopric of Derry and Irish Society*, i, 231; B.L., Harl. MS 2138, ff 185-9. Account should also be taken of garrison soldiers.
[144] P.R.O., S.P. 63/259, ff 223v-4.
[145] Perceval-Maxwell, *Scottish migration*, pp 303-8; N.L.I., MS 2559, p. 217.
[146] For salmon exports to the Straits in 1638-9 see Moody, *Londonderry plantation*, p. 348.

Norway[147] In October 1637 Charles Moncke, surveyor-general of the customs, found at Derry 'more ships from foreign parts and England than in all the northern ports besides'.[148] A cargo of tobacco ('4,000 wt.' i.e. 2 tons), entered in September 1644 from Barbados, possibly a wartime stray, may provide a glimpse of a recent transatlantic dimension in trade.[149] If so, then the possibility of such trade, put forward in 1609 with reference to Newfoundland as an inducement to the Londoners,[150] had come to some fruition. Exports of at least linen yarn and wool appear to have expanded considerably by the 1630s.[151] To the more important question of the share of Derry in Irish trade as a whole the answer can only be approximate. Calculations based on customs returns for various half years between 1632 and 1635 and in 1641 place it in the range of from 3% to just over 5%.[152] In the light of these estimates, the document printed as Table II would seem to fit Derry tolerably enough within the over-all framework.

Though the degree of urbanisation achieved was limited, in fulfilling the various functions they did, Ulster plantation towns in this period underwent developments of very great significance.

[147] N.L.I., MS 2559, p. 215.
[148] B.L., Harl. MS 2138, f. 185.
[149] N.L.I., MS 2559, p. 215.
[150] *Cal. S.P. Ire., 1608–10,* p. 209.
[151] P.R.O., S.P. 63/259, ff 217v–20v. Average exports of linen yarn over the five years 1635–9, some 106 packs per year, can only be compared with the total from the port book of 1614–15, 31¾ packs. (I owe this latter figure to Mr Donald Woodward). Wool exports, for Derry and Coleraine jointly, over the period 1632–40 were more than double their 1614–15 quantity.
[152] Leeds City Council Libraries, Archives Dept., TN/P07/1/16–18; P.R.O., S.P. 63/259, f. 225. The corresponding figures for Coleraine were 0.3–1% and for Dublin 24–38%. Officials at Derry and Coleraine were said, however, in 1637 to under-value the book of rates (B.L., Harl. MS 2138, f. 187v).

Table I

Proposed towns 1609	Proposed towns 1611	Towns incorporated
Dungannon	Dungannon	Dungannon 27 Nov. 1612
Clogher		Clogher c. 1629–34
Omagh	Omagh	
Loughinsholin		
Mountjoy	Mountjoy	
	Strabane	Strabane 18 March 1613
		Augher 15 April 1613
Limavady	Limavady	Limavady 30 March 1613
Dungiven		
	Coleraine	Coleraine 28 June 1613
Derry	*Derry*	Londonderry 29 Mar. 1913
Lifford	Lifford	Lifford 27 Feb. 1613
Ballyshannon	Ballyshannon	Ballyshannon 23 Mar. 1613
Killybegs		Killybegs 14 Dec. 1615
Donegal	Donegal	Donegal 27 Feb. 1613
Raphoe		
Rathmullan	Rathmullan	
Dowagh in Innishowen		
Lisgoole		
Castleskeagh ⎤		
middle way between ⎟		
Lisgoole and ⎟		
Ballyshannon ⎦		
	Enniskillen	Enniskillen 27 Feb. 1613
Cavan	*Cavan*	Cavan 15 Nov. 1610
Belturbet	Belturbet	Belturbet 30 March 1613
midway between ⎤	Lough Ramor	
Kells and Cavan ⎦		
Armagh	Armagh	Armagh 26 March 1613
Mountnorris	Mountnorris	
Charlemont	Charlemont	Charlemont 28 April 1613
Tandragee		

Italicisation indicates that incorporation had taken place by this time.
(I am very grateful to the editor of *Studia Hibernica* for permission to reprint this from no. 11 (1971), p. 79).

Table II

A CONTEMPORARY SYNOPSIS OF IRISH CUSTOMS RETURNS, PROBABLY LATE 1630s

Rates or Magnitudes	Ports	Proportion per cent
I	Dublin	41
II	Cork	10
III	Waterford	7
	Galway	7
IV	Limerick	5
	Kinsale	5
	Youghal	5
V	Drogheda	3
	Londonderry	3
	Carrickfergus	3
VI	Ross 1½	1
	Wexford	1
	Dundalk	1
	Baltimore	1
	Sligo	1
Under Rate or Minute	Killybegs	½
	Dungarvan	½
	Donnaghadee	½
	Strangford	⅓
	Coleraine	⅓
	Dingle	⅓

This table (P.R.O., S.P. 63/276, ff 30–30v) which is undated requires more critical attention than is appropriate here. It is headed as follows:
Comparing together the proceed of the duty for six years of this last farm received from the several ports of Ireland. They may be thus ranked in classes according to their worth respectively and will at a medium be found to bear each to other very near these proportions expressed in whole numbers without fractions for more clearness of apprehension.
It is endorsed 'Dr Woods remarques concerning the exports and imports of Ireland', and, in a later hand, P. 12, F. 337.5.
A transcript of this Crown-copyright record in the Public Record Office appears by permission of the Controller of H.M. Stationery Office. I am grateful to Professor M. Perceval-Maxwell for bringing it to my attention.

Armagh 1770: Portrait of an Urban Community

Leslie Clarkson

I

Economic historians habitually borrow baggage from the social sciences. This article's particular portmanteaux are labelled 'urban characteristics' and 'community studies', and before proceeding with a portrait of Armagh in 1770 a little must be said about both concepts.

The first borrowing—'urban characteristics'—is second hand. Until the recent resurgence of urban history in Britain and North America, histories of towns usually concentrated on their legal and physical features; and, insofar as they studied urban dwellers, dealt principally with leading citizens. Towns are now seen, more fashionably, as places possessing special demographic and social characteristics and fulfilling particular administrative, cultural and economic functions. These are paths pioneered by sociologists along which urban historians have followed.[1] In painting this portrait of late eighteenth-century Armagh, I have been guided by recent work on pre-industrial towns in England.[2]

The second sociological borrowing—'community studies'—is more direct but necessarily more selective, for sociologists, in the manner of their craft, have identified nearly one hundred different

[1] See the discussion by Stephen Thernstrom, 'Reflections on the new urban history' in *Daedalus*, 100 (1971), pp 359–75.
[2] E.g. Peter Clark and Paul Slack, *English towns in transition 1500-1700* (London, 1976); The Open University, *Course A322: English urban history, 1500-1780* (Milton Keynes, 1977).

meanings of 'community'.[3] The definition most appropriate to our purpose is that a community is 'an area of social living marked by some degree of *social coherence*. The bases of community are *locality* and *community sentiment*.'[4] It will be argued here that in 1770 the inhabitants of Armagh had a strong sense of belonging to a distinct locality and were united in pursuing specifically urban functions. This is not to suggest that Armagh's citizens consciously articulated community sentiments, nor is the existence of forces cutting across the sense of community denied. Nevertheless, this paper will hope to show that the people of Armagh possessed sufficient in common to permit us to speak of an urban community.

So much for concepts: now for evidence. This portrait is drawn principally from a census of the population of Armagh taken in 1770 by the Rev. Dr William Lodge on behalf of the archbishop.[5] Its purpose was probably to distinguish the numbers of Catholics, Presbyterians and members of the Established Church in the city and, as far as can be judged, Lodge did his work well.[6] Within each street Lodge grouped the inhabitants—there were 1948 in all—into 499 households, most of which contained a simple nuclear family; households containing several families or extended families were unusual.[7] Here is important, although not surprising, evidence about the structure of community in Armagh: its basic unit was the household. This contained the family in which individuals lived and died; and which was also the agency through which property was transmitted from generation to generation, and the institution within which much of the economic life of the town was conducted.[8]

Another feature of the census is worthy of note. Normally the only person for whom full information was given—christian name, sex, occupation and relogous denomination—was the head of the household. Other members were noted, not by name, but by their relationship to the head; occupations and denominations were recorded only if different from those of the head.[9] Since almost

---

[3] Alan Macfarlane, *Reconstructing historical communities* (Cambridge, 1977), p. 2.
[4] R. M. MacIver and C. H. Page, *Society: an introductory analysis* (London, 1950), p. 9. Italics in original.
[5] Armagh Public Library, 9/5/20.
[6] The compilation of the census and its reliability are discussed in my two articles: 'Household and family structure in Armagh City, 1770' in *Local Population Studies*, no. 20 (1978), pp 14–31; 'An anatomy of an Irish town: the economy of Armagh, 1770' in *Irish Econ. and Social Hist.*, v (1978), pp 27–45. Lodge made no attempt to survey the population of the whole parish of Armagh.
[7] Clarkson, 'Household and family structure', loc. cit., pp 19, 29.
[8] Clarkson, 'The economy of Armagh', loc. cit., pp 30–1.
[9] Thus a typical entry runs: Market Street, John McLaghlin and wife; barber; five children; Presbyterian. From this we can distinguish a single family household comprising seven people and two generations. All may be assumed to be Presbyterians.

eighty per cent of household heads were males,[10] it follows that Lodge focussed attention on men. We may regret that women and children in our portrait are shadowy figures, but we may be sure that we are presenting the true position in 1770. In Lodge's time society was composed of households and families, the public face of which was sternly masculine.

Several sources have been used to supplement the census of 1770. These include the Church of Ireland parish register for the 1750s and the 1770s. Unfortunately the crucial years 1758–75 are missing and the register casts little light on Catholics and Presbyterians.[11] Another source is the *Belfast News-Letter,* giving vivid but brief glimpses of a few Armagh citizens. The corporation book for the period 1738–1818[12] provides further evidence, as do estate records and contemporary and near-contemporary descriptions of the town in the *Irish House of Commons Journals,* the works of Arthur Young, Sir Charles Coote and, most valuable of all, James Stuart. Stuart published his *Historical Memoirs of the City of Armagh* in 1819, but he was born and educated in the city, and knew many inhabitants whose memories stretched back to 1770 and beyond.[13] The modern anthropologist has his note book containing his interviews: the historian of Armagh has the gossipy pages of Stuart recounting many intimate details of the lives of its people. From Stuart and other sources we can cull information for about one-quarter of the householders appearing in the census, a small proportion, admittedly, but adequate to give depth to our portrait.

II

Before examining the urban functions making Armagh a community, three objections to the argument must be considered. The first is that Armagh was not one community, but three: Church of Ireland, Presbyterian and Catholic, possessing different values and beliefs, influenced by different traditions and even hostile to

[10] Clarkson, 'Household and family structure', p. 27.
[11] The Church of Ireland register runs from 1751 to 1758 and from late 1775 to 1805 (baptisms and marriages); and from 1750 to 1758 and from September 1770 to 1805 (burials) (P.R.O.N.I., T679/140). There are no Presbyterian registers for Armagh for the period 1729–96 and no Catholic registers before 1796.
[12] In the Armagh Public Library; partial transcripts in Public Record Office, Northern Ireland.
[13] Stuart was the son of Benjamin Basnett Stuart of Scotch Street who died in 1778 (J. Stuart, *Historical memoirs of the city of Armagh* (Newry, 1819), p. 417). Benjaman Stuart was probably 'Mr Stewart' a linen merchant of Scotch Street listed in the census. The Stuart family were related to the Ogle family who were prominent in Armagh (ibid., p. 511).

one another. The second is that there were class divisions, based on economic differences, undermining the unity of society. The third is that many inhabitants of Armagh were recent arrivals to the city and as newcomers felt themselves to be outsiders and not part of a community.

The most obvious fragmenting force was religion. The history of Armagh from the early seventeenth century created a dichotomy between Catholics and Protestants that was reflected in Lodge's labelling of households according to denominations. As Table I shows, nearly forty-two per cent of households were Catholic, thirty-two per cent Church of Ireland, and the remainder Presbyterian.

Table I

HOUSEHOLDS BY DENOMINATION

	Number	*Per Cent*
Church of Ireland	156	31.7
Presbyterian	132	26.8
Catholic	204	41.5
	492	100.0
Not known	7	
	499	

Although the city was physically small, there were clearly defined Catholic and Protestant districts. Fifty-four per cent of Catholic households were in just three streets, Callen, Irish and Castle. On the other hand, there were six streets, Market, Little Meeting, Church, English, Scotch and New (the present Thomas and Ogle), dominated by Protestants. In general, Protestants were clustered around the commercial centre and Catholics were more numerous on the peripheries. There was no significant differences in the geographical distribution of Church of Ireland and Presbyterian households.

There were occupational differences between Catholics, the Established Church and Presbyterians, as can be seen from Table II. Catholics monopolized labouring, supplying sixty-one out of seventy labourers in Armagh. Conversely, adherents of the Church of Ireland provided thirty out of thirty-five people in government and the professions. Presbyterians were more concentrated in manufacture and trade, although their dominance here was less clear-cut than was the case with Catholics in labouring and the Established Church in the professions. Some of the reasons for these occupational differences are obvious. Law and traditions alike

84

Leslie Clarkson

largely reserved government and the professions to the Church of Ireland and made Catholics an economically deprived group. The Presbyterian prominence in manufactures and trade is harder to explain. In part it was merely the consequence of their relative insignificance in labouring and the professions, but it is tempting to see here some manifestation of the Protestant ethic.

Table II
PROPORTION OF HOUSEHOLD HEADS IN FOUR OCCUPATIONAL
CATEGORIES, BY DENOMINATION[14]

	Church of Ireland Per cent	Presbyterian Per cent	Catholic Per cent
Manufacturing	21.6	31.7	17.2
Transport and trade	19.2	34.7	24.0
Government and the professions	19.2	7.8	2.5
Labouring	2.6	3.8	29.9

Catholics and Protestants differed also in the structure of households and families. These differences are summarised in Table III which shows that, although Church of Ireland households were on average larger than Presbyterian and Catholic households, the

Table III
THE STRUCTURE OF HOUSEHOLDS AND FAMILIES
BY DENOMINATION[15]

	Church of Ireland	Presbyterian	Catholic
Mean household size	4.12	3.90	3.81
Mean number of kin, servants and other persons per household	0.43	0.10	0.04
Mean size of conjugal family unit	3.69	3.80	3.77
Proportion of one-person households	17.3%	12.9%	8.8%
Proportion of families comprising parents and child(ren)	49.4%	50.0%	58.8%

conjugal family unit was slightly smaller. Church of Ireland households contained more servants and resident kin than either Presbyterian or Catholic; but Catholics had more households composed exclusively of parents and children and fewer one-person households.

[14] The occupational classifications are considered in detail in Clarkson, 'The economy of Armagh', loc. cit., pp 33–40, 44–5.
[15] For a detailed analysis and definitions see Clarkson, 'Household and family structure', loc. cit., pp 11–31.

Two conclusions can be deduced from these differences. First, Church of Ireland households were richer than the rest. They could afford to employ servants and support co-resident kin to a greater extent than the others. Second, the Catholic population was probably younger than the Protestant population. Generally speaking, people living alone were either widowed or unmarried adults and therefore relatively elderly; while members of conjugal families were usually adults of child-bearing or near child-bearing age, together with young children or adolescents. Thus Catholics were relatively under-represented among the elderly and over-represented among the young. The significance of these differences in age structure will be considered later.

There were, therefore, noticeable differences between the denominations but they did not, I think, create separate communities. The geographical segregation, for example, was not complete. The three Catholic streets of Callen, Irish and Castle, also contained about seventeen per cent of the Protestant population; while sixteen Catholic families lived in the mainly Protestant Scotch Street. Similarly, except for the professions and labouring, Catholic and Protestants shared many occupations. To give a single example, the city contained fourteen Church of Ireland publicans, fifteen Presbyterian, and sixteen Catholic. A larger proportion of Presbyterian householders were publicans than was the case with either Church of Ireland households or Catholics—a slightly unexpected outcome of the Protestant ethic. Finally, differences in household structures should not be exaggerated, for among all denominations the nuclear family household was the most common.

But what were the consequences of more fundamental divisions of belief and tradition between Catholics and Protestants? Surely these split Armagh into two, if not three, hostile communities? In fact, Armagh was remarkably free from overt sectarian conflict. There were riots in Scotch Street in 1718; and in 1771 several citizens were indicted for riot.[16] Otherwise, disturbances periodically affecting the surrounding countryside seem not to have seriously bothered the city. On one occasion, for example, in 1764, the Oakboys 'sallied forth in a desultory excursion' towards Armagh, but were met by Thomas McCann, the sovereign who addressed 'them with a kind of pleasant, lively and playful eloquence, peculiar to himself'. Thereupon they cheered him, 'adorned his hat with oaken boughs' and returned home.[17] Later, in 1788, during the

16 P.R.O.N.I., T808/14937, 14951.
17 Stuart, op. cit., p. 441, note.

86

conflicts between the Peep-of-Day Boys and the Defenders, a corps of Volunteers was raised in Armagh, but there was little trouble in the city itself.[18]

It is perhaps not surprising that the tensions between the denominations only rarely erupted into violence. It has been pointed out, for example, that what is remarkable during the recent bitter history of Northern Ireland is not how much violence has been directed against civilians, but how little. The explanation offered is that warring factions possess values in common, mitigating the forces dividing them: a common humanity, a common Christianity—albeit differently perceived[19]—a shared set of beliefs in the importance of family and kin, a shared identity with a particular place.[20] There is an echo here of a passage in a letter written in August 1788 by Lord Charlemont, commander of the Volunteers, to the Armagh corps, exhorting them to deal impartially with Catholics and Protestants 'and to consider their fellow-subjects, of every denomination, as their countrymen and bretheren'.[21] More practical instances of shared interests were Protestant gentlemen lending arms to Catholic tenants in order to defend their property against the Peep-of-Day Boys; and a Protestant shopkeeper in Armagh selling weapons to Catholic Defenders.[22]

Individuals sometimes crossed the religious barriers and established close links with people of other denominations. There were fifteen families in 1770 of mixed donominations, including six of Church of Ireland-Catholic marriages, and six of Church of Ireland-Presbyterian marriages. The remaining examples were of children belonging to a different denomination from their parents. There is also evidence in the parish register that Catholics and Presbyterians sometimes had their children christened in the Established Church. In the 1750s there were eight fathers of baptised children who match with Catholic householders in the census of 1770, and seven others who seem to be identical with Presbyterians.[23] These 'cross-christenings' may have occurred for

[18] Ibid., p. 561. In 1786 a group of Peep-of-Day Boys attacked a Catholic house in Armagh but were dispersed by Protestant neighbours (Account of sectarian disturbances in County Armagh, 1784–91, by John Byrne (P.R.O.N.I., T1722/1, p. 24)).

[19] Cf. the remarks of Byrne: 'It is not five years ago [i.e. in the early 1780s], since all the social virtues that attend human happiness in this life, were displayed by a union of sentiments in this county with two classes of christians, who envied each other for no other crime than for the mode of worship by which they addressed their benign Creator' (P.R.O.N.I., T1722/1, p. 20).

[20] Elliott Leyton, 'Oppositon and integration in Ulster' in *Man*, n.s., ix (1975), pp 185–98.

[21] Quoted in Stuart, op. cit., p. 561.

[22] P.R.O.N.I., T1722/1, pp 24–5.

[23] P.R.O.N.I., 679/140. The Catholics were Henry Conner (6-10-1756), Thomas Conner (2-9-

social prestige; or because, among Catholics, there was a belief that baptism should follow quickly after birth and that a Church of Ireland sacrament was better than no sacrament at all. The most intriguing examples of cross-denominational contacts were the five public renunciations of faith by Catholics in Armagh cathedral between 1750 and 1758. So small a number might be interpreted as evidence that the Church of Ireland lacked proselytizing zeal or, alternatively, that Catholics generally remained resolute in their faith. But the case of Thomas McCann suggests that faith might be subordinated to other interests. The McCanns were an old Irish family originally inhabiting north County Armagh. Thomas publicly renounced the errors of Rome in October 1751 and was received into the Church of Ireland. Within a few years he was launched on a public career which saw him elected burgess in 1755, and sovereign of Armagh four years later. He was sovereign again in 1764, 1767, 1769, 1773, 1775, and continuously from 1777 until his death in 1795.[24] The highest municipal office was closed to him as a Catholic, but as a member of the Established Church the way was clear. Just as Henry IV of France thought Paris was worth a mass in 1593, so Thomas McCann evidently thought Armagh was worth a recantation in 1751. Still, memories were long. When, thirty-five years later, he ordered a group of Defenders to put down their weapons, they objected 'to surrender to the Magistrate of Armagh, and swore they would never surrender to Papist McCann'.[25]

Even had denominational barriers remained inviolate, Armagh would not have been less a community. It is a normal feature of all societies that individuals combine together in groups such as churches, trade unions or clubs whose members share common interests which are not shared by outsiders. Members of groups do not cease to be members of the wider community, for as individuals they have functions outside the group and interact with people from other groups.[26] Thus Catholic butchers in eighteenth-century

1753), John Davy (9-6-1757), Peter McGuire (1-9-1753, 4-12-1756), John Rice (3-5-1751), Anthony Shannon or Shenan (23-10-1751), Robert Wainwright (31-1-1754, 19-5-1758), George Wilton (22-1-1753, 6-7-1754, 4-8-1756, 5-6-1758). Thomas McCann also had a child baptised before formally renouncing the Catholic faith (see below). The Presbyterians were William Crossley (19-5-1754), George Geough (1-11-1755, 22-7-1757), William McCully (15-2-1752), William McGeough (26-2-1756), James Simpson (7-7-1757).
[24] P.R.O.N.I., T679/140; T808/15318; Stuart, op. cit., pp 476-7; Edward McLysaght, *Irish families: their names, arms and origins* (Dublin, 1957), p. 72.
[25] P.R.O.N.I., T1722/1, p. 56.
[26] See Ronald Frankenberg, *Communities in Britain: social life in town and country* (Harmondsworth, Mx, 1966), pp 18-19.

Armagh sold meat to customers of all creeds—since there were ten Catholic butchers in 1770 they could hardly have confined their trade to the Catholic households.[27] Similarly Presbyterian publicans traded side by side with Catholic and Church of Ireland publicans, united in slaking the thirst of men if not in the service of God. All denominations combined in the economic life of the town and shared in other activities that made Armagh an urban community.

III

Now to the other reasons for doubting whether Armagh was a community. The first is that the population was divided into classes based on economic differences. There were great extremes of income in Armagh. In 1770 Lodge noted that thirty-six households were 'poor' or 'very poor': sixteen Church of Ireland, seventeen Catholic, but only three Presbyterian. At the other end of the spectrum, Dr Greuber, headmaster of the Royal School, received a salary of £400 a year, and Thomas McCann, the long-serving sovereign, earned enough from his business interests to support a household of fifteen people, including five living-in servants, and to employ a daily man-servant who lived in a house of his own.[28]

Differences in income do not in themselves create class distinctions, although economic differences can cause class cleavages in other ways. Sociologists sometimes distinguish three classes based on the relationship of individuals to the means of production: those who live on rent or capital, those who are self-employed, and those who work for wages.[29] In practice these classifications do not get us far, for they become blurred as soon as individuals in Armagh are considered. The town did not contain many property owners. Apart from the archbishop and vicars choral, the principal ones lived elsewhere, including Thomas Townley Dawson Esq. and Lord Dartrey who between them owned more than forty-five per cent of the houses in 1767. Another property owner, Thomas Ogle, with twenty-three houses, did live in Armagh, but in addition to rents, his

---

[27] Clarkson, 'The economy of Armagh', loc. cit., p. 32.

[28] Ibid., p. 39. McCann lived in English Street with his wife, eight children, and five servants, next door to Dr Greuber and his wife who kept seven living-in servants. The Lodge census does not state McCann's occupation, but the Freeman's Register gives it as soap boiler and chandler in 1746 (P.R.O.N.I., T808/14932).

[29] Frankenberg, op. cit., p. 257. Not all sociologists accept that class is based on economic divisions. See McIver and Page, *Society: an introductory analysis,* pp 349–50.

income came from a marble quarry.[30] Much property in Armagh was leased in perpetuity and then sublet. Thus John Burges, an attorney, had many sub-tenants on land held from the See of Armagh. In 1799 his rents from thirty-eight properties in the city totalled £479, while his head rents cost him £90. His income from rents probably considerably exceeded the fees he earned from his legal practice.[31]

The majority of people in Armagh obtained income neither from rents nor wages, but from the profits of self-employment. Out of 471 people with identifiable occupations in 1770, only 143 were wage-earners, most of these being either labourers or servants. There were also thirty-five professional people who received fees or salaries, men like Arthur Greuber and John Burges.[32] It is obviously absurd to think of such people as belonging to the same class as labourers and servants, for they were the social superiors of even the wealthiest tradesmen.

The whole concept of economic class is inappropriate to eighteenth-century Armagh. It is more realistic to regard the community as stratified by status. At the top were the gentry—although there was nobody in Armagh, apart from the archbishop, above the rank of esquire—and at the bottom labourers, servants and paupers. Status was determined by religion (Church of Ireland above, Catholics below), the possession of property, occupation (the professions ranking above trade and trade above manual labour), wealth, birth, and a conventional view of which individuals ranked high or low. Far from dividing the community, the social hierarchy bound it together by a system of rights and obligations. Armagh, it seems, possessed what Peter Laslett has called, when discussing pre-industrial England, a 'one-class society'.[33]

The remaining objection to portraying Armagh as a unified community is that it was inhabited by recent migrants from the countryside lacking the bonds of kinship and neighbourliness that existed in old settled societies, and without 'the sense of participation that comes with living in an integrated society'.[34] In order to test this hypothesis it is necessary to examine closely the indi-

[30] Map of the City of Armagh, by Robert Livinston (P.R.O.N.I., T2933/3/250); Stuart, op. cit., pp 443, 447; *Commons jn. Ire.,* 1761–2, vii, xcv.
[31] Papers relating to the Burgess estates (P.R.O.N.I., D/1594/82). Most of this property was in his possession in 1770.
[32] Clarkson, 'The economy of Armagh', pp 33, 35. Although Burges had a large rent income he still practiced as a lawyer in 1770. See *Belfast News-letter,* 9 Jan. 1770.
[33] Peter Laslett, *The World we have lost* (2nd ed., London, 1971), chapter 2.
[34] The quotation comes from Louis Wirth, 'Urbanism as a way of life' in *American Journal of Sociology,* xliv (1938), pp 1–24, which has stimulated my thinking in this section.

viduals listed in the Lodge census and try to establish how long they had been in Armagh. We need also to look beyond the household units in which Lodge grouped the individuals to discover what ties of kinship existed.

Clues to patterns of settlement are offered by the Church of Ireland parish register for the 1750s. This covers the whole parish of Armagh although the events relating to the city itself are clearly distinguished from those of the surrounding townlands. The register suggests that the Church of Ireland population failed to grow during the 1750s. As Table IV shows, burials exceeded baptisms in five out of the seven years, 1751–7, and they probably did so in 1750 as well. Table IV overstates the true excess of deaths over births in

Table IV[35]

ANNUAL NUMBERS OF BAPTISMS AND BURIALS IN THE CHURCH OF IRELAND, ARMAGH CITY, 1750–58

	1750	*1751*	*1752*	*1753*	*1754*	*1755*	*1756*	*1757*	*1758*
Baptisms	—	34[2]	34	29	38	29	24	35	15[4]
Burials	60[1]	53[3]	32.	51	29	34	112	42	—
Surplus of baptisms (+) or burials(—)	—	—19	+2	—22	+9	—5	—88	—7	—
Burials as percentage of baptisms	—	156	94	176	76	117	467	120	—

1. April to December.
2. Eleven months only; January missing.
3. Eleven months only; January excluded. Total for 1751, including January, 66.
4. Seven months only; register ends 6 August 1758.

Armagh because the burial figures were inflated by the presence of Catholics and Presbyterians, who were more likely to be interred in Church of Ireland graveyards than immersed in Church of Ireland fonts. Nevertheless, deaths probably did outnumber births even among the Church of Ireland population during the period 1751–7, and there can be no doubt at all about the excesses of mortality in 1750, 1751, 1753 and 1756.[36] Assuming that the demographic

[35] Armagh Parish Register (P.R.O.N.I., T679/140).
[36] The question of the extent to which Catholics and Presbyterians used the Church of Ireland burial ground requires further investigation. An analysis of burials for 1750 and 1751 shows that of surnames common both to the register and to the census of 1770, forty-two per cent

91

experience of Catholics and Presbyterians was no better than that of Church of Ireland adherents, the population of the city declined.[37] The position in the 1760s is unknown for the register is blank, but when entries resume, average annual baptisms were twenty-seven per cent higher between 1776 and 1786 than they had been in the 1750s[38] Such an increase suggests that the base population had grown and also that the age-structure of the population had probably shifted in favour of the child-bearing age groups. Even allowing for a fall in mortality from the levels of the 1750s, it is most unlikely that natural increase alone could have produced a larger and more fertile population, for nearly two-thirds of deaths in the 1750s had been of children (see Table V), so depriving the community of potential parents for the 1770s and '80s. The evidence, instead, points to a considerable influx of people from the countryside during the 1760s; the city surveyed by Lodge in 1770 must have contained many recent arrivals.

Table V
CHILD MORTALITY AS A PROPORTION OF TOTAL MORTALITY IN ARMAGH CITY, 1750–57[39]

	Per Cent		Per Cent
1750	65	1754	62
1751	77	1755	47
1752	56	1756	80
1753	71	1757	52
		Average 1750–7	64

It is not difficult to see why they came. The linen industry was becoming increasingly important in South Ulster from the mid-eighteenth century, stimulating the business of the linen markets, including Armagh, so increasing the demand for labour.[40] The city was an important road centre and its economy received a further

were exclusively Catholic or Presbyterian. Subtracting this proportion from the burials, we are left with a total of 205 for 1751–7. There were also baptisms of twenty-three non-Church of Ireland children during the period (see note 22), giving a net total of 200 baptisms. Only on the unlikely assumption that approaching one-half of burials were of non-Episcopalians, can the Church of Ireland population be shown to have had a surplus of baptisms over burials. For a brief discussion of Catholic burial practices see Maureen Wall, *The penal laws, 1691–1760* (Dundalk, 1976), pp 57–8.

[37] Unless of course it was replenished by migration from the countryside. But the surge of burials in 1750–1, 1753 and 1756 also occurred in the rural parts of Armagh parish and elsewhere in south Ulster (I am grateful to Miss Patricia Worthington for supplying me with this information).

[38] Births to soldiers' wives and of foundlings have been excluded.

[39] Burials were classified in this period by the curate of Armagh as: child, young man or woman, middle-aged man or woman, old man or woman, and—occasionally—very old man or woman.

[40] Clarkson, 'The economy of Armagh', loc. cit., 28, 43; W. H. Crawford, 'Economy and society in south Ulster in the eighteenth century' in *Clogher Record*, viii (1975), pp 245–7.

boost from the building boom instigated by Archbishop Robinson after 1765, and there was a vigorous demand for building workers. In September 1770, for example, the Dean of Armagh advertised for a 'number of Masons and Bricklayers' and offered work throughout the winter at good wages. Armagh, indeed, seems to have been a considerable labour market in the building industry, for in July the church authorities had recruited bricklayers and carpenters in the city for building work at Killyman, County Tyrone.[41] To support the skilled craftsmen, labourers were required; they may not have answered advertisements, but heard, through word of mouth, of jobs to be had.

Plausible explanations of migration can thus be offered but it is less easy to spot who migrants were. A clue is provided by considering their likely demographic characteristics. Migrants are typically young men and women of marriageable age, who might, indeed, migrate in order to earn enough to get married, or because they had married and needed an income to support the inevitable family. The labouring group in Armagh fit this description remarkably well. Fifty-five out of the seventy labouring households consisted of a married couple with a child or children, and another thirteen households contained a couple without children.

The labourers were mainly Catholics, but there must have been many migrants among the Protestant population as well, for the increased baptisms in the 1770s were chiefly of members of the Established Church. Protestant migrants did not usually become labourers but were diffused throughout the economy. Many may have been young women, daughters of Protestant farmers, perhaps, sent into domestic service in the city,[42] once there adding to the stock of marriageable girls.

The problem of migration can be approached from another direction by trying to compare the size of the migrant group with the longer settled members of the community. Once more the parish register yields useful information which is summarised in Table VI. More than seventy per cent of the individual fathers named in the 1750s do not appear in the census of 1770; although their grown-up children and re-married widows may still have been in the city. It is remarkable, though, that almost thirty per cent of fathers can be identified with a fair degree of confidence a decade or more later,

[41] *Belfast News-letter,* 17 July 1770, 18 Sep. 1770.
[42] The majority of living-in servants appear to have been Protestants. See Clarkson, 'The economy of Armagh', loc. cit., pp 31–2.

either by their own presence or the presence of their widows, for the normal process of mortality would have removed many of them by 1770.[43] Table VI, in fact, is evidence of considerable stability in the community of Armagh.

Table VI

FATHERS RECORDED IN THE PARISH REGISTER, 1751–8

		Per Cent
Total number of different fathers	159	100
Still in Armagh in 1770	19	11.9
Probably in Armagh in 1770, or widows were in Armagh in 1770	28	17.6
Cannot be traced in 1770	112	70.4

A similar picture of stability comes from an analysis of the names of men who sat on the grand juries that governed the affairs of the city. In the two decades 1750–69, a total of ninety-one different individuals served as jurors. Just over half were mentioned by Lodge in 1770, and another dozen can be identified through surviving relatives. Only thirty-two had totally disappeared in 1770.[44] Furthermore, the names of the jurors suggest a solid core of long established families: Burleigh, Cust, Dobbin, Gardiner, Hamilton, Johnston (twelve households of them), McCann, McKew, McKinstry, Ogle and others. The high death rate in the city did not seriously erode the core, for mortality was concentrated among children. It removed individuals from family units, but the families themselves survived for a long time.

These old established Armagh families were linked together by bonds of kinship. At first sight kinship ties appear weak, for the community was composed chiefly of households containing the nuclear family only. But appearances are deceptive; as Michael Anderson has written, 'kinship does not stop at the front door. There are few functions which can be performed by a co-residing kinsman which he cannot perform equally well if he instead lives next door, or even up the street'.[45] This was the pattern in Armagh, but it makes

[43] An indication of the magnitude of the possible losses from mortality can be gained by using the Princeton model life tables. Assuming: (a) that fathers were aged between twenty and forty-nine; (b) that they were distributed throughout the age range as indicated by the model life tables; (c) that the rate of population growth was zero; (d) that the death rate was stable at 43.76 per 1000; (e) that all entries occurred in 1755; then, using the 'model west male life table', we would expect twenty-seven or twenty-eight of the 159 fathers to be still alive in 1770. An assumed death rate of 33.25, all other assumptions remaining unchanged, would leave thirty-two or thirty-three in 1770. These calculations take no account of the ageing of surviving fathers (A. J. Coale and Paul Demeny, *Regional model life tables and stable populations* (Princeton, New Jersey, 1966), pp 126–7, 132–3).

[44] List of Armagh City grand jurors (P.R.O.N.I., T636, pp 106–10).

[45] Michael Anderson, *Family structure in nineteenth century Lancashire* (London, 1971), pp 56–7.

94

kinship connections difficult to detect for the main clues are shared surnames, inadequate indicators of kinship since related families may not have the same name, and a common name is not necessarily evidence of relationship.

The Church of Ireland population possessed twenty-one shared surnames (as well as 101 individual family names) from which it is possible to identify at least nine sets of related households with reasonable confidence. For example, Thomas Campbell, senior, an innkeeper of Market Street, had a son Thomas, junior, who kept a shop further down the same street; Thomas, senior, was probably also father of Edward Campbell who lived next door with his wife. Very unusually for Armagh, Edward had no stated occupation, although his wife was a shopkeeper, and it is tempting to believe that he worked in his father's public house. To take another example, there were clearly both economic and family links between the household of Widow Edge and her son, a nailer by trade, in Church Lane, and John Edge, another nailer who lived with his wife and five children in Callen Street. Widow Barnes, sextoness at the cathedral, was probably mother of Robert, living nearby, who was cathedral organist. Another ecclesiastical network was formed by the households of the Rev. Richard English, curate of Armagh, situated in Abbey Street, and Widow English and Mary English, neighbours in Pound Hill. The Pound Hill houses had been built earlier in the century by Archbishop Boulter for widows of the clergy.[46]

Among Presbyterians there were twenty-two shared family names from which at least seven kinship networks can be discerned. The most important, economically, was the Dobbin connection consisting of two households in English and Scotch Street. The precise nature of the family relationship between Thomas and Leonard Dobbin is not clear—they may have been uncle and nephew—but their business connections were intimate and extensive, embracing soap-boiling, candle-making, distilling, shopkeeping, the dispensing of medicines, and money-lending.[47] The three McCreery households next door to one another at the corner of Big Meeting Street and the street leading to the common were almost certainly related, as were the two Goodfellow families six houses apart in School Lane; Michael and Barnabas Goodfellow were two of only nine Protestant labourers in the whole of Armagh.

Catholic kinship connections are particularly difficult to untangle, for there were forty-two shared Catholic surnames, some of them

[46] Stuart, op. cit., p. 427.

[47] *Belfast News-letter,* 30 Oct. 1770; Indictments at Armagh assizes (P.R.O.N.I., T636, p. 88).

stretching over five households. However, it seem likely that Brigid and Widow Vallily living next door but one to each other in Callan Street were related in some way; and William, Henry, and John Rice, living in different houses in Irish Street with their wives and children were surely connected, for they were all butchers. Likewise, Widow Whittington, public house keeper of Abbey Street—and the only Catholic in Armagh to employ a servant—was possibly the mother of Edward, who kept a public house in Irish Street.

There is a significant contrast between Catholics as a whole and the seventy labourers, a mainly Catholic sub-group, who had only eight shared surnames. The best way of showing the contrast is to express the total number of different names in a group as a proportion of the number of households in the same group. This is done in Table VII.

Table VII
THE NUMBER OF DIFFERENT NAMES IN A GROUP EXPRESSED AS A
PERCENTAGE OF THE NUMBER OF HOUSEHOLDS IN
THE SAME GROUP

Group	Per Cent
Church of Ireland	78
Presbyterian	75
Catholic	68
Labourer	87

The proportion for labourers is considerably higher than for Catholics as a whole, and larger also than for the Protestant population. Admittedly this is a crude measure, but it clearly suggests connections were weaker among labourers than among the rest of the community. I have argued that most labourers may have been newcomers to Armagh; they may also have felt themselves to be only loosely integrated into the life of the city.

IV

I have now concluded the case against claiming that Armagh was a community. The religious denominations seem to constitute groups that are perfectly compatible with the existence of a wider community. The objection based on class is no objection at all, for the concept of class is anachronistic when applied to eighteenth-century Armagh. On the other hand, the city contained migrants who seem not to have been fully absorbed into the community. But I turn now to examine those forces forging the inhabitants of Armagh—notwithstanding their differences in religion, status and origins—into an urban community.

The city of Armagh was incorporated in March 1613, but the charter did not define its limits. In practice the city was contained within the townland known as 'Corporation', an area of 1,100 acres bounded by the river Callen to the west, and the Scotch Street river to the east. In Lodge's time large parts of this area were still not built on, and the city consisted of seventeen streets radiating like spokes of a wheel from a central hub formed by the hill where the cathedral stood.[48] The population in 1613 had been incorporated into a commonalty and additional freemen, including Catholics, were elected by the commonalty until 1771. Elections then ceased, possibly because the freedom conferred few if any privileges.[49]

The charter also provided for the election of twelve burgesses. They served for life, chose their own replacements, often did not live in Armagh and were, in fact, frequently Church of Ireland clergymen nominated by the archbishop as lord of the manor of Armagh. The burgesses elected the members of parliament, the sovereign, and the freemen;[50] but effective government was exercised by a grand jury of twenty-three men selected yearly by the sovereign from the panel of names of inhabitants. The pool of jurors was not large and the city was virtually run by an oligarchy. Catholics were ineligible as jurors during the 1750s and '60s. There was no legal basis for the authority of the grand jury, but the system worked because it was generally acceptable to the city's inhabitants.[51]

Legally the city of Armagh was ill-defined. Rather, it was more a state of mind—a feeling of belonging—on the part of its citizens. That there was a sense of civic pride is clear. When Archbishop Robinson came to Armagh in 1765 he found, in Arthur Young's phrase 'a nest of mud cabbins',[52] and forced his tenants to rebuild with stone and slate. Despite the expense caused to his leaseholders he won public approval.[53] In June 1770, for example, a house in Scotch Street was advertised to let with 'a most pleasing Prospect of the Town, and of the Primate's improvements'.[54] Even before

---

[48] *First report of the commissioners appointed to inquire into the municipal corporations in Ireland,* H.C. 1835 (27) xxvii, appendix, pt. i (hereafter *Report*), p. 671; Stuart, op. cit., pp 471, 640–6; P.R.O.N.I., T2933/3/250.

[49] Armagh corporation minute book, 1738–1818 (P.R.O.N.I., T808/14932); *Report*, p. 672. The report is wrong in suggesting that Catholics were excluded from the freedom. At least six were admitted between 1758 and 1771.

[50] *Report*, pp 671, 672–3; List of Burgesses of Armagh (P.R.O.N.I., T808/15318).

[51] *Report*, pp 672–3, 676; Stuart, op. cit., p. 473; List of Armagh city grand jurors (P.R.O.N.I., T636, pp 106–10).

[52] Arthur Young, *A tour in Ireland . . . 1776–9* (London, 1780), I, 104.

[53] Stuart, op. cit., p. 451.

[54] *Belfast News-letter,* 26 June 1770.

Robinson arrived in Armagh, Thomas Ogle improved the city's communications in 1759 by constructing the street that bore his name; and in 1763 a group of citizens, at their own expense, raised an ancient stone cross 'from the rubbish in which it was buried' and placed it on a plinth in Market Street.[55]

Community sentiment depended on more than pleasing prospects, convenient thorough-fares, and restored ancient monuments: it came as well from the performance of functions peculiar to an urban community. The chief of these was, I believe, economic. I have examined the economy of Armagh in detail elsewhere,[56] and it is necessary here only to emphasise the salient features. Armagh was a finishing and distribution centre, processing the products of the surrounding countryside, providing marketing services for local farmers and linen weavers, and linking the county of Armagh to the wider world of Dublin, London, and beyond. Three-quarters of its occupied population were engaged in manufacturing, distribution and the service industries. Of the rest, fifteen per cent were labourers and the remainder professional men mostly associated with the cathedral and schools. Agriculture played a little part in the life of the city.

An important part of Armagh's economic function was to introduce to the city and county the goods and tastes of the outside world. Thus, in February 1770, Robert Scott of Market Street, an apothecary, announced in a newspaper advertisement that his wife 'is lately returned from Dublin, from whence she has furnished her shop with a Variety of Articles, the best she could get, in the Millinery, Haberdashery and Grocery Business; and is determined to sell them as cheap as she can'.[57] The following month Robert Gardiner, who had an ironmongery business, offered for sale a range of imported metal wares, as well as 'Hops, Writing Paper and Paper for Rooms, Clover Seed, Gun Powder and Shot, great Variety of China Ware, and Several other Articles too tedious to mention'.[58]

The city had other roles to play in relation to the countryside. One was political. The county assizes were held in Armagh and I have already noted how, on two occasions, Thomas McCann, as magistrate, rode out of the town to quell agrarian and sectarian unrest in the county; and how the Volunteers were organized in the city. A regiment of regular soldiers was also stationed in Armagh

[55] Stuart, op. cit., pp 509–10.
[56] Clarkson, 'The economy of Armagh', loc. cit., pp 27–45.
[57] *Belfast News-letter,* 2 Feb. 1770.
[58] Ibid., 27 Mar. 1770.

during the 1780s, maintaining law and order in the county, and, incidentally, creating havoc among the baptismal entries in the parish register.

Another urban function was cultural, a term employed here to refer to Armagh's role as an ecclesiastical, educational, and social centre. As ecclesiastical capital of Ireland, Armagh's influence was nation-wide for its Protestant archbishop was primate of all Ireland and during much of the eighteenth century, head of the 'English interest'. Robinson was less a political prelate than some of his predecessors, spending more time in the city and more money and energy making it one of the most elegant of Irish towns. Even so, he was probably a remote figure to most of his flock. The influence of the Church of Ireland, instead, was exercised through the person of the curate of the cathedral church of St Patrick. Standing on the summit of the hill at the centre of the city, the church physically dominated the community and extended pastoral care over a huge parish stretching almost from the borders of County Tyrone to County Monaghan.[59] People came from all corners of the parish to be married, baptised and buried; and sometimes from places more distant, such as Monaghan town, Limavady and, occasionally, Dublin.

The influence of Armagh over the other denominations was less obvious. The Catholic archbishop, Anthony Blake, lived mostly in County Galway, was at loggerheads with his clergy, and, in any case, was paralysed for a considerable part of his long reign. When he died in 1786 the diocese 'was disorganised by professed anarchy'. His coadjutor bishop and eventual successor, Richard O'Reilly, lived in Drogheda[60] and there was no resident priest in Armagh, although a chapel had been built in 1750.[61] The Presbyterian community was in the care of William Campbell, a skilful defender of Presbyterianism, advocate of an Irish college for the training of ministers, but a 'rather monotonous and prolix' preacher.[62] One of his congregation, William McGeough, helped introduce Methodism into south Ulster. When John Wesley visited Armagh in 1767 the sovereign ordered him not to preach, but McGeough allowed him to use his garden. Wesley returned to Armagh several times subsequently, each time as guest of McGeough.[63]

[59] In 1770 the parish of Armagh included also what later became the parishes of Eglish, Grange, and Lisnadill and contained more than 150 townlands, (*General valuation of rateable property in Ireland. Union of Armagh* . . . (Dublin, 1864), pp vii–xii).
[60] Stuart, op. cit., pp 407–9.
[61] Clarkson, 'The economy of Armagh', loc. cit., p. 30.
[62] Stuart, op. cit., pp 493–7.
[63] Ibid. pp 501–3.

Armagh's importance as a centre of education was connected with its religious functions, for both the Royal and the Charter schools were established in order to secure the Protestant faith. The former drew its pupils from throughout Ireland and during the headmastership of Arthur Greuber (1754–86) only a quarter of its boys came from the city or county of Armagh. When they left most of them entered the professions, usually via Trinity College, Dublin, in all parts of Ireland. The school's most famous pupil in Greuber's time was Robert Stewart, Lord Castlereagh, although it would be fanciful to see the influence of Armagh extending to the Congress of Vienna.[64] The influence of the Charter school, by contrast, extended nowhere at all, for its pupils were orphans or children of the city's poor. And it had no famous old boys, only insubordinate young ones, like Michael Higgins, aged fifteen, who absconded in March 1770: 'a pretty faced Boy with a handsome Head of White Hair tied with a black Ribband; he had a good deal more to say for himself than is true'.[65]

The clergy, teachers and substantial tradesmen of Armagh created a demand for the services of watchmakers, wigmakers and barbers, printers and musicians. There were a score of such people in Armagh in 1770, whose clientele must have included many country gentry. Mr Moorehead, for example, a dancing master, and 'notable [violin] teacher of those days' attracted pupils from Tandragee, and probably elsewhere.[66] Armagh was particularly well supplied with medical practitioners, well in excess of the needs of the city alone. The half dozen apothecaries offered a range of services, including 'various operations of Surgery performed, and the necessary Medicines administered'. Those who could not afford their prices could go to 'Mrs Gillespy in Armagh' who sold 'medicines and ointments for scurvy, dropsy, tooth ache, eyes, lips, etc.', supplied to her by Robert Agnew, druggist of Killyleagh, County Down.[67] For treatment of the poor there was an infirmary established in 1767 by public subscription.[68]

The new hospital played an important part in the social life of Armagh. During the summer, assemblies 'conducted in the Genteelest Manner' were held at the sessions house 'for the Benefit of the

---

[64] *Register of the Royal School, Armagh,* compiled by M. L. Ferrar (Belfast, 1933), pp 8–16.
[65] Stuart, op. cit., p. 541; *Belfast News-letter,* 6 Mar. 1770.
[66] E. Estyn Evans (ed.), *Harvest home: the last sheaf. A selection from the writings of T. G. F. Patterson* (Dundalk, 1975), p. 175.
[67] *Belfast News-letter,* 2 Feb. 1770; 26 Oct. 1770. In the Lodge census, Mrs Gillespy appears as 'Widow Gillespie', a public-house keeper of Scotch Street.
[68] Stuart, op. cit., pp 533–4.

County Hospital'. With tickets at 2s 8½d a time, attendances must
have been confined to the comfortably-off members of society.[69]
For the lower orders there were entertainments of other kinds
widely advertised in the press. In June, for example, 'the Sieur Rea'
came from Belfast to display his 'philosophical experiments' and
'magical card deceptions'. But the big event of 1770 was the
exhibition in October of the *Microcosm,* recently displayed in
Dublin to 'universal approbation'. It was a machine composed of 'a
Vast Variety of Figures moving in the most lively Manner' designed
to appeal to those with a taste for 'the GRAND, the UNCOMMON,
and the BEAUTIFUL'. Admission was one shilling (no half prices
for children or servants) and a copper plate print was available at
the exhorbitant cost of 2s 2d.[70] Finally, for those whose tastes or
purses stretched neither to the grand nor the uncommon, there was
a race-course where the Mall is now, the scene of 'periodical sports
of the peasantry, who assembled at the races [which] not infrequently
terminated in gambling, drunkenness, and riot'.[71]

V

This portrait has tried to view Armagh as a community, both in the
sense of its being a distinct locality, and of its fulfilling specifically
urban functions. In approaching Armagh in this way concepts have
been deliberately borrowed from the discipline of sociology. Such a
method carries with it dangers. For one thing, sociology is not
famed for the beauty of its prose, while history still has claims to be
literature. More seriously, sociology is often justly accused of being
unhistorical; concepts developed in the study of modern societies
may be inappropriate when applied to earlier times. There is also the
difficulty that sociological theory is changing, contradictory, and
sometimes confusing; the naive historian looking for a suitable
vehicle may well drive off in last year's superseded model.

Still an outdated model is better than no model at all in helping
the historian to make sense of his evidence.[72] In the present case
concepts such as 'urban functions' and 'community' help us to focus
attention away from what towns look like, or what they were,
legally; and towards what towns did, and how they were constructed

[69] *Belfast News-letter,* 6 June 1770, 31 Aug. 1770.
[70] Ibid., 25 Sept. 1770; 12 Oct. 1770.
[71] Stuart, op. cit., p. 552.
[72] On this point see Lawrence Stone, 'History and social sciences in the twentieth century' in
C. F. Delzell (ed.), *The future of history* (Nashville, Tennessee, 1977), p. 19.

socially and demographically. Eighteenth-century Irish towns received a bad press from George O'Brien from which they have still not fully recovered. Commercially, he claimed that they took away more than they 'added to the economic efficiency of the country'. Socially, the 'better class [of townsmen was] composed of a crowd of drunken idlers, usually middlemen; while the lower class generally contained an altogether disproportionate number of beggars'.[73] Even the most obsolete sociological model can take us further than this.

Adam Smith knew better. Writing in the *Wealth of Nations* six years after William Lodge counted the inhabitants of Armagh, he explained how towns contributed to the improvement of the country: by marketing the produce of the rural areas; by spreading money and urban attitudes throughout the countryside; and by providing order and good government.[74] If, as historians, we would be more inclined to think of towns in this way, we would be in a better positon to understand the difficult problems of Ireland's economic and social development in the eighteenth century.

[73] O'Brien, *Econ. hist. Ire., 18th cent.,* pp 368, 370.
[74] Adam Smith, *An inquiry into the nature and causes of the wealth of nations* (Everyman edition, London, 1910) i, 362–3.

Urban Politics in Ireland 1801-1831

Peter Jupp

Apart from the abolition of the Irish parliament, the most radical provisions of the Act of Union were those that set out the future representation of Ireland at Westminster. Hitherto the Irish House of Commons had consisted of 300 M.P.s, of whom 234 were returned by the boroughs, 64 by the counties and 2 by Trinity College. It was therefore similar to the British House of Commons in that the majority of M.P.s were returned by the boroughs. By the terms of the Union, however, the balance between county and borough representation was reversed. Thus of the 100 Irish M.P.s at Westminster, 64 were to be returned by the counties, 1 by Trinity College and only 35 by 33 retained boroughs. 84 boroughs were totally disfranchised and 31 of the retained boroughs became single-member constituencies. The future parliamentary representation of Ireland was thereby based upon the county as opposed to the borough constituencies.

The question of which boroughs should be disfranchised and which should continue to return M.P.s was resolved by a compromise. Pitt was well-disposed towards the idea of parliamentary reform in Ireland but had no wish to give undue encouragement to the parliamentary reformers in Britain. The government therefore selected for representation at Westminster the 33 most populous and wealthy boroughs irrespective of the franchise upon which their members would be returned. This ensured that there were no rotten boroughs but set aside the question of how many were 'open' or 'close' as a result of the peculiarities of their franchise. There were in fact 6 different borough franchises after the Union although for present purposes these may be divided into two categories. The first consists of 28 constituencies in which the vote was exercised at the time of the Union either exclusively or primarily by members of the corporation. The second consists of 5 constituencies in which the vote was based solely upon a property qualification.[1] The general effect of these measures upon the political future of the Anglo-Irish ascendancy was to enhance the importance of the surviving borough constituencies, and particularly of those where the vote was exercised by members of the corporation. The primary reason for this was the removal of the weight of representation from the boroughs to the counties. As a result of the Relief Act of 1793 Catholics were able to vote on the same terms as Protestants, a provision that was likely to have its most dramatic effect in those county and borough constituencies where the population was predominantly Catholic and where the franchise was based upon a low property qualification. The ascendancy therefore faced the prospect of a majority of Irish M.P.s managing a large and predominantly rural Catholic vote—a prospect that enhanced the significance of those   borough constituencies where the more restricted corporation franchise offered a greater degree of security to the Protestant interest. It is to the parliamentary and municipal history of the 28 towns and cities in this category—the potential bastion of the ascendancy—that this paper is directed.

At the time of the Union their parliamentary and municipal affairs were managed by Anglo-Irish interests of varying degrees of complexity.[2] In 11 constituencies the parliamentary franchise was either vested by charter or had been limited by tradition to the provost, the burgesses and the odd freeman of the corporation. In most cases they were 13 in number, being restricted to the provost and the burgesses, but in a few it was either more or less as a result of vacancies not being filled or because there was uncertainty as to the terms of the charter of incorporation. The exact number, however, is academic as all 11 electorates were under the management of one

---

[1] The 5 constituencies in this category were Downpatrick, Lisburn and Newry where the vote was vested in the £5 householders; Dungarvan, where it was vested in the £5 householders and 40s freeholders; and Mallow where only the 40s freeholders voted.

[2] This generalisation and many of those that follow are drawn from the histories of the Irish constituencies and the biographies of the Irish M.P.s that I have contributed to the official *History of Parliament, 1790–1820,* to be published by H.M.S.O.

or two families who in effect selected the M.P.s and supervised municipal affairs.[3]

Most, although not all these families owned considerable property in their respective boroughs but as the exceptions suggest, the possession of property was not necessarily the means by which they maintained their interests.[4] These can be more readily found in the traditions of municipal politics. Thus in the majority of constituencies the provost and burgesses elected replacements to their own number, a tradition which enabled individual families to establish a superior position within the corporation and then to sustain it almost indefinitely.[5] In the other constituencies burgesses were supposedly elected by the freemen but as the latter were normally admitted to that status by the burgesses the same process of self-election and the same tradition of self-perpetuating patriarchies or oligarchies prevailed.[6] The dominant interests in these constituences were therefore virtually impregnable and remained so for most of this period. They continued to nominate the M.P.s and took no steps to increase the degree of local, and where it was possible, Catholic participation in corporate affairs. In fact the only notable change in their parliamentary history after the Union was that some 'patrons' willingly sold their seats to nominees of the prevailing government and opposition at Westminster, many of whom turn out to be British and not Irish.

In a further 9 constituencies it was generally accepted that the freemen could vote with the provost and the burgesses. The precise reasons for this are somewhat obscure. The parliamentary commissioners who studied the Irish borough franchises in 1831 and 1833 certainly found the subject perplexing and were not enlightened by their perusal of the relevant charters. The subject

---

[3] The 11 constituencies and the heads of their leading interests were as follows: Armagh, the Primate of the Established Church; Bandon, Lords Shannon and Bandon and after 1807, the Duke of Devonshire; Belfast, Lord Donegall; Carlow, Lord Charleville; Dungannon, Lord Northland; Ennis, Sir Edward O'Brien and James and subsequently William Vesey Fitzgerald; Enniskillen, Lord Enniskillen; New Ross, Robert and subsequently Francis Leigh and Charles Tottenham; Portarlington, Lord Portarlington; Sligo, Owen Wynne; Tralee, Sir Edward Denny. The three constituencies where the vote was not specifically restricted to the provost and burgesses were Enniskillen, New Ross and Portarlington.

[4] Lord Charleville, for example, owned little property in Carlow, see *First report of the commissioners appointed to inquire in to the municipal corporations in Ireland,* (hereafter cited as *Report M.C.(I)),* H.C. 1835, xxvii, appendix, pt. 1, 167. *Parliamentary Representation: Boundary Reports (Ireland),* (hereafter cited as *Parl. Rep. (I)*), H.C. 1831–2 (519), xliii, 18.

[5] Armagh, Belfast, Dungannon, Ennis, Enniskillen, New Ross, Portarlington, Sligo and Tralee, see *Report on M.C.(I),* H.C. 1835, xxvii, supplement, sect. ii, 48; sect. iii, 50; sect. iv, 52; sect. v, 54; sect. vi, 56.

[6] Bandon and Carlow, ibid., sect. i, 46; sect. ii, 48.

remains perplexing and perhaps the most that can be ventured at this stage is that the charters of these constituencies did not specifically restrict the franchise to the provost and burgesses and that there had been occasions when freemen voted in reasonably conspicuous numbers.[7]

In theory such a franchise was sufficiently wide to have produced electorates that reflected local interests and to have prevented the constituency from becoming 'close'. In practice, however, their electorates while larger in number were as unrepresentative in composition and as subject to management by individual families as was the case in the 'burgess' boroughs. The reasons for this can once again be found in the rules and regulations of the corporations, and particularly those relating to the creation of freemen. Thus with the exception of Youghal the power to create freemen was vested in the burgesses thereby enabling the dominant interest in the corporation to create and sustain a subsidiary interest among the freemen. Furthermore, with the exception of Londonderry, freemen were admitted only by special favour of the corporation and not by right through being the son of a freeman, by being an apprentice or by having married into a freeman's family.[8] This meant that the burgesses were not restricted in their choice of freemen. Finally, there was no residence qualification. Patrons therefore established a dominant interest among the burgesses, a process normally completed by the Union, and when necessary strengthened it by the admission of honorary and often non-resident freemen, a process clearly evident in this period. Thus parliamentary enquiries conducted between 1829 and 1833 showed that the vast majority of freemen in these constituencies were admitted by special favour and that approximately half were non-resident. They also stated that only a tiny proportion were Catholic.[9]

These successive stages of management are clearly visible in individual constituencies. Thus on 6 May 1798 Lord Loftus and

---

[7] The 9 constituencies and the heads of their leading interests were as follows: Athlone, William Handcock, 1st Lord Castlemaine; Cashel, Richard Pennefather; Clonmel, John, and after 1806 William Bagwell; Coleraine, Lord Waterford; Dundalk, Lord Roden; Kinsale, Lord de Clifford; Londonderry, Lord Caledon and Lord Waterford; Wexford, Richard Nevill and Lord Ely—Cpt. Henry Evans took over Nevill's interest on the latter's death in 1822; Youghal, Lord Shannon until 1822 and then the Duke of Devonshire.

[8] *Report on M.C.(I)*, H.C. 1835, xxvii, supplement, sect. i, 46; sect. ii, 48; sect. iv, 52; sect. v, 54; sect. vi, 56.

[9] *Returns of the number of persons registered as freeholders and admitted as freemen within the last eight years in every city and town ... in Ireland*, H.C. 1829 (253), xxii, 25–258; *Returns of the number of freemen in each corporate town in Ireland*, H.C. 1829 (254), xxii, 261–7; *Parl. Rep. (I)*, H.C. 1831–2 (519), xliii, 1–145.

Richard Nevill came to an agreement 'that a cordial union shall exist between them in the borough of Wexford' by which each would return an M.P. and choose alternately the mayor, burgesses and an equal number of freemen 'each party to act as trustees for the other'. At the Union, when one of the Wexford seats was abolished, they agreed upon alternate nomination to the survivor and this was confirmed by an exchange of correspondence in June 1806. In fact the agreement between the two parties lasted until 1829 when only 20 of the 152 burgesses and freemen were said to be resident in the town. Moreover in 1833 the municipal commissioners discovered that the officers of the corporation could not remember a Roman Catholic having been admitted as a freeman prior to 1830.[10]

Thus for the greater part of this period the parliamentary representation of these constituencies was managed by Anglo-Irish families acting when necessary with almost wholly Protestant and often predominantly non-resident freemen oligarchies. The seats for Athlone, Cashel, and Dundalk were usually sold by the prevailing family interest to outsiders while those for Clonmel, Coleraine, Kinsale, Wexford and Youghal were reserved for one of their own number. In the unusual case of Londonderry where there was a large and mainly resident freeman electorate, Sir George Fitzgerald Hill was returned without a contest from 1802 until he retired in 1830. This was largely due to the fact that in addition to being closely connected with one of the dominant family interests he also proved to be a competent spokesman of the local business community.[11]

In the final 8 constituencies, including the largest and wealthiest towns and cities in Ireland, the vote was vested in both the burgesses, the freemen and those freeholders whose property was assessed as being worth at least 40s per annum. As all but Carrickfergus contained predominantly Catholic populations and as Catholics were able to vote as freemen or freeholders their electorates could have been broadly representative of their respective communities. At the time of the Union, however, they all had predominantly Protestant freemen electorates, the number of

[10] *Report on M.C. (I)*, H.C. 1835, xxviii, appendix pt. 1, 624–5; *Parl. Rep. (I)*, H.C. 1831–2 (519), xliii, 146. Neither 'patron' owned much property in Wexford.
[11] In 1829 it was estimated that there were 380 resident and 270 non-resident freemen in Londonderry, see *Returns of the number of freemen in each corporate town in Ireland*, H.C. 1829 (254), xxii, 4; Sir George Fitzgerald Hill (1763–1839) married a neice of Lord Waterford and was a commissioner of the Irish Treasury, 1806–16. In 1825 he claimed that 'For thirty years past no one resident gentleman has been more actively connected with the concerns of the north than myself.' Hill to Peel, Feb. 1825 (B.L. Add., MS 40373, f. 175).

freeholders amounting in one case to no more than 28% of the total electorate and in all other cases to considerably less than that.[12] In other words the corporations had not been willing, or had not been requested to admit Catholics as freemen and little advantage had been taken of the possibility of registering them as freeholders in those constituencies where they formed the majority of the population. Moreover although the freeman electorates were in general considerably larger than those in other boroughs, they were all subject to various degrees of management by Anglo-Irish families that had established a strong influence within the governing bodies of the corporations and who deployed the same means as their counterparts elsewhere to sustain it. In fact at the time of the Union the only significant difference between these boroughs and the 'freeman' boroughs was that in the former the prevailing interests tended to be more numerous, more competitive and more broadly based. In the untypical case of Galway, one interest—that of the Daly family—was predominant. In all the others, however, at least two and sometimes three or four interests took a leading part in parliamentary and municipal affairs. Thus in the early years of the Union elections were contested or arranged between Lords Donegall and Downshire in Carrickfergus; between Lords Desart and Ormond in Kilkenny; between the Fosters, Hardmans, Smyths and Ogles in Drogheda;[13] and between the Alcock, Bolton, Carew and Newport families in Waterford. In Cork and Dublin which were each to retain two M.P.s and which possessed the largest of the urban electorates there were several families which traditionally attempted to win a seat. In the case of Cork they had to contend with the changing moods of an inner group of 500 freemen known collectively as the Friendly Club. In Dublin, on the other hand, the return depended principally upon the disposition of the 25 guilds that dominated the affairs of the exclusively Protestant corporation.

The composition of these interests can be gauged by the size of the governing bodies of the corporations. The smallest was that of Galway with 21 members; one of the largest that of Limerick with 60. In the case of Limerick where Lord Gort's interest carried elections until 1820, his near relations at one time filled 7 seats on the common council.[14] He therefore had to construct his interest

---

[12] Deduced from an analysis of *Returns of the number of freeholders registered . . . for every county and county of a city in Ireland* (1795–1803) *Commons' jn.*, lviii, 1105–1116 and *Returns of the number of electors who polled at the contested elections in Ireland since 1805*, H.C. 1829 (208), xxii, 1–11. Cork City had the highest proportion of freeholders.
[13] A. P. W. Malcomson, *John Foster* (Oxford, 1978), pp 159–191.
[14] *Report on M.C. (I)*, H.C. 1835, xxvii, appendix pt. 1, 361–2.

from the large number of other aldermen and burgesses. It was Protestant oligarchies of this broadly-based kind that were the chief competitors in the 'freeman-freeholder' constituencies, the competition between them being based upon the traditional means of influencing large electorates such as money, tactical manoeuvres and propaganda; and often revealing elements of conservative, liberal and radical opinion within the Protestant community.

In fact the Anglo-Irish interest in all 28 constituencies was pluralistic. It rested upon both the possession of property and the deployment of the various rules and traditions of the corporations. It was these latter considerations which determined the size and composition of individual interests and which would have been the staple topic of local political discussion between those anxious to use conventional means of maintaining or obtaining some vestige of influence.

The relationship between these various types of Protestant oligarchy and the economic and social circumstances of the towns and cities whose parliamentary and municipal life they managed was uneasy at the time of the Union and was brought under increasing pressure by subsequent developments. Most of the towns had grown in population and commercial prosperity during the latter half of the eighteenth century and most either maintained their status in these respects or improved upon it in the course of this period. In the case of the 'burgess' and 'freeman' boroughs, for example, only a handful appear to have stagnated during the early nineteenth century.[15] In the case of the majority, on the other hand, growth in population and commercial prosperity appears to have been modest in the market towns such as Armagh, Athlone and Ennis; notable in the ports such as Coleraine, Dundalk, Londonderry and Wexford; and spectacular in the case of Belfast.[16] Sligo, which had an electorate of 13 burgesses, is an example of the scale of developments. There the population appears to have doubled between 1801 and 1831 when it was approximately 15,000. The general level of commercial activity also seems to have increased, largely through improvements to the harbour. 65 vessels entered the port in 1800 and produced revenues of just over £6,000. By 1830 the total

[15] Bandon, Dungannon, Cashel and New Ross.
[16] My conclusions on this aspect of the subject are drawn principally from the reports and statistics on individual towns and cities in *Parl. Rep. (I)*, H.C. 1831–2, (519), xliii; *Report on M.C. (I)*, H.C. 1835, xxvii, xxviii; and A. Marmion, *The ancient and modern history of the maritime ports of Ireland,* (London, 1860).

number of vessels using the port had risen to 540 and revenues had increased to over £74,000.[17]

In the case of the 'freeman-freeholder' constituencies, a similar pattern of varied growth and improvement is apparent. With the exception of Carrickfergus all were important commercial centres with reasonably broadly-based economies. Most profited from an increasing provision trade with Britain and were able to cope with both the sudden depressions in certain industries caused by the cessation of Union protecting duties in the 1820s and with the fluctuating demands of the British market. Waterford is an example of the general pattern. The population rose to about 28,000 in 1821 and then remained static. It had been a centre for the manufacture of woollen goods but this declined in the 1820s, no doubt as a result of the removal of protection. Its prosperity depended, however, upon the curing of provisions and its import and export trade. The estimated value of exports rose from £1.3m in 1807 to £2.1m in 1829 and the figures for individual foodstuffs suggest considerable flexibility within the provisions trade. Thus while the export of beef, pork, oats, barley, oatmeal and rapeseed declined between 1807 and 1829, that of bacon, butter, lard, wheat and flour increased substantially. Perhaps the most visible sign of this improving commercial prosperity was the foundation of the chamber of commerce in 1815, one of the significant number established in the larger towns and cities during the course of the early nineteenth century.[18]

The developing economies of Irish towns presented the prevailing political interests with a range of problems. Electorates were already unrepresentative of those engaged in local trade and commerce and were likely to become more so—particularly in the southern and western towns where a high proportion of merchants and tradesmen were Catholic. In addition the corporations were ill-equipped to cope with the growing demands of urban life. Many of them had let their property at low rents during the course of the eighteenth century and had become increasingly dependent financially upon tolls and customs levied upon the sale of goods at markets and fairs. They were therefore open to a number of charges: of political exclusiveness; of incompetence as a result of not having sufficient resources to provide the local justice, the policing, the paving, the lighting and sanitation required by an increasing population and an expanding commerce; and of discrimination as a

[17] Marmion, *Maritime ports of Ireland*, p. 428; *Parl. Rep. (I)*, H.C. 1831–2, (519), xliii, 127.
[18] Marmion, op cit., pp 557–566; *Report on M.C. (I)*, H.C. 1835, xxviii, appendix, pt. 1, 616–7.

result of the fact that their own members were exempted from the taxes they levied upon local trade.

The Union aggravated their problems. The creation of single-member constituencies ran in many cases against the grain of their economic prospects. The measure also left several Protestant interests aggrieved and heightened the chances of expensive and resource-sapping competition between the 'ins' and the 'outs'. In addition the removal of parliamentary representation to Westminster opened up promising opportunities for those hitherto excluded from urban politics. Catholics in the professions or in business could look forward to a more sympathetic, although not necessarily a more informed hearing in the British as opposed to the Irish parliament. Moreover as the Irish urban economy was so dependent upon the decisions of British governments and the state of the British economy it became increasingly important for local commercial interests to be represented adequately at Westminster.

In the course of this period the corporation oligarchies came under increasing pressure from local and national interest groups that varied considerably in composition and intent. In the sphere of municipal as opposed to parliamentary affairs there appear to have been two different developments. The first was most apparent in the fast expanding or larger towns and consisted of the establishment by local acts of parliament of new, and usually more broadly based bodies than the corporations to deal with various aspects of expansion. This was a development which had a long history but which, from the evidence compiled by the commissioners who investigated Irish corporations in 1833, had increased in pace during this period. In Sligo, for example, the task of regulating and improving the civic and commercial amenities of the town was vested by a local statute of 1803 in 60 commissioners elected by £20 householders. Their duties were to regulate the markets; to improve the port and harbour; to construct new docks and quays; to regulate the pilotage; and to levy a rate upon all houses of the annual value of £5 to meet their expenses.[19]

In Belfast a substantial range of local affairs such as street cleaning, lighting, policing, tending to the poor and improving the port were vested by 1831 in bodies other than the corporation, some of which were elected by various classes of ratepayers. From 1816,

---

[19] 43 George 3, c. 60; Marmion, *Maritime ports of Ireland*, p. 427.

for example, 12 of the Belfast police commissioners were elected annually by inhabitants assessed for rates at £4 or more.[20] The composition and intentions of the groups who sponsored these developments require more attention than I have yet been able to give them, but from such evidence as I have looked at, I hazard the guess that they consisted of alliances between wealthy inhabitants and M.P.s who were conscious of the inability of the corporations to cope with expansion and who were anxious to establish alternative institutions that could do so. If this guess proves to be accurate then this development was not so much an attack upon the corporations as an expressions of interest in civic improvement and a recognition that this should be based upon more representative institutions.

The second development had a different origin and consisted of a growing dissatisfaction on the part of tradesmen and the poorer classes with various functions of the corporations. One of these was to provide a cheap and speedy measure of local justice, particularly with regard to disputes over debt. In many cases it appears that the corporations failed to provide this essential service with the result that by the end of this period the whole question of local justice had become a serious source of local grievance—particularly in the market towns. The most contentious function, however, proved to be the levying of tolls and customs. These local taxes upon trade affected town and countryside alike and were pocketed by both corporations and private individuals. Thus in 1826 it was estimated that there were over 2000 toll franchises and that they produced revenues to their owners of more than £1m.[21] The evidence suggests that they were a particular source of grievance in the towns and it is not difficult to see why this was so. Thus tolls were levied upon goods entering a town; upon their sale at markets and fairs; and also upon the weighing of them by the municipal cranes. The charge for weighing a featherbed in Cashel, for example, was 5d although the weighmaster sometimes reduced it to 3d in the case of exceptionally light featherbeds.[22] In addition methods of toll collection were alleged to be somewhat inelegant. Sir John Newport once remarked, for example, that:

It was the practice for the toll-collectors of the Irish markets to stand at the entrance of the market place, with a huge bludgeon in one hand and a prayer book in the other. He imposed the oath upon the vendor of the

---

[20] *Report on M.C. (I),* H.C. 1835, xxviii, appendix, pt. 1, 702–5, 714, 726.
[21] *Parliamentary Debates,* n(ew) s(eries), xiv, 441.
[22] *Report on M.C. (I),* 1835, xxviii, appendix, pt. 1, 472.

goods in a summary way; and if he met with resistance, he took the law into his own hands, and the bludgeon became his instrument of vengeance.[23]

The result of this state of affairs was that in the latter half of this period there was widespread local movement supported by a national campaign inspired by Thomas Spring Rice, M.P. for Limerick City, to press for the reduction or abolition of tolls. By 1832 the movement had met with some success and in at least 9 towns (Armagh, Athlone, Carlow, Dundalk, Ennis, New Ross, Portarlington, Wexford and Youghal), had led to a reduction or abolition.[24]

The pressure upon the prevailing corporation interests was most keenly felt, however, upon their control of parliamentary representation. Inevitably this pressure was exerted first in the larger constituencies where the freeholder franchise offered the best prospect of successful opposition to the established parties of freemen. Thus during the course of this period the predominantly Protestant freeman electorates were confronted in all but two constituencies with the growth of a freeholder electorate which in each case was largely Catholic in composition. The exceptions were Carrickfergus and Waterford where, for somewhat different reasons, the electorate continued to be drawn from the freemen. In the largely Protestant town of Carrickfergus this was due to the fact that at the Union the freeman electorate probably consisted of the vast majority of the adult male population. As the total population of Carrickfergus did not increase to any significant degree during the next 30 years this led to a situation in which the competing interests had no untapped or new reserves of local opinion to call upon. Parliamentary and municipal elections were therefore contested within a large electorate which showed little change in religious and social composition, a situation which led eventually to the expenditure of money and the possession of liberal opinions being of equal importance to successful candidates.[25]

In Waterford, where Protestants were in a minority, Catholics were admitted in small numbers to the freedom of the corporation after 1793. Furthermore, both Catholics and liberal minded Protestants appeared to be appeased when Sir John Newport was

[23] *Parliamentary Debates,* n.s., xiv, 444.
[24] *Reports on M.C. (I),* 1835, xxvii, appendix, pt. 1, 113, 132–6, 168–9, 253, 313; xxviii, appendix, pt. 1, 562–4, 629, 680–3; appendix, pt. 2, 898–901; *Parliamentary Debates,* n.s., xiv, 439–50, n.s., xv, 30–34.
[25] In 1802 Carrickfergus had a population of c. 8000 and an electorate of c. 650. In 1831 the population stood at c. 8700 and the electorate at 851. Of the latter number 683 were resident freemen and 39 were freeholders. It was anticipated that the Irish Reform Bill would reduce the electorate, see *Parl. Rep. (I),* H.C. 1831–2 (519), xliii, vi–vii.

returned on petition in 1803 following a judgement of the House of Commons that only resident freemen could vote in Waterford elections. Newport was a local banker renowned for his expertise in national finance and for his support of municipal reform and Catholic emancipation. The Commons' decision in favour of residency enhanced his reputation and from then until 1831 he proved to be the unchallenged representative of commercial and liberal opinion in the city and one of the acknowledged champions in the southern counties of moderate municipal reform.[26]

In the other six constituencies, however, predominantly Catholic freeholder electorates grew rapidly in number. The development occurred first in Cork, Drogheda and Galway between the general elections of 1807 and 1812. It then spread to Kilkenny and Limerick and eventually affected Dublin in the late 1820s. The overall effect was startling. In 1812 ·the total number of freemen in these constituencies outnumbered freeholders by approximately 4:1. By 1831, when the overall electorate was much larger, the freemen had only a narrow majority.[27]

The reasons for this dramatic increase in the freeholder vote cannot simply be ascribed to an assertion of strength by the urban Catholic community either against the Protestant oligarchies or in favour of additional Catholic relief. Protestant parties that were opposed to the prevailing corporation interest had every reason to develop an alternative electoral base especially amongst voters whose economic and social status suggested that their votes could be easily won by a general expression of liberal sentiment or by proprietorial pressure. Thus in nearly every case the expansion of the freeholder vote can be linked with candidates who had lost ground with the freemen. In Cork it proved to be the flamboyant and radical 'Kit' Hely-Hutchinson who was defeated by a government inspired coalition between his opponents at the 1812 election.[28] In Drogheda in was Henry Meade Ogle;[29] in Galway, the 'well meaning' but 'indolent' Valentine Blake whose family influence in the town had been surrendered to the Dalys;[30] and in

---

[26] *Commons' jn.*, lviii, 26; lix, 36; between 1790 and July 1826, 305 Catholics became freemen out of a total of 1314 admissions, *Report on M.C. (I)*, H.C. 1835, xxvii, appendix, pt. 1, 616–7; in 1831 there were 900 voters of whom 750 were resident freemen and 80 were freeholders, *Parl. Rep. (I)*, H.C. 1831–2(519), xliii, vi–vii. Sir John Newport (1756–1843) was a close friend of Lord Grenville and served as chancellor of the Irish Exchequer 1806–7.

[27] *Returns of the number of electors who polled at the contested elections in Ireland since 1805*, H.C. 1829 (208), xxii, 1–23; *Parl. Rep. (I)*, H.C. 1831–2 (519), xliii, vi–vii.

[28] Christopher Hely-Hutchinson (1767–1826), a younger brother of Lord Donoughmore and a distinguished soldier.

[29] Henry Meade Ogle (c. 1762–1823), member of a Drogheda mercantile family.

[30] Valentine John Blake (1780–1847) of Menlough Castle, Co. Galway.

Limerick it was Lord Glentworth, the son of the Earl of Limerick whose corporation interest had been eclipsed by that of Lord Gort.[31] In fact Kilkenny was the only constituency in which the expansion of the freeholder vote cannot be linked with a candidate whose interest amongst the freeman had declined or was under pressure and this was probably due to the fact that the two corporation interests—those of Lords Ormond and Desart—had formed an alliance when the Union reduced the city to the status of a single-member constituency.[32]

As for the freeholders they appear to have been ideally suited to play the role of mercenaries in an internecine battle between the 'ins' and the 'outs' of the corporation. Most of them registered their property qualification at between 40s and £10 and appear to have consisted of a substantial number of tenant farmers working small-holdings in the suburbs. Thus of 1615 40s freeholders registered in Limerick between 1816 and 1824, 815 were tenant farmers, the rest being tradesmen, weavers, labourers and in the solitary but intriguing case of one William Lysaght, a sportsman. Furthermore it is significant that the Vereker family which managed the prevailing interest in the Limerick corporation was landlord to some 11% of the poorer freeholders and that Lord Limerick, who was his corporation rival, was landlord to some 12%.[33] In other words the interests at loggerheads within the Protestant freeman electorate had potentially important tenant interests within the Catholic freeholder electorate. It is likely that the situation in Limerick applied elsewhere and it is certainly the case that by 1829 (when the 40s freeholders in the towns were not disfranchised like their counterparts in the counties) a substantial proportion of urban freeholders were poor tenant farmers, many of whom held leases that were not automatically renewable.[34]

Yet there does seem to be sufficient evidence to suggest that in course of time the growth of the freeholder vote in these constituencies came to reflect a popular enthusiasm on the part of both Protestants and Catholics for a range of political and economic reforms. This included the disfranchisement of honorary and non-resident freemen and therefore the enfranchisement of local merchants and tradesmen; Catholic emancipation; and eventually

[31] Lord Glentworth (1789-1834). He never became an M.P.
[32] In 1812 a William Collis stood as an opponent of the Ormond and Desart interests. This may have been Lieut. William Collis (1788-1866), a relative of the Knight of Kerry.
[33] *Returns of the number of persons registered as freeholders within the last eight years in every city and town . . . in Ireland,* H.C. 1829 (253), xxii, 20-119.
[34] Ibid., pp 1-261.

economic reforms and a new borough franchise that would produce more representative borough electorates.

The Protestant contribution to these local alliances opposed to the prevailing corporation oligarchies and in favour of reform was not limited to the candidates who acted as their initial spokesmen. Thus it is significant that in Cork and Dublin and until 1826 in Drogheda, substantial numbers of freemen voted with the candidates favoured by the freeholders. 'Kit' Hely-Hutchinson's successful attempt to recapture his seat for Cork City in 1818, for example, was due to his receiving approximately 30% of the votes of more than 1000 freemen in addition to the overwhelming support of the freeholders.[35] The same division between the freemen of Dublin secured the return of the reform candidates, Robert Harty and Louis Perrin, at the general election of 1831.[36] This suggests that there was a stratum of liberal Protestant opinion in these constituencies although it was probably tentative in character. Cork and Dublin were two-member constituencies which enabled 'corporation' and 'freeholder' candidates to be returned in harness. This encouraged what might be termed cross voting. When there was a straight fight between such candidates for one seat, the freemen tended to close ranks in order to resist the return of a freeholder candidate.

As for the Catholic contribution to these alliances it consisted in the first place of active leadership and management of the freeholders by lawyers, businessmen and in some instances, the clergy. In Cork, for example, Hely-Hutchinson's return in 1818 was due in large measure to the efforts of the Reverend Peter England, the parish priest of Bandon and a prominent member of his re-election committee. This committee appears to have been founded soon after Hely-Hutchinson's defeat in 1812 and included Protestant and Catholic members. According to England it was primarily responsible for registering the Catholic freeholders that contributed

[35] The poll produced the following result:

	C. Hely-Hutchinson	Sir N. Colthurst	M. Longfield
Freemen	638	665	535
Freeholders	583	194	189
	1221	859	724

See *Returns of the number of electors who polled at the contested elections in Ireland since 1805,* H.C. 1829 (208), xxii, 7.

[36] The poll here resulted in:

	R. Harty	L. Perrin	F. Shaw	G. Moore
Freemen	1011	1005	1408	1405
Freeholders	932	930	160	157
	1943	1935	1568	1562

See *Freeman's Journal,* 8 June 1831.

to Hely-Hutchinson's re-election and as a tribute to their efforts his candidate's long victory procession was headed by a trumpeter and then two freeholders carrying wands, wearing laurel and mounted on two white horses. These symbols of peace were significant. Hely-Hutchinson's opponents claimed that his victory was due to the coercion of the Catholic voters. The Reverend England retaliated by acknowledging the part they had played but pointed out that they had been joined by substantial numbers of Protestant voters. He therefore claimed that the victory was a symbol of a new era in Cork politics in which liberal Catholics and Protestants would work together. Thus the two 'peaceful' freeholders were followed in the procession by Catholic *and* Protestant members of the re-election committee and then by the band of the City of Cork Militia conveyed in a replica of a ship. This was presumably a symbol of Hely-Hutchinson's military career and the importance of shipping to Cork. The band played a suitably ecumenical sequence of tunes: 'See the conquering hero comes'; 'God save the King'; 'St Patrick's Day'; 'Garryowen'; 'Morgan Rattler'; and 'I'll follow my own vagary O'. Hely-Hutchinson brought up the rear.[37]

In Galway and Limerick commercial interests appear to have been prominent. In Galway the committee of freeholders which sponsored Valentine Blake's opposition to the patron's candidate in 1812 seems likely to have represented the interests of Catholic tradesmen who were excluded from membership of the corporation and who had formed independent guilds to represent their interests following the Relief Act of 1793.[38] In Limerick, Lord Limerick's campaign to overthrow Lord Gort's corporation interest was based upon the 'Friends of the Independence of Limerick'. This body received legal advice from Daniel O'Connell, financial support from the chamber of commerce in which Catholic merchants were prominent, and substantial individual contributions from such businessmen as O'Connell's friend, Edmund Ryan. It was said that the 'Independents' spent £30,000 in what eventually was a successful campaign against Lord Gort.[39]

---

[37] *Report of the proceedings at the election for the city of Cork,* (Cork, 1818), passim but particularly pp 34, 43–4, 79–80. *The Dublin Correspondent* (13 July 1818) referred to it as 'a unique election' in which 'the distinctly Protestant member (M. Longfield) espouses Catholic emancipation and the favourite candidate of the Roman Catholic (C. Hely-Hutchinson) polls a triumphant body of Protestants'.

[38] *Dublin Correspondent*, 3, 16 Oct., 6 Nov. 1812; *Commons' jn.*, lxviii, 19–579; *Parl. Rep. (I)*, H.C. 1831–2 (519), 77–9.

[39] M. Lenihan, *Limerick; its history and antiquities* (Mercier Press reprint, Cork, 1967), pp 361, 398, 414–9, 430–447, 461–6, 482; B.L., Add. MSS 38568, f. 207, 40221, f. 221, 40261, f.

As for the Catholic freeholders it seems probable that once brought into the electoral battlefield they soon identified themselves in the heat of war with the causes that their leaders, and particularly their Catholic leaders, supported. Thus at the Cork City election of 1818 many expressed concern for their future if they voted against the wishes of their landlords or employers.[40] Yet the poll book for this election reveals considerable uniformity in their voting behaviour and as the campaign for Catholic emancipation and electoral and municipal reform matured this proved to be the general case in these constituencies.[41]

The municipal objects of these alliances can to some extent be measured by the results that they achieved. In this respect the spotlight fell upon Galway, Kilkenny and Limerick where the prevailing corporation interests were maintained by the creation of honorary and non-resident freemen and by resistance to the admission of local residents on claims of birth, marriage or apprenticeship. In the case of Limerick the 'Independents' secured legal judgement in 1812 that freemen could only be admitted upon claims of right and this was followed in 1825 by an act of parliament which remodelled the corporation and enforced residency upon the freemen.[42] In the same year the Kilkenny Corporation also agreed under duress to admit freemen by virtue of birth, marriage and apprenticeship[43] and in 1826 the issue was raised in a general form when Sir John Newport introduced a motion to disfranchise non-resident freemen by repealing the Newtown Act.[44]

The *cause celèbre*, however, was that of Galway. There the Daly family managed the prevailing corporation interest but found itself confronted after 1812 with a rising Catholic freeholder electorate which reflected the wish of the local Catholic tradesmen to become freemen. The problem for both parties was that freedom was specifically reserved to Protestants by a local act of the Irish parliament—the Galway Act of 1717.[45] The Dalys could not legally expand their corporation interest by admitting Catholics as freemen

---

104, 40271, ff. 77, 93; *Commons' jn.*, lxxiii, p. 7, lxxiv, p. 22; Maurice R. O'Connell (ed.), *The Correspondence of Daniel O'Connell*, (Shannon: Irish Univ. Press, 1972-), i, p. 462, ii, p. 618.

[40] *Report of the proceedings at the election for the city of Cork*, (Cork, 1818), pp 43-4.

[41] Ibid., passim; the freeholders who voted singly produced the following result:

C. Hely-Hutchinson	Sir N. Colthurst	M. Longfield
542	193	185

[42] *Report on M.C. (I)*, H.C. 1835, xxvii, appendix, pt. 1, 352-3; 4 George IV c. 126.

[43] *Report on M.C. (I)*, H.C. 1835, xxvii, appendix, pt. 1, 542-3.

[44] *Parliamentary Debates*, n.s., xiv, 1247-53; the motion was defeated 76 v 38.

[45] 4 George 1, c. 15.

and Valentine Blake, the freeholders' spokesman, could not satisfy the aspirations of his supporters by securing it for them. Eventually the question arose as to whether the Relief Act of 1793 had repealed the Galway Act and therefore enabled Catholics to vote as freemen. In 1821 the King's Bench adjudged that it had not, with the result that the issue of the Galway franchise passed out of the hands of the Dalys and a beggared Blake and became the stock in trade of pro-Catholic politicians in both Ireland and Britain. In 1830 Spring Rice brought forward a bill to repeal the offending section of the Galway Act but found it opposed by the Duke of Wellington's government which sought instead to repeal the whole of it thereby taking the law relating to the admission of freemen back to a statute of Charles II. This would have placed the privilege in the hands of the governing body of the corporation which was then managed by the Dalys.[46]

The Galway franchise bill and the government's subtle amendment died with the dissolution of parliament in July 1830 but with the Whigs safely in office in the following year Spring Rice re-introduced his measure to the accompaniment of a massive number of petitions presented to parliament from all quarters of Ireland, and including some from Britain. The bill soon became a symbol of the underlying issues in Irish municipal politics and following extensive debates engaging all sections of the Commons, was eventually passed on 15 October 1831.[47]

The general political objects of the freeholder interests can be gauged by the policies of the candidates which they supported. Thus in each case and in each constituency these included further Catholic relief, and after this had been achieved in 1829, a number of economic and political reforms. At the 1830 election these varied considerably and included proposals to reform the corporations and the courts, expressions of opposition to increases in taxation, and in the case of Maurice O'Connell, the freeholders's candidate in Drogheda, support for the secret ballot and the enfranchisement of all taxpayers. In fact the sole unifying force in their campaigns was Daniel O'Connell who made an extensive tour of Ireland during the course of the election and publicly endorsed all the freeholder

---

[46] *Report on M.C. (I)*, H.C. 1835, xxvii, appendix, pt. 1, 321–3; *The Mirror of Parliament*, 1830, i, 665; iii, 2570–77. The *Mirror of Parliament* gives a much more comprehensive coverage of the parliamentary debates, 1830–32, than Hansard. Thomas Spring Rice (1790–1866) was a nephew of Lord Limerick and M.P. for Limerick City, 1820–32. James Daly (1782–1847), the 'patron' of Galway, was a close friend of Robert Peel, the government's home secretary.

[47] 1, 2 William IV, c. 49. The petitioning campaign can be traced through the indexes of *The Mirror of Parliament*, 1828–32. Over 100 were presented between 1830 and October 1831, considerably more than were presented from Ireland in favour of parliamentary reform.

[48] *Freeman's Journal*, 2, 14, 22, 29, 30, 31 July and 2, 3, 4, 6, 7, 9, 10 August 1830.

candidates in these constituencies.[48] O'Connell was also busy during the election in the following year, although on that occasion the future of the Whigs and their reform bills proved to be an additional unifying theme. Thus despite widespread misgivings in Ireland about the provisions of the first Irish reform bill, all the candidates favoured by the freeholders supported the general idea of parliamentary reform in both Ireland and Britain.[49]

In due course the development of alternative electoral interests to the prevailing Protestant oligarchies in the larger constituencies was matched by a similar development in the smaller 'burgess' and 'freemen' boroughs. For most of this period the prevailing interests were left undisturbed and were able to return M.P.s without opposition. Thus there were only 2 polls at the 202 elections that took place in these constituencies between the Union and the 1826 general election, a statistic which gives a general indication of the placidity of local politics as far as parliamentary representation was concerned.

However, following the Catholic Relief Act of 1829 and the intensification of the movement for municipal and electoral reform in both Ireland and Britain, oppositon interests emerged in at least half of the twenty constituencies. These varied in constitution and objectives. In the midland market towns of Armagh, Athlone and Carlow they appear to have consisted of Protestant and Catholic tradesmen who were frustrated with the unrepresenative character of the prevailing corporation interest. In Athlone, for example, a liberal club consisting of local residents petitioned parliament on four occasions between 1829 and 1830 in favour of the vote being vested solely in resident freemen and at the 1830 and 1831 elections supported the candidacy of a liberal reformer against the patron's nominee. These were the first contested elections in Athlone since the Union.[50]

The basis of such opposition in other constituencies was of a different complexion. In the western towns of Ennis and Tralee attempts to get reform candidates O'Gorman Mahon and Nicholas

---

[49] The pro-reform candidates at the 1831 general election were as follows: in Cork, the Hon. J. Boyle and D. Callaghan; in Drogheda, T. Wallace; in Dublin, R. Harty and L. Perrin; in Galway, J. J. Bodkin; in Kilkenny, N. P. Leader; in Limerick, T. S. Rice. Supporters of parliamentary reform were returned in Carrickfergus and Waterford.

[50] *Freeman's Journal,* 6, 10 Aug. 1830, 31 Apr., 12 May 1831; *Dublin Evening Packet,* 10, 14 Aug. 1830; *Commons jn.,* lxxxiv, 387–8, lxxxv, 212, 270, 505, 513–14; lxxxvi, 32, 40, 42, 76, 94–5, 273, 385. *Report on M.C. (I),* H.C. 1835, xxvii, appendix, pt. 1, 124–37. The reform candidate at Athlone was James Talbot.

Philpot Leader returned, derived from local Catholic frustration with the corporation and rested on the claim that the vote should belong to all the male inhabitants.[51] In the northern towns of Coleraine and Londonderry candidates went forward in 1830 to represent the dissatisfaction of the resident freemen with the superior number of non-residents.[52] In the southern ports of Wexford and Youghal contests also took place in 1829 and 1830 between established interests and opponents who seem to have represented local opposition to the unrepresentative condition of the corporations. In Wexford the contest led to a House of Commons' ruling that the vote should be exercised by resident apprentices and tradesmen and by way of a retaliation on the part of the corporation, to the decision to give the freedom of the town to any citizen who wished to claim it. This led in turn to a much enlarged resident electorate and to the return of Charles Walker, a reform and repeal candidate, at the 1831 election.[53] As for Youghal, a candidate stood there as a representative of local Protestants against the interest of the Duke of Devonshire.[54] This may have been a local example of a general Protestant reaction to the course of events in the corporation constituencies during the agitation for Catholic emancipation and municipal and electoral reform. Dr Malcomson has pointed out that in Drogheda the freemen closed ranks after 1826 to overcome the possibility of being overwhelmed by the freeholders.[55] However, the problem for the Protestant interest as a whole became more acute when it was discovered in March 1831 that under the terms of the proposed Irish reform bill non-resident freemen would be disfranchised thereby leaving the vote in the hands of the existing resident freemen as well as the £10 householders.[56] The implication of these provisions was that in many of the corporation boroughs there would be a substantial increase in the Catholic vote with the result that in some there was a sudden rise in the number of freemen during the course of the next 15 months.[57] O'Connell spotted the

[51] *Freeman's Journal,* 14 Aug. 1830, 14 May 1831; *Commons' jn.,* lxxxiv, 404–5.
[52] *Freeman's Journal,* 18 Aug. 1830, 29 Apr., 12 May 1831; *Commons' jn.,* lxxxvi, 77, 81, 87, 603, 635.
[53] *Parl. Rep. (I),* H.C., 1831–2 (519), 139–44; *Commons' jn.,* lxxxiv, 412 5, lxxxv, 175; lxxxvi, 26; *Freeman's Journal,* 6 May 1831.
[54] *Report on M.C. (I),* H.C., 1835, xxvii, appendix, pt. 1, 104–14; *Parl. Rep. (I),* H.C. 1831–2 (519), 145–50; *Freeman's Journal,* 14 Aug. 1830.
[55] A. P. W. Malcomson, *John Foster,* p. 185.
[56] The first Irish reform bill was introduced rather tardily on 24 March 1831.
[57] *Return of the number of freemen created in each corporate town in Ireland returning members to parliament from 1 March 1831 to 20 May 1832,* H.C. 1831–2 (550), xxxvi, 1–6.

development and in its final form the Irish reform bill disqualified honorary freemen admitted after 30 March 1831.[58]

To conclude: the attempt to make generalisations about local politics invites the charge that constituencies are laws unto themselves and that they cannot therefore have a collective history. Furthermore the historian who assumes that the parliamentary or municipal contests of this period were caused by differences of opinion can all too easily overlook the possibility that they derived from nothing more than a common desire to engage in a ritualistic drama in which the contestants were obliged to perform comedies and where the verdict of the audiences was determined by the versatility of the leading actors and the depth of their financial resources. Anyone who has studied individual elections and constituencies will be aware of the force of this argument.

Yet it is possible to suggest that the theatrical features of urban politics in Ireland rested—as in all good theatre—upon an element of serious contention. The terms of the Union encouraged the Anglo-Irish ascendancy to regard the enfranchised corporation towns as potential bastions of the Protestant interest and also emphasised that the collective control of them should be maintained. Individual 'patrons' also had good reason to maintain their interests particularly as it proved to be the policy of British governments to regard the Irish borough seats as pawns that could be captured by money or patronage for the sake of the parliamentary battle at Westminster.

However, the Union took place at a time when many of the enfranchised towns and cities were growing in size and commercial prosperity. The uneasy relationship between close Protestant oligarchies and the needs of the expanding towns resulted in some cases in the establishment of alternative and more broadly based institutions to the corporations; and a widespread agitation against the latter's right to levy tolls and customs. In the sphere of parliamentary politics the prevailing interests in the largest constituencies were confronted after 1807 with the rapid growth of the freeholder electorates that were largely Catholic in composition. These were sponsored by alliances between Protestants and representatives of the Catholic middle class, and in due course became identified with such causes as municipal reform, Catholic emancipation and after 1829, economic and electoral reforms. After a long period of

[58] 2, 3 William IV, c. 88, clause ix.

comparative peace these issues were reflected to varying degrees in about half the smaller constituencies leading to a situation at the time of the debates on the Irish reform bill in 1831 when a majority of the prevailing corporation oligarchies were under pressure from local interest groups. As it happened the final version of the bill failed to satisfy any particular party. Its restrictions upon the freeman franchise annoyed the conservative section of the ascendancy while the Catholic spokesmen regarded the £10 rate for householders as set too high. In this respect it was, perhaps, a typically 'English' measure.

That these developments and these issues could have been a common feature of urban politics in Ireland is not altogether surprising. After all, they were a common feature of politics in those other parts of Europe where the urban responsibilities entrusted to the landed classes in earlier times began to conflict with the aspirations of the bourgeoisie.[59]

[59] I would like to record my thanks to Mr and Mrs Rowan of 92 Malone Road, Belfast for allowing me to consult material in their possession relating to Cork city politics.

The Economic and Social Structure of Nineteenth Century Cork

Maura Murphy

In 1737, Cork was described as the second city of the Kingdom. Its trade was flourishing and its population progressively increasing, so that by the late 1790s it was believed that it would soon rival Liverpool as a centre of commerce.[1] But the nineteenth century saw a reverse of fortune: by 1851 the city's population had reached its pre-twentieth century peak of 85,000, but decline had already set in. By 1861 the population had reverted to its 1820 level of 80,000; ten years later it had fallen to under 79,000, and by 1901 it had dropped to 76,000—i.e. 5% less than its 1820 level.[2] Contemporaries claimed that the decline in the city's population was checked only by the constant inflow from the rural areas. As almost every person in Cork today has country connections, nineteenth century commentators were no doubt correct in attributing such importance to the rural influx. But the destruction of Irish census schedules in 1922 and the extremely unsatisfactory nature of local catholic church registers[3] prevents any attempt to quantify the country inflow. The printed census figures are very poor substitutes, for while they record the number of Cork citizens born in the thirty-one other counties of Ireland, they fail to distinguish between those born in Cork city itself and those born in Cork county—the very region from which the majority of immigrants could be expected to come.

---

[1] Alexander the Coppersmith, *Remarks upon the religion, trade, government, police, customs, manners and maladys of the city of Corke* (Cork, 1737; Tower Books reprint, Cork, 1974), p. 1; *Pilot*, 10 Dec. 1830.
[2] *Census of Ireland*, 1821-1901.
[3] Catholic baptismal and marriage registers for nineteenth century Cork give no indication of parties' occupations and in most cases give no address.

Economic and Social Structure of Cork

Of the counties charted, the census shows that those bordering on Cork—i.e. Kerry, Limerick, Tipperary and Waterford—accounted for the greatest level of immigration to Cork city, varying between 46% of all immigration in 1841 and 31% in 1891.[4] The inflow from Dublin city and county was as high as that from individual Munster counties, and much higher, in fact, than that from Waterford and Clare. The number of Dublin people in Cork, however, was never as high as the number of Cork people in Dublin. As the century passed, the level of immigration into Cork city generally rose. Just before the Famine, some 6% of Cork's population had been born outside the city; by 1901, this figure had risen to 14%. The most dramatic rises in non-local born population took place in the 1840s and 1880s. Between 1841 and 1851 the country-born population of the city rose by over 3,000; between 1881 and 1891 it rose again by 2,000. The rise in the 1840s reflected, no doubt, the rural famine influx, while that of the 1880s was attributed to the distress in the rural areas which drove many into the city in search of work.[5]

Cork had never been an industrial city. It was a commercial centre, described in 1846 as 'a city of great trade' exporting grain, butter, provisions, hides, whiskey and livestock, and acting as victualling centre for British ships bound for the West Indies and other transatlantic ports.[6] Cork's commercial status was reflected in the composition of its town council which, during the course of the

Table I[7]

COMPOSITION OF THE CORK TOWN COUNCIL, 1841–99

	1841	1853	1863	1871	1883	1898	1899
Merchants	23	23	23	27	23	29	24
Retailers	10	5	3	3	3	4	5
Vintners	1	1	2	1	2	3	2
Master tradesmen	4	2	3	2	3	4	4
Legal and professional men	6	13	14	13	6	7	6
Gentlemen	4	4	6	8	7	4	5
Manufacturers	16	8	5	4	5	—	—
Journeymen	—	—	—	—	—	—	7
Others	—	—	—	2	7	5	3

[4] *Census of Ireland,* 1821–1901.
[5] *Third report of His Majesty's Commissioners for enquiring into the housing of the working classes* (for Ireland), [C 4547] H.C. 1884–5, xxxi, qs 23680–88.
[6] *Connor's Cork Directory for the Year 1828* (Cork, 1828); *Slaters' National Commercial Directory of Ireland* (Manchester, 1846).
[7] F. Jackson, *The county and city of Cork post office general directory for 1863 1842–3* (Cork, 1843); Robert H. Laing, *Cork Mercantile Directory for 1863* (Cork, 1863); Fulton & Co, *The*

nineteenth century, was dominated by merchants. Of the 56-strong council, never fewer than 23 seats were held by merchants; and this although Cork's position as a commercial centre was actually declining as the century passed.

The two main sources for tracing the changes in Cork's occupational structure during the nineteenth century are the printed census returns and the local trade directories. The census figures trace the fluctuations in the different occupational sectors as a whole. The directories chart the expansion and contraction of the master and employer sector. The census figures will be examined first, and basing calculations on the occupational groupings suggested in a recent study of quantitative methods,[8] the occupational structure of Cork over the period 1841 to 1901 appears as in Table II following:

Table II[9]

(i) Proportion of Males employed in each Occupational Sector in Cork City (1840-1900), as percentage of total occupied male population.

	1841	1851	1861	1871	1881	1891	1901
Agriculture	9.99	7.94	3.64	3.78	3.98	3.15	2.86
Mining	0.07	0.37	0.03	0.10	0.12	0.10	0.18
Building	7.95	6.81	6.73	7.10	7.79	8.53	9.17
Manufacture	40.88	27.23	22.88	23.67	19.14	19.57	19.15
Transport	1.60	8.37		10.77	10.76	14.33	15.29
Dealing	10.29	10.51	9.31	10.75	11.22	11.95	11.47
Industrial Service	18.50	27.56	31.32	25.81	25.59	18.51	23.22
Public Serv. & Professions	3.63	3.86	13.72	10.15	14.15	14.48	15.69
Domestic Serv.	4.16	3.81	2.63	2.03	2.59	3.06	2.30
Indefinite	3.36	3.14	1.51	5.77	4.76	6.70	0.66

(ii) Proportion of Females employed in each Occupational Sector in Cork City (1840-1900), as percentage of total occupied female population.

	1841	1851	1861	1871	1881	1891	1901
Agriculture	0.42	1.63	0.22	0.39	0.11	0.21	0.26
Manufacture	30.89	41.10	26.54	21.08	21.93	24.94	28.09
Transport					0.07	0.16	0.10
Dealing	13.68	16.23	17.75	14.85	11.85	14.14	19.01
Indust. Serv.	0.99	1.60	1.92	1.49	0.77	1.02	0.25
Public Serv. & Professions	2.39	3.10	3.08	2.49	2.83	5.29	7.76
Domestic Serv.	49.19	48.14	43.62	39.86	57.27	40.00	41.87

City of Cork Directory 1871 (Liverpool, 1871); Francis Guy, *Almanac and Directory,* 1883 (Cork, 1883); *Guy's Directory of Munster 1890-* (Cork, 1890-); *Cork Examiner* (hereafter *CE*), 6, 18 Jan 1899.

[8] Maura Murphy, 'Nineteenth century Cork; The working classes', forthcoming in *Cork Hist. Soc. Jl*, (1979-80).

[9] This table is compiled from the data available in the printed census tables for Cork City, 1841-1901.

Thus, between 40% and 70% of Cork's male population was engaged in gainful employment during the nineteenth century, while among females the proportion so employed varied between 34% and 40%. As Table II suggests, female labour in Cork was concentrated mainly in domestic service, dealing and manufacture. Towards the end of the century the proportion of women working in the public service and professional sectors rose slightly due to the increase in the number of teachers, nuns, midwives, clerks and office workers. But such occupations were generally confined to a limited educated sector of the population, and by the early twentieth century the occupational structure of Cork's female population had changed little from what it had been before the Famine.

In the male working population the changes were more marked. As Table II suggests, certain occupational sectors expanded while others contracted. Agriculture, which in 1841 had employed 10% of all adult males, employed less than 3% in 1901, while the employment potential of the manufacturing sector fell from over 40% in 1841 to less than 20% in 1901. Expansion took place in three sectors: a dramatic expansion in the case of the transport and public service sectors, and slight expansion in the building sector. In the dealing, industrial service and domestic service sectors, employment potential remained relatively stable.

Though nineteenth century Cork was not an industrial centre, at least one-fifth of its occupied population, both male and female, worked in manufacture. And this figure could be increased by the inclusion of that portion of the industrial service sector who worked as labourers in the city's mills, factories and foundries. But the employment potential of the city's manufacturing sector contracted sharply during the course of the century. In 1841 just over 8,000 men worked in manufacture: by 1851 this number had plummeted to under 6,000 (a 25% decrease in ten years) and by 1901 it had dropped to just over 4,000—half its pre-Famine level. In the female manufacturing sector the trend towards decline was less marked. Some 3,500 strong in 1841, it numbered just over 3,200 in 1901. And during the period 1841–51 (the time of greatest decline for the male manufacturing sector) the female manufacturing sector had risen by a dramatic 35% to reach over 5,000 in 1851. This rise was due to the efforts of the short-lived post-Famine manufacture revival movement which throughout Ireland as a whole fostered domestic industry (knitting, lace-making, net-making and artificial flower manufacture) among the women of the poorer classes.[10] But this

[10] CE, Jan., 7, 23 May, 27 June 1851; 12, 23 Jan. 1852.

movement soon petered out, and by 1861 the number of Cork women employed in manufacture had fallen to 2,500, stabilizing thereafter around 3,000.

During the course of the nineteenth century not all trades and occupations in the manufacturing sector declined, nor did all those in the building sector expand. As Table III below indicates, of the thirty principal male occupations in the manufacturing and building sectors, eleven had more members in 1901 than they had in 1841. This, however, did not necessarily mean that those trades were prospering. Several trades whose numbers had risen, e.g. the painters, bakers and coachmakers, were dogged by unemployment. Their rise in numbers was attributed to the influx of non-union country tradesmen, a rise which simply resulted in the flooding of the market by surplus labour.

Table III[11]

	1841	1851	1861	1871	1881	1891	1901
Farriers	3	24	34	37	28	32	43
Printers	116	143	181	191	189	227	184
Engineers	183	142	116	333	242	232	298
Coachmakers	76	68	147	158	161	139	179
Saddlers	140	99	117	97	—	81	76
Shipwrights	91	153	166	111	74	44	43
Builders	51	47	47	48	59	156	212
Carpenters	603	500	645	603	522	612	586
Masons	241	324	300	256	250	284	214
Stonecutters	98	114	117	116	154	93	98
Slaters	150	125	123	90	50	60	35
Plasterers	101	49	55	88	121	111	135
Plumbers	259	226	282	301	102	146	201
Painters					247	276	341
Cabinetmakers	218	175	227	142	124	129	120
Weavers	325	160	113	25	7	3	—
Hatters	98	63	56	37	26	18	—
Tailors	748	551	635	543	484	457	425
Shoemakers	1,398	1,216	1,078	702	590	510	425
Ropemakers	109	90		64	34	23	14
Bakers	253	367	353	348	322	290	274
Tobacco-workers	20	63	77	140	106	254	216
Tanners	288	258	89	137	96	101	36
Brushmakers	45	59	55	39	25	25	11
Coopers	725	551	638	564	442	397	275
Blacksmiths	316	231	322	273	213	172	147
Nailors	131	105	98	78	49	23	7
Sawyers	163	173	172	95	65	55	93

[11] *Census of Ireland*, 1841–1901.

The census figures dealt with here include both employers and employees and therefore do not clarify the sequence of growth and decline in the Cork employer sector. For this one must turn to the trade directories which, it must be emphasised, hide as much as they reveal. Not until the 1870s is there a fairly continuous run of Cork trade directories extant. There is no Cork directory known to this writer for the 1830s, and for the intervening decades we rely on erratic publications, some produced locally, others in Britain. The accuracy of these directories is questionable. They concentrated, naturally enough, on listing the more prominent employers in the city, ignoring many of the small backstreet businesses and small masters who formed a sizeable part of the Cork employer class. For instance, *Pigot's Directory* for 1824 listed forty master coopers in the city, though we know from the evidence of the local journeymen coopers' society that there were at least ninety masters in the city.[12] Moreover, directories produced by different publishers frequently contradicted each other's figures. The locally published *Aldwell's Directory* for 1844–5, for instance, listed forty-five blacksmiths, twelve brushmakers, fifty-two coopers and twenty-one engineers, while the Manchester-published *Slaters' Directory* for 1846 listed these classes as thirteen, five, thirty-four and ten respectively.[13]

Even when such discrepancies are taken into account, however, the trade directories remain our best source of information on the fluctuation of the city's employer numbers and business structure. Interestingly, the directories show that in spite of Cork's progressive decline as a manufacturing centre, employer numbers in most sectors remained relatively stable. There were, of course, as Table IV suggests, certain marked areas of decline, mainly in those areas of manufacture where mechanization and importation were squeezing out the old local handcrafts. Such areas were cabinetmaking, coopering, brush and hat manufacture, the leather trade, and all textile-related industries.

In these sectors the decline in employer numbers, as documented by the trade directories, was accompanied by a corresponding decline in total trade numbers, as traced by the census returns. But in some sectors where total trade numbers fell sharply, the employer numbers remained relatively stable. Thus, while the census showed

12 *Pigot's National Commercial Directory of Ireland* (Dublin, 1824); *Cork Mercantile Chronicle*, 21 Jan. 1832.
13 Alexander Aldwell, *The county and city of Cork post office general directory 1844–45* (Cork, 1844); *Slaters' National Commercial Directory of Ireland, 1846* (Manchester, 1846).

that the total number of shoemakers in Cork fell from 1,400 in 1841 to 425 in 1901, the directories indicated that during the same period the number of master shoemakers rose from 78 to 88.[14]

Table IV[15]

NUMBER OF EMPLOYERS IN VARIOUS TRADES IN CORK CITY, 1824–1906, AS INDICATED BY LOCAL TRADE DIRECTIONS

	1824	1846	1856	1863	1875	1886	1891	1906
Bakers	51	59	66	53	51	52	49	54
Blacksmiths	9	13	32					6
Blockmakers	4	4	6	2		2	1	
Bookbinders	5	9	12	11		8	6	6
Bootmakers	50	78	162	85	48	43	30	88
Brassfounders	6	75	11	4	5	3	3	3
Brewers	5	5	4	5	5	6	6	4
Brushmakers	6	5	10	6	2	2	2	2
Builders	18	27	31	57	36	19	20	26
Butchers	17	86	103	96	73	52	65	91
Butter Merchants		42	72	78	86	69	70	57
Chemical Manufacturers		2			2	5	5	3
Cabinetmakers		34	38	29	18	10	14	17
Coachmakers	7	12	11	13	8	9	11	12
Coal Merchants		15	18	28	34	15	17	21
Coopers	40	34	94	29	8	10	10	10
Corkcutters	5	6	8	6	4	7	9	10
Corn Merchants		34	98	53	49	32	28	
Distillers	8	8	6	5	2	3	3	2
Dyers	14	9	10	7	6	4	3	2
Bleachers		2	2	1	1			
Sailcloth manufacturers	2	2	2					
Woolcombers	19	8	7					
Wool Manufrs	10	2	4	5	6	4		6
Cotton Manufrs	10	3	3		2		1	
Frieze Manufrs	3							
Hosiers	4	3	9	16	18			
Tape Manufrs	6							
Flax & Hemp Manufacturers					2			
Engineers	4	10	12	8	6	10	14	10
Engravers	3	9	11	6	9	5	6	6
Grocers	93	108	148	156	99	69	100	120
Hatters	20	8	14	13	10	6	5	2

[14] *Pigot's National Commercial Directory of Ireland* (Dublin, 1824); Slater, op. cit. (1846); *Slaters' Royal National Commercial Directory of Ireland* (Manchester, 1856); Robert H. Laing, op. cit. (1863); Guy & Co, *Guy's County and City of Cork Directory, 1875–6* (Cork, 1875); *Guy's Directory of Munster,* 1886, 1891, 1906.
[15] *Census of Ireland,* 1841–1901.

Table IV (*Continued*)

NUMBER OF EMPLOYERS IN VARIOUS TRADES IN CORK CITY,
1824–1906, AS INDICATED BY LOCAL TRADE DIRECTIONS

	1824	1846	1856	1863	1875	1886	1891	1906
Ironfounders	5	6	5	6	5	6	12	22
Leather Sellers		21	19	14	14		8	8
Machine makers		7	8		4	5	6	9
Merchants		52	67	15		13	20	16
Millers	10	21	16	16	9	8	8	8
Painters	24	43	56	15	18		17	24
Plumers				20	18	19	20	29
Pawnbrokers	34	35	38	37	30	21	19	18
Printers	2	12	18	15		14	14	11
Provision merchants		40	37	21	52	42	65	65
Publicans		286	418		448	315		
Ropemakers	10	15	15	11	6	10	5	6
Saddlers	16	18	24	25	17	10	14	15
Sailmakers	1	2	14	4	4	5	5	3
Sawmillers						8	11	8
Shipbuilders		2	3	2	2		2	
Salt Works		9	10	8	6	6	7	10
Tailors	23	48	91	56	37	35	49	55
Tanners	28	33	26	21	12	8	17	8
Timber Merchants		9	13	20		12	12	9
Tobacco Manufacturers		12	9	7	6	5	5	5
Wine Merchants		58	76	46	45	19	57	

As the available figures show, the sharpest decline occurred among those least able to resist it, the journeymen. But there was apparent lack of stability, too, in the ranks of the employers. Though certain large city business concerns like the breweries, distilleries and provision stores remained in the same families for generations, the smaller concerns remained in individual families for much shorter periods i.e. from one to three generations. In order to chart the longevity of small business establishments, this writer made an examination of Cork trade directories at approximately ten-year intervals—1824, 1846, 1856, 1867, 1875, 1884, 1891 and 1906. What emerged from this examination is summarized in Table V, which documents the survival rate of houses in each of 7 trades.

As indicated by this table, longevity was not a general feature of small business concerns in nineteenth century Cork. The vast majority of businesses survived less than twenty years, and, if the

Table V[16]

SURVIVAL RATE (IN DECADES) OF INDIVIDUAL ESTABLISHMENTS
IN EACH OF SEVEN CORK TRADES, 1824–1906

Trade Establishment	10 yrs and under	20 yrs	30 yrs	40 yrs	50 yrs	60 yrs	70 yrs	80 yrs
Bakers	166	45	30	11	3	1	1	1
Brushmakers	14	2	2	—	1	—	—	—
Cabinetmakers	63	5	6	1	3	2	—	—
Coachmakers	22	8	5	2	2	2	—	—
Coopers	119	26	9	2	1	—	—	—
Shoemakers	264	13	35	9	5	—	—	1
Tailors	115	34	13	10	5	2	2	—

trade directory indications are correct, relatively few businesses passed on from father to son. Those concerns which survived over forty years were obviously passed on in the family line, but these form a very small proportion of all concerns listed in the local directories between 1824 and 1906. There is, in some cases, it is true, a persistence of certain surnames within individual trades. Much of the city's coach-making business was in the hands of the Busbys, Eddens, Johnsons, Julians and Williams; the coopering trade displayed such names as Codys, Cronins, Deyos, Drinans, Hickeys and Hollands; cabinetmaking was linked with the Cox's, Dees, Lesters and Notts; and so on. The same persistence of surnames extended to the ranks of the journeymen, for though records of this section are scanty in the extreme, it is possible from time to time to encounter surnames which are easily linked with their relevant trade. Such continuity of surnames was, of course, largely due to the rule favoured by all trade unions, of admitting to the trade only those whose fathers were already members. However, this rule was becoming increasingly difficult to enforce, and as early as the 1830s the problem of 'illegal apprentices' was a major worry to all the city's trade societies.[17] Perhaps this incursion of trades by those not traditionally connected with them accounts in part for the great variety of surnames appearing in the ranks of masters and employers from the 1840s onwards. In the ranks of the coopers, for instance, the old traditional and largely Protestant names—Bath,

---

[16] See note 14 above.
[17] *Cork Constitution*, (hereafter *CC*), 9 Mar. 1834; *CE*, 20, 23 Apr., 7 May 1855; Cork Coopers' Society Minute Book, 7 Jan. 1875; 21 Apr. 1887; 10 May 1888; Cork Typographical Society Minute Book, 12 May, 25 July 1888 (Minute Books held by Cork Archives Council).

Burgess, Cottrell, Fair, Paine—were disappearing, to be replaced by others, obviously Catholic. A similar trend was noticeable among the cabinetmakers and shoemakers.

All this raises the question: How did men become masters? If, as the trade directories suggest, so few businesses passed on from father to son, from where did the new masters come? Did they rise from the ranks of the journeymen themselves? The existence of surnames common to the ranks of both masters and men suggests that the transition from journeymen to master was, if not usual, at least possible. A study of the journeymen coachmakers' society list for 1812 shows three surnames which by the 1830s belonged to the master section.[18] The records of the local societies of printers, coopers and plumbers make occasional references to members' progression to the position of masters, or list as journeymen individuals who later appeared in the trade directories as masters.[19]

Nor was the transition from journeyman to master a one-way process: masters falling on hard times could revert to the position of journeymen. In one case, at least, we have definite evidence that a master coopering family of the 1850s had, by 1890, fallen on the ranks of the journeymen. The individual in question, one King Giltinan, appeared in the 1856 trade directory as a master cooper, carrying on his business in Crowley's Lane. In 1892 either this same man or, more probably his son, was listed in the minute book of the local journeymen coopers' society as a journeyman prone to cause trouble at meetings.[20] The coopers' and plumbers' societies, in fact, had special provisions in their rules for the admission of reduced masters as society members—a point indicating that such reverses of fortune were not altogether uncommon.[21]

Though the usual avenue of entry into the rank of master was apparently through the journeyman body, it seems also that it was possible for a man with sufficient capital to become a master in a trade in which he had no traditional roots. This would apply mainly in trades requiring little craft skill, e.g. the baking trade. There is no indication of how common a mode of entry this, in fact, was but there is one recorded case—possibly exceptional, possibly representative—where it did happen. This involved one Michael

[18] Cork Coachmakers' Minute Book, 1812–25 (Vehicle Building and Automative Museum, Holyhead Road, Coventry).
[19] Cork Plumbers' Society Minute Book, 1 May 1868; 15 Oct. 1870 (Cork Archives Council); Cork Typographical Society Minute Book, 5 Apr. 1890.
[20] Slaters' . . . Directory, 1856; Cork Coopers' Society Minute Book, 28 Nov. 1892.
[21] Cork Coopers' Society Minute Book, 13 June 1888; 14 June 1892; Cork Plumbers' Society Minute Book, 15 Oct. 1870.

Downing, a baker who appeared in the Cork bankruptcy court in 1896. He had no background in the trade, but had emigrated to America sometime in the 1870s, returning to Cork in 1881 on money raised by his sister in a local loan office. He joined her in the old clothes business, and earning the then enormous sum of twenty to thirty pounds a week, he saved sufficient money to set up in 1892 as a master baker. His bankruptcy four years later resulted from business inefficiency caused by his growing addiction to drink.[22]

It is not possible to decide how typical a 'new' master was Michael Downing in his entry to a trade in which he had no roots. Had alcoholism not prevented him, he might have become firmly established in the trade, and his mode of entry would have been obscured forever from the prying researcher. In one thing, however, Downing does appear typical i.e. he operated on relatively little capital. The question of capital—or the lack of it—leads to much debate in Irish economic history. In the history of nineteenth century Cork, as of other centres, much research must yet be done into the structure and financing of business concerns. The points suggested in the following pages are no more than suggestions— questions to raise further questions.

While the major businesses of the city, the distillers, brewers and big factories, had few obvious financial worries, the great majority of smaller employers kept their businesses running on the minimum of capital. Business records in Cork, alas, have had a survival rate of almost nil, so that other sources must serve as evidence. There is, in the first place, the evidence of the local trade societies. These regard the small employers, especially those risen from the ranks of the journeymen, as the worst culprits in cutting wage rates to make ends meet. In 1855, for instance, the coopers' society complained of the employment of cheap non-union labour in their trade, mainly by small masters—'men of small or equivocal capital'.[23] Thirty years later, in 1886, a similar situation existed in the tailoring trade, and in this case the divide between small and big masters had actually been formalized by a classification into first and second class masters. The first class employers (those with long-established businesses who drew their custom from among the county gentry and the city's upper classes) paid their men what was known as the first class log. The smaller second class employers, many of whom were ex-journeymen, were allowed by the local tailors' society to pay a lower

---

[22] Cork Bankruptcy Court Records, 1896/84 (Cork Archives, Council Rooms, City Court House, Cork).
[23] *CE,* 19 Jan. 1855.

rate, in order that by so economizing they might firmly establish themselves in the business. By the early 1890s, three of these second class masters were believed by the tailors' society to have made enough money in the trade hence-forward to pay the first class log. A long and bitter strike followed the masters' refusal to pay the higher rate, a refusal based on the contention that their means were insufficient to allow such an advance. The journeymen, of course, paid no attention to these excuses, but subsequent events showed that the second class masters were indeed, as they had claimed, operating on limited capital. By 1912, five of the city's second-class employers had become bankrupt.[24] It should be added, however, that two of the city's first class master tailors had also become bankrupt by the same time. Of all Cork's manufacturing sector, the tailoring sector had, in fact, the greatest number of bankruptcies in the period 1890–1916, followed closely by shoemakers and dealers and by bakers and cabinetmakers.[25] Most, though not all, of those appearing in the Cork bankruptcy court belonged to that group of employers which the local trade directories showed as staying in business for less than two decades, i.e. they belonged to the largest single group of small masters in the city. Even where such men did not actually find themselves in the bankruptcy court, their swift disappearance from the trade directory columns would seem a fairly sure sign that their financial means had been exhausted.

Yet another aspect of trade directory evidence pointing to the unstable financial basis of small businesses in Cork, is the almost constant changing of addresses. Very few business concerns kept the same address for longer than ten years. The main exceptions were the obviously stable and long-lived concerns like Keane and Turnbulls' tailoring house which continued at the same address in the Grand Parade from 1829 to the early twentieth century.[26] Other concerns moved from house to house in the same street or to a different street—the direction of the move generally showing whether business was prospering or declining. A move from one of the minor streets to Patrick Street indicated a rise in fortune: a move in the opposite direction boded ill for the business.

Entry into the master section of certain trades required very little capital. We know that in nineteenth century London, a

---

[24] *CE,* 27 Mar., 10 Apr., 19 May 1893; Cork Bankruptcy Court Records, 1895/81; 1897/17; 1898/113; 1899/148; 1906/230; 247; 1910/311; 1912/303; 1916/365.
[25] Cork Bankruptcy Court Records, Index.
[26] *CC,* 14 May 1829.

man required as little as between one and three pounds to set up in the furniture or footwear industry. Thereafter, he made his business pay by renting a single cheap room as depot, and by employing sweated outworkers at low rates of pay.[27] From the mid-century onwards, sweated outworkers were widely employed in Cork's tailoring and cabinetmaking trades, and the tradition was much older in the shoemaking trade. In the 1820s and 30s journeymen shoemakers collected leather from the masters and made up the boots in their own homes, receiving very little money for long hours of labour.[28]

With the exception of the afore-mentioned master baker, Michael Downing, who went into business with something over £160, we have no evidence of the actual amount of capital at the average small master's disposal. Those who went bankrupt had little or no money left when their means were recorded, so there is little worthwhile information there. But what is significant is the fact that some apparently had never opened a bank account during their entire business career, possibly another indication of lack of capital, or, at least, of lack of understanding of financial matters.[29]

Those who went bankrupt late in the nineteenth century generally blamed their misfortunes on trade depression and on the increasing competition of the big general stores which were invading the tailoring, cabinet making and footwear market.[30] As early as the 1850s complaints had been raised in Dublin and Cork against these 'monster houses',[31] and their progressive takeover of the market is seen in their accelerating entry into the master lists of the trade directories. The firms of Cashs, the Munster Arcade and the Queen's Old Castle, big Cork business houses only today disappearing, all set up their own tailoring workshops and furniture factories, as well as acting as agents for imported goods. As long as such firms preserved the manufacturing side of the business, they gave work to the local journeymen, and though they presumably injured the trade of the small masters, there were few open complaints against them on that score. The worst invaders of the market, from the local manufacturing sector's viewpoint, were the importing warehouses. These were becoming particularly common

---

[27] Gareth S. Jones, *Outcast London: a study in the relationship between classes in victorian society* (Oxford, 1971), p. 31.
[28] *Royal Commission on the state of the poorer classes in Ireland, first report*, Appendix C, [35] H.C., 1836 xxx, pp 27–28.
[29] Cork Bankruptcy Court Records, 1892/31A; 1893/41; 1897/102.
[30] Ibid. 1895/91; 1898/113, 125.
[31] *Irish Trades Advocate*, 27 Sept. 1851.

in the furniture and footwear trade from 1870 onwards. They were set up with relatively little capital, and most of their goods were imported—furniture from Belfast and English centres, footwear from the great centres of the trade at Leicester, Northampton, Kettering and Bristol.[32]

Yet, though these large general stores and importing warehouses were becoming increasingly common, the small master manufacturer remained very much part of the scene, and was no less prominent in the Cork business structure of 1900 than he had been in 1820. Perhaps, paradoxically, the survival of the small master sector was due to its very instability. Men rose and fell on the journey-master see-saw as the dictates of fortune decided, and relatively few made sufficiently large fortunes to transfer to the big employer sector. The continued survival of the small master class, employing from four to twenty men, meant that in a large section of Cork manufacturing industry, the intimacy of the small workshop milieu was never displaced by the factory system. Throughout the century this close master-man relationship survived in different forms. In some trades men lodged with their masters, and in others masters acted as money-lenders to their men (though this practice was not always conducive of good relations).[33] Small masters were not inevitably more popular with their men than were the largescale employers, for some of the worst offenders against trade union principles were those small masters who had graduated from among the ranks of the journeymen, and who were themselves former trade union members.[34] But individuals varied, even within the one trade. Thus while among the bakers the small masters were among the worst offenders against the sanitary regulations and the employment of union labour, they were also the most favourable to the abolition of night work in the trade. They themselves worked in the bakehouse and had first-hand experience of conditions in the trade, whereas the big employers were removed from the shop floor and had less sympathy with the grievances of the journeymen.[35] In the tailoring trade similar variations of attitude were apparent: in the great tailoring strike of 1870 the main opponents of the tailors' union were the large merchant-tailors like Cleburnes and Keane and Turnbulls, while the smaller employers had no quarrel with their

[32] Cork Bankruptcy Court Records, 1893/41; 1896/82; 1898/125.
[33] Sean Daly, *Cork: a city in crisis* (Cork, 1978), pp 199–200; *Southern Reporter*, 9 Nov. 1826; *CE*, 25 Nov. 1881.
[34] *CE*, 20, 23 Apr., 7 May 1855.
[35] *CE*, 23, 25, 26, 28 Aug., 18, 20, 22 Sept., 2, 6 Oct. 1890.

men.[36] Two decades later, the situation was different. When a further major tailoring strike broke out in 1893, the union's main opponents were the smaller second-class employers, while the erstwhile villains of the piece (Keane and Turnbulls and Cleburnes) were held up by the union as examples of the model employers.[37]

If this picture of Cork's trade structure as one of small struggling masters is largely correct, what influence did this structure have on political and social developments in the city? Did it make for labour conflict, for political and social radicalism and class consciousness? Or did it hinder such developments? Perhaps the best way to approach these questions is to look at the various political and social movements which took root in Cork city during the course of the nineteenth century. Basically, there were three different types of movement: the political, the economic and the social. Chief among the constitutional political movements were O'Connell's repeal campaign of 1830–46, and the movements for Home Rule and land reform in the period 1880–1900. In between came the militant and mainly underground organisations, the Confederate Clubs of 1848, the Irish Democratic Association of 1849–50, and the Fenian movement which, through different phases and faces, maintained a continuous existence from the late 1850s into the twentieth century. Of the economic movements, perhaps the most significant, and certainly the most continuous, was the development of trade unionism among skilled and unskilled workers, and the related conflicts between workmen and employers. The socio-political movements, whose inspiration was drawn mainly from England and the continent, were not basically nationalistic but had as their ultimate objective class changes in society. Chief among these movements were Chartism (with which the Irish Democratic Assocation had connections), the Internationale of 1867–72, and the Irish Republican and Socialist Party of 1898–1903, of which James Connolly was the leading light. And cutting across all these movements, nationalist, economic and social, was the ever-present element of local politics, i.e. politics which were really concerned with the mutual rivalries and animosities of local individuals and groups. In the mid-century, John Mitchel spoke disparagingly of what he termed 'the puddle of Irish politics',[38] and this description was perfectly apt for Cork, where family and individual squabbles frequently had more political relevance than had the broad national

[36] Sean Daly, op. cit., p. 20.
[37] *CE,* 23 Aug. 1892; 10 June, 25 Aug. 1893.
[38] Malcolm Brown, *The politics of Irish literature* (London, 1972), p. 239.

issues of the day. This, perhaps, was becoming less evident as the century passed, but it was particularly noticeable in the 1830s and 40s. At that time, a local Repealer, Michael Joseph Barry, wrote to Thomas Davis to ennumerate the chief family factions in Cork City:

There is Joseph Hayes, Alderman—singularly clever, equally intemperate, thoroughly impractical, hating everybody in general, and the Murphy family in particular. (He) cannot, I presume, do the entire work of the city himself, and will not, I am convinced, work with anyone else . . . There are the Murphy and Lyons parties, having their origin in trading rivalry. The , influence of each is extensive; but from their great number, wealth, perfect union among themselves, and the various branches of trade in which they have nearly a monopoly, the Murphy family has a much more extended influence than the Lyonses. The former, too, are backed by the great body of the clergy, from their connection with the bishop, and have all the doubtful and dishonest professors of liberal politics on their side.[39]

These local rivalries helped to a great extent to shape the Cork response to national issues, particularly in the period 1830–50, the 'age of Reform', when repeal of the Union and the reform of the municipal corporations occupied the public mind not alone in Cork, but in every urban centre in Ireland. In the early 1830s, Cork society was divided into two main political groupings, O'Connellites and Anti-O'Connellites or tories. Neither of the two groups was homogenous, but the O'Connellites were by far the more fragmented group, including in their ranks men as socially divided as the city's biggest merchants and poorest labourers, and as politically apart as mild reformers and red hot repealers. The O'Connellites of the mercantile class had their stronghold in the Cork Chamber of Commerce which, during the 1820s, had played a major role in the local campaign for Catholic Emancipation. In the 1830s and 40s it monitored the collection of the O'Connell tribute and the repeal rent, supervised the registration of voters, and arranged entertainments for O'Connell and his lieutenants on their visits to Cork. But in 1832 there emerged a new radical group to challenge the chamber of commerce. This was the Cork Trades Association, initially an artisan body set up to foster local manufacture,[40] but later opening its ranks to a wider social group than artisans, and turning its attention to politics. It became the most vociferous exponent of repeal in Cork, and concentrated its

[39] Charles Gavan Duffy, *Thomas Davis: memoirs of an Irish patriot, 1840–46* (London, 1870), p. 164.
[40] *Cork Mercantile Chronicle,* 27 June 1832.

attention on abusing the chamber of commerce for being lukewarm in the cause of repeal. This was, in fact, a fair criticism, for most of the chamber members were not repealers at all. They were political pragmatists and hard-headed businessmen, favourable to liberal reform in certain areas, but unwilling to join a popular agitation which might injure their business prospects. Such an attitude was regarded as traitorous by the repeal enthusiasts of the Cork Trades Association. But though the quarrel between the Trades Association and the chamber of commerce was ostensibly political, its real basis was social and economic. Just before the Trades Association launched its most virulent attacks on the chamber of commerce,[41] the Association had opened its ranks to a non-artisan element which included shopkeepers, vintners, small manufacturers and clerks. Such individuals were, in fact, far more committed to repeal than were the merchants and big manufacturers of the chamber of commerce, but many were simply using the repeal issue as a vehicle for their own commercial jealousies. It was significant that the severest criticism of the chamber men came not from the very small men, but from the employers and business men in the no-man's land between the chamber and the small masters, i.e. from among those who believed themselves entitled to a place in the chamber, and who were yet without sufficient means to enforce their claim.[42]

Under the provisions of the Municipal Reform Act of 1840, this class became the city's new burgess body. Municipal reform was one of the most significant stages in the politicization of the Irish middle classes, for as Catholic Emancipation and the Reform Act of 1832 had drawn them into the field of parliamentary government, so municipal reform opened to them the hitherto closed field of local government. But, in Cork at least, municipal reform also revealed clearly the deep social divisions within the ranks of the Catholic middle classes. From 1840 onwards, class antipathies and commercial jealousies between the major merchants and manufacturers on the one hand, and the shopkeeping and small master class on the other, took the form of public squabbles between the reformed town council and the burgesses.[43] The two groups were not, of course, mutually exclusive, for town councillors were themselves drawn from the ranks of the burgesses. But the big merchants dominated

[41] Ibid., 14 Nov., 26 Dec. 1832.
[42] One of the most bitter critics of the chamber of commerce at this time was William Ring, a small distiller from the city's North Side.
[43] Maura Murphy, 'Municipal reform and the repeal movement in Cork, 1830–44', in *Cork Hist. Soc. Jn.,* lxxxi (1976), pp 1–18.

the council; they were more likely to attain the rank of alderman than the 'small men' who, though elected each year, were likely to be much further down the poll than the merchants, brewers and distillers of the city.

The burgess class (shopkeepers, vintners, pawnbrokers and small masters) were the most politically active class in the city. They formed the backbone of the campaign against Ministers' Money in the 1840s, the Irish Manufacture Movements of the period 1832–52, the local Land League branch of the 1880s, and, of course, of the various burgess associations which regularly appeared and disappeared each decade from 1840 to 1900. This political activeness of the Cork shopocracy and small masters was perhaps typical of their class, not alone in Ireland, but also in England, where small masters tended to be social radicals.[44] In the Irish context, or at least in the Cork context, nationalism took the place of social radicalism. The shopkeepers and small tradesmen who, for example, in Leeds, formed the backbone of Chartism,[45] were to be found in Cork in the ranks of the repealers, the Confederate Clubs of '48, and the Fenians. The shoemakers who fostered Chartism in the Scottish villages[46] were most prominent through Ireland, and no less so in Cork city, in the Fenian ranks.[47]

Nationalism both replaced and hindered the growth of social radicalism in Cork. The constitutional nationalist movements, in particular, were tailored to enforce rather than challenge the existing social order, for the structure of membership accurately reflected the social gradations of the city. This was particularly true of the repeal movement, in which the liberal representatives of the merchant and manufacturer class filled the top positions, while in the subordinate positions of authority, e.g. as repeal wardens and collectors of the repeal rent, were the shopkeepers and small masters. The journeymen and labourers formed the anonymous rank-and-file. Even when militant nationalism emerged in 1848, the social structure of leadership and membership was not immediately upset. Though the large-scale merchants and manufacturers held aloof, the leadership of the Confederate Clubs of '48 was largely middle-class and propertied. In certain cases, club presidents were actually the employers of the men who formed the rank-and-file of their clubs. The Hegarty Brothers, leading tanners on the city's

[44] John Foster, 'Nineteenth century towns—a class dimension' in H. J. Dyos (ed), *The Study of Urban History* (London, 1966), p. 291.
[45] Asa Briggs, *Chartist studies* (London, 1959), p. 72.
[46] Ibid., p. 275.
[47] Irish Crimes Records, 1865–70, Fenianism: Index of Names (S.P.O.I.).

Maura Murphy

north side, headed the Wolfe Tone Club, in which tanyard porters formed the mass of the membership. In other cases, the club president was the immediate landlord of the club members, while yet other presidents were young professional men of advanced political ideas: the Cork merchant families' younger generation who had been educated mainly at Trinity College, Dublin.[48] These individuals were, in a sense, social orphans, for their Trinity education had divorced them from their family commercial background, while as young revolutionary intellectuals they had little in common with the small shopkeepers, tradesmen and labourers who formed the rank-and-file of the clubs. Their alienation from their own class was, however, temporary. As soon as the prospect of revolution became a reality in 1848 they abandoned all militancy, and emerged from short prison sentences as highly respectable and conservative citizens. The diehard portion of the clubs, disillusioned by their leaders' about-face, reconstituted themselves as the Irish Democratic Association to perpetuate the separatist militancy of '48 and combine with it some commitment to radical social change. The Irish Democratic Association was perhaps the closest nineteenth century Ireland got to a socially radical movement. It was the only movement which habitually used what might be termed 'the language of class', directing its criticism against the middle classes.[49] Yet, such anti-middle class feeling was less a 'class thing' than a nationalist one. The middle classes were condemned not because of any alleged exploitation of the worker or abuse of social privilege, but because they had failed to support the nationalist movement of 1848. Moreover, the Irish Democratic Association's leaders were themselves middle class men (albeit of very modest means), shopkeepers, and master tradesmen, men with a certain stake in the community, and many of them being employers of labour. The same was true of the Fenian movement from 1860 on, for though the majority of the rank-and-file were men of little or no property (journeymen, labourers, clerks and shopboys), small masters and shopkeepers were prominent among the leading men, and at least three of these individuals had already been involved in the Confederate Clubs and the Irish Democratic Association.[50]

---

[48] *Southern Reporter,* 30 May 1848; *CC,* 6 June, 25 July, 3 August. 1848; *Griffith's Valuation, Borough of Cork,* 1852.
[49] *Irishman,* 15 Sept. 1849; 12 Jan., 9 Mar., 23 May 1850.
[50] The three most prominent individuals associated with the 1848 Confederate Clubs, the Irish Democratic Association, and the Fenians, were James Mountaine (Master shoemaker), William O'Carroll (Master baker), and Brian Dillon (Publican).

No movement could be highly radical if property owners and employers, no matter how humble, held in it positions of authority. The nationalist movement in Cork, therefore, was far from radical. Only the Irish Democratic Association had briefly raised the class issue, and for the remainder of the century social issues never entered the field of popular nationalist politics. Nothing illustrates so well the non-radical nature of Cork politics as the absence of Chartism from the city in the 1830s and 40s, and the highly unfavourable reception which met the Internationale in 1872 and the Irish Republican and Socialist Party in the early 1900s. In the latter two cases, the movements in question at least made some attempt (though unsuccessful) to establish themselves in Cork, but in the case of the Chartist movement there was apparently no such attempt, and this, ironically, though Fergus O'Connor had been the darling of the masses in city and county in the early 1830s.

Why did Chartism not prosper in Cork? It seems to the present writer that if ever a social movement like Chartism was to catch on in Cork, the most likely period for this to happen was in the 1830s and 40s before the social upheaval of the Famine and the political disillusionment following the fiasco of '48. The explanation for the absence of Chartism from Cork is most likely to be found in the social and economic make-up of the city. How did Cork's social structure compare with that of the English cities in which Chartism flourished? In England, Chartism was reputedly strongest in single-industry towns, like the textile centre of Manchester, and in centres of decaying domestic industry, like the hosiery town of Leicester. Cork, as the trade directories suggest, failed to fit the mould of a single-industry town, for its manufactures were varied and generally small-scale. Cork was perhaps nearer to the model of a centre of decaying domestic industry, for its hosiery, cotton weaving and woolen weaving industries were, by the early 1830s, almost extinct. Decay had set in as early as the mid-1700s, but the worst blow was the 1826 textile slump in England which resulted in the dumping of cheap factory-produced textiles on the Irish market. Cork weavers thrown out of employment were temporarily employed on local relief works at the rate of a shilling a day, and a scheme was started to emigrate young single men of the trade to the textile centres of England.[51] Many of these individuals went to Manchester, one of the strongest centres of English Chartism. The view that exiled Irish formed the backbone of Chartism in English cities is now being challenged,[52] so it cannot be claimed that the exiled Cork weavers

[51] *Southern Reporter,* 15 June, 4, 9, 11 Nov. 1826; 10, 15, 20, 24 Feb. 1827.

[52] J. H. Treble, 'O'Connor, O'Connell, and the attitudes of the Irish immigrants in the north

espoused in Britain the radicalism they had failed to adopt at home. On the other hand, the Cork weavers, as part of the local populace, were, before their final collapse as a trade, quite a turbulent body. In 1772 they caused major disturbances in the city in protest against the importation of cloth from Dublin and England, and they were still prominent in major trade union disturbances in the early 1820s.[53] By the early 1830s, however, whatever spirit of rebelliousness they had was dead. Their trade was not simply decaying: it was extinct, and their spark of independence crushed. By 1850 they were held up by the city's employers as the classic models of respectable and peace-loving artisans

well deserving of the solicitude and sympathy which had been manifested towards them; for while enduring the keenest pangs that the most severe privations could inflict, they had notwithstanding, borne their sufferings with manly fortitude and the most exemplary patience, and had been at all times distinguished for their peaceable and orderly demeanour. In silence and sorrow they had meekly submitted to their sad lot, without commiting crime, or disturbing society by clamour, riot or agitation.[54]

Decaying trades might prove socially radical or at least prone to riotous behaviour, but dead trades were without resilience of any kind. The failure of Cork's domestic trades to espouse Chartism, therefore, was due to the fact that the process of trade decay had gone too far to allow any hope from such a movement. If their exiled fellows in Manchester turned Chartist (and this writer has no proof that they did) then perhaps it was because they had been removed from the local context and transferred to one where employment prospects were marginally better and despair warded off for a time.

It is interesting to compare the expectations of the masses which followed Chartism in Britain and those who looked for repeal of the Union in Cork and the rest of Ireland. Asa Briggs cites the bread-and-butter expectations of the Trowbridge Chartist who promised his audience 'plenty of roast beef, plum pudding and strong beer by working three hours a day'.[55] A Cork street ballad of the 1830s paraphrased the same hope in relation to repeal:

The tradesmen and labourer that's now in poverty,
Will sit in their parlour and sing melodiously.

of England, 1838–48' in J. Butt and I. F. Clarke (eds) *The Victorians and social protest: a symposium* (Newtown Abbott, Devon, 1973).
[53] Sean Daly, op. cit., p. 271; State of the Country Papers (S.P.O.I.) 1822, 2345/81.
[54] *CE,* 16 Oct. 1850; 14 Feb. 1851.
[55] Asa Briggs, *Chartist studied,* p. 10.

We'll have mutton, beef and bacon, with butter, eggs and veal,
And religion will come again to welcome the Repeal.[56]

Chartism in England, especially among domestic outworkers, was characterised by an intense longing for the past. In Cork of the 1830s the same longing for a return to the golden age of plenty was very much a part of the popular support for repeal, particularly among the distressed handloom weavers of Blackpool and Glasheen. During the parliamentary election of 1832, canvassers on the popular side were told by a woman whose father had once been a master weaver on the city's North Side:

I will show you my father's machinery, lying idle, my family in rags ... The labour of my father's hands, twenty-five years ago enabled me to carry an ostrich feather in my hat. Our apprentices were then fed like kings. Their master is now worse off than a beggar, for he is ashamed to beg.[57]

Perhaps as effective as extreme trade depression in discouraging the rooting of Chartism in Cork was the socal structure of the local artisan class. Researchers have shown that in England Chartism did not flourish in the small workshop milieu. Where the small workshop dominated the trade structure, close master-man relations tended to prevent the feeling and articulation of class tensions which fostered Chartism among outworkers and factory operatives. Equally important, the prospect (however remote) of a journeyman progressing to the rank of master would discourage the desire for change in the social structure. In Cork, as the trade directories suggest, the prevalence of the small workshop system in many craft trades possibly helped to prevent the feeling and articulation of class rivalry, at least within the ranks of the skilled trades, though such rivalries did exist between the skilled workers on the one hand and the unskilled labourers on the other.

How relevant were political issues to the organised workingmen of nineteenth century Cork? In the age of O'Connell such issues were of major concern to the Cork trade societies and mortality societies, as they were to those of every other Irish town at the time. Indeed, the period 1830–48 is one of the most fascinating political periods to study, precisely because organised working men had not yet learned to separate trade unionism and nationalism. It is in the study of this period that one can see most clearly the individual

[56] 'A Speedy Repeal', sung in Buttevant, Co Cork, Sept. 1843. 'Outrage Reports' (S.P.O.I. 1843 CSO/RP 6/17767).
[57] *Cork Mercantile Chronicle,* 28 Nov. 1832.

artisan's or labourer's subjection to a triple political pressure: that of his immediate landlord; that of his employer; and that of his fellow workmen. In the euphoria roused in 1832 by the seemingly imminent granting of repeal, parliamentary reform and abolition of tithes, political activity in Cork reached a peak which it would never again attain. In the general election of 1832, the newly-augmented voting force[58] was mobilized on behalf of two repealer candidates, and the enforcement of election pledges on candidates, voters and non-voters alike, ensured that the principle of repeal triumphed. During that election the various trade societies of the city called on all their members to work for the return of the repeal candidates, either by voting for them or by 'persuading' others to do so. The strong, cohesive nature of the trade society as a political and social entity is seen in the fact that society secretaries could so definitely state the expected political behaviour of the membership, and in the fact that in at least one society members refusing to obey the election directive were ostracized by the remainder of the trade.[59] At the same time, tradesmen and labourers came under pressure from their immediate landlords, who guaranteed to the election committee that they would secure the votes of their tenants for the popular candidates. This practice, if exercised by a country landowner on behalf of a tory candidate would have been loudly condemned by the O'Connellite press, but it was looked upon as quite correct and reasonable when exercised on the popular side.[60]

The exact nature of employers' political influence on their men is less clear, but there is little doubt that it was exercised on both sides of the political divide, i.e. by tories and O'Connellites alike. Following the popular victory of the 1832 election, it was suggested that workingmen who had voted or canvassed on the repealer side should be presented with medals testifying to their efforts. Such medals were not simply tokens of gratitude: they were really political identification badges which would vouch for a man's political integrity when he looked for work, for

possession of such a medal would be an introduction and a recommendation to the poor tradesman or labourer that sought employment.[61]

---

[58] The 1832 Reform Act increased the Cork City electorate from 2,500 to 4,300. See *Number of persons entitled to vote at the elections of members for cities and boroughs in Ireland etc* H.C. 1830 (522), xxxi, 321; and *Registered electors II Ireland. Number registered under the Reform Act etc.*, H.C. 1833 (177), xxvii, 289.

[59] *Cork Mercantile Chronicle,* 24 Oct. 1832.

[60] Ibid., 24 Oct., 21 Nov. 1832; *CC,* 18 July 1837.

[61] *Cork Mercantile Chronicle,* 23 Jan. 1833.

Similarly, the collection of the O'Connell tribute and the repeal rent was greatly dependent on the co-operation of individual employers, who took up contributions from their workmen. The tories saw this practice (perhaps correctly) as an exploitation of those who could not well refuse their employer's demand without endangering their employment. In 1840, the tory *Cork Constitution* quoted one workingman's objection to the mode of collecting the tribute:

I was witness now, to as great a piece of barbarity as ever you heard of—sixpence a week stopped from poor labourers earning only four-and-sixpence a week. Sure, if the people wanted to give the man [O'Connell] anything, they ought to leave it to themselves.[62]

The big city businesses owned by O'Connellites indeed gave large sums towards the tribute, but whether or not a portion of these sums was taken up from the workmen is not now clear. In the case of small masters and their men, however, an en-bloc contribution was more common. A typical entry in the published subscription list for 1845 illustrates both the intimate employer-men relationships of the small workshops and the way in which this social contact led to political cohesion:

Mary Coughlan, Hatter . . . £1
Her Workmen:
J. Ainsworth; H. Murphy;
Thomas Bowles; J. Twomey . . . 5s each.[63]

If the mutual political commitments of employers and men were as common as this suggests, then it made sense for employers to seek as workmen those of their own political persuasion, and this would usually mean of the same religious persuasion. Employee recruitment along sectarian lines would apply less in cases where an employer's religious and political loyalties did not follow the traditional pattern, e.g. where a Protestant employer was an O'Connellite, or (much less frequently) where a Catholic employer was tory in politics. The big Cork brewers, Beamish and Crawford, were such a case: Protestant in religion, they were nonetheless among the foremost adherents of O'Connell in Cork. Recruitment on sectarian lines also applied less in cases where a workforce was largely unskilled, e.g. in the big provision stores, in the shipping companies, and later in the railways. Most of the big employers in

[62] *CC,* 10 Nov. 1840.
[63] *CE,* 18 Nov. 1845.

Maura Murphy

these sectors were Protestant, but their manual unskilled workforce was over 90% Catholic.[64] The recruitment of a workforce on the lines of religious creed was more common in small establishments and among skilled manual workers and white collar workers. Already in the early 1830s the local Protestant Operative Society had called on all Protestant employers in the city to engage only workers of their own faith.[65] The extent to which such advice was followed is not certain, but as late as 1870 it was claimed that the local wine merchants, Woodford Byrnes, employed only Englishmen and Protestants in the more lucrative positions in their firm.[66] In the late 1880s, the printing staff of the conservative *Cork Constitution* was largely Protestant,[67] and into the early twentieth century certain job-printing houses in the city preferred to recruit their staff on sectarian lines.[68]

It was only natural that employers of the minority faith should give employment preference to men of their own creed. Yet perhaps it is incorrect to see employment on a sectarian basis in the Cork context as a totally deliberate policy. Certain trades and occupations, it so happened, were more Protestant (or less Catholic) than others. And this, it would seem, was due not to employer manipulation but to two other factors: the survival of certain eighteenth century occupational trends, and the structural differences between one trade union and another. In the first case, at least three trades, coopering, weaving and shoemaking, owed their relatively strong Protestant nature in the first half of the nineteenth century to the fact that during the eighteenth century their master section had been organized in chartered guilds. The guilds were exclusively Protestant bodies, which, as their members became reduced in circumstances, merged with the journeyman body, thus increasing the Protestant ratio of these trades.[69] The survival of the old sectarian-political structure was evident even in the 1830s, when the poll-book for the 1835 election (the latest surviving Cork-City poll-book known to this writer) showed that the enfranchised portion of the coopering trade had the greatest number of freemen,

[64] *Census of Ireland*, 1871–1901. Among labourers in Cork City, the Catholic proportion varied between 98% and 99%.
Proceedings of the select committee on the sale of intoxicating liquors on Sunday (Ireland) Bill, H.C. 1877 (198), xvi, 1.
[65] *CC*, 9 Aug. 1832.
[66] Sean Daly, op. cit., pp 51–2.
[67] *CC*, 2 Dec. 1887.
[68] Evidence of the writer's father.
[69] Sean Daly, op. cit., pp 254–270.

and that the trade voted overwhelmingly for the tory candidates.[70] Interestingly, too, the local Union Workhouse Registers during the latter half of the nineteenth century show a considerable number of Protestant shoemakers in their columns.[71] It is unfortunate that not until 1871 did the printed census returns differentiate between Catholics, Protestants and Dissenters on an occupational basis. By that time, those trades reputedly strongly Protestant during the early century had levelled out to match the general ratio of 80% Catholic to 20% Protestant.[72] But other trades had even by the period 1870–1901 a higher than average Protestant membership. These were the printers, engineers and boilermakers, among whom the proportion of Protestant members was as high as 40%. It would seem that in these cases the higher Protestant ratio was due to the amalgamated structure of the relevant trade unions. Cork trade unionism was divided (as was that of other Irish centres) between local societies and branches of English-based amalgamated unions. The trade societies operating on the local principle showed extreme intoversion in all their dealings, doing their utmost to prevent the invasion of the Cork labour market by tradesmen who had served their apprenticeships outside the city. The branches of amalgamated unions, on the other hand, allowed a controlled traffic of union members into the city from other Irish centres and from cross-channel, while, in return, Cork union members frequently sought work in Britain. Even without formal amalgamation, of course, the tramp system allowed for constant communication between Cork trade unions and those of other centres, but as tramps could stay only a night or two in the city, the tramp system did not allow for a permanent infusion of English-born (and probably Protestant) artisans into the city's trade structure. Amalgamated unionism, on the other hand, allowed for this infusion.

The proportion of English and Protestant members in the Cork trades never exceeded forty per cent, yet it did have a definite effect on the political behaviour of the trade societies concerned. Local societies like the coopers and carpenters were stongly and arrogantly nationalistic (though becoming less so as the century passed). But trades with British connections and with the ac- companying membership of mixed political and religious views, did their best to avoid all political entanglements. The Cork Typo-

[70] *People's Press*, 17, 24, 31 Jan., 7, 14 Feb. 1835. Following the defeat of the popular side in the 1835 election, the *People's Press*, a local radical publication, published the election poll over a period of weeks, to expose tory voters to the odium of the popular side.
[71] Cork Union Workhouse Registers, 1850–80 (Cork Archives Council Rooms).
[72] *Census of Ireland*, 1871–1901.

graphical Society, which though not formally amalgamated with the Typographical Association in Britain had close working relationships with that body, was the most successful in avoiding political entanglements. From 1843 until 1880 it took no part in any political demonstration in the city, and thereafter, even at the height of the Parnellite excitement, it maintained its political neutrality. It refused, as a body, to contribute to nationalist causes, and in 1887 it strongly resisted the local Trades Council's politically motivated boycott of the conservative *Cork Constitution,* pointing out that such a boycott would injure the society members working in that office more than it would discommode the *Constitution's* pro-prietors.[73] As the century passed, even those trade unions which were openly committed to nationalism, however, did not allow political loyalties to stand in the way of trade union objectives, and they judged an employer not on the intensity of his political commitment, but on the wages and conditions he gave his workmen. Agreement on political matters did not necessarily bring in its train harmony on trade issues, and a number of the most commited nationalists among the master tradesmen of the city found themselves at loggerheads with their workmen over breaches in trade union rules.[74] By the 1880s the nationalist members of the local trade societies and of the Trades Council had begun to articulate much more clearly than heretofore their dissatisfaction with local nationalist employers and town councillors who acted against trade union interests, and a similar attitude was evident amongst those trades unionists commited to the British connection. In 1888, during a lockout in the office of the *Cork Constitution,* one of the locked-out men spelt out his priorities clearly: 'He was a Unionist in politics, but he was first and always a trades unionist'.[75]

It has been said that 'the essential precondition of class con-sciousness is that people *think* it possible to change things'.[76] There is little evidence that many citizens of nineteenth century Cork thought thus along social lines. Positive thinking of this sort was confined to the field of nationalism and trades unionism: nationa-lists wished to cut the link with England and their belief in the possibility of success made them active in that cause. Trade

[73] *CC,* 2 Dec. 1887; *CE,* 3 Dec. 1887.
[74] William O'Carroll, master baker and Fenian, opposed the bakers' union's campaign against night work in 1861, and in 1886 the Fenian master cooper, Cornelius P. O'Sullivan, was brought to book by the coopers' society for employing non-union men. Sean Daly, op. cit., p. 283; Cork Coopers' Society Minute Book, 4 May 1886.
[75] *CE,* 4 June 1888.
[76] Foster, op. cit., p. 288.

unionists considered it possible to maintain or raise wages or to exclude non-union labour by means of the strike, and the number of strikes in the city, particularly in the later decades of the century, showed that they were prepared to put this belief into action. But there was no widespread belief that the social structure could or should be altered. Only before the Famine were such beliefs expressed, and then only by the ignorant and largely inarticulate masses who placed their hopes equally in O'Connell and the prophecies of Colmcille and Pastorini. In 1837 the election of two O'Connellite candidates in the city election led to the spreading of wild rumours among that populace that 'there's no more cattle nor corn to be sent from Cork for the next seven years, that the people may eat the meat and bread', and that 'no more tithes are to be paid, and no more people are to be hanged'.[77] The popular street ballads expressed similar hopes, though less forcefully as the century passed. But the ballads and the prophecies were the hopes of the unorganised masses. The organised section of the working classes had different objectives: the improvement or maintenance of wages and working conditions within the existing social context. And even in this field there was little unity, certainly nothing like a unified labour movement. Artisans vigilantly guarded against the incursion of their crafts by unskilled men, and were frequently openly hostile to the unionization of the unskilled: to such an extent, in fact, that in 1890 an exasperated organizer of the city's unskilled labourers complained that:

It was the old, old story, that whenever a movement was started to help the working men, the greatest clog upon it were the Trades of Cork . . . [who] think more of their own ambition than of harmony and the working mens' improvement.[78]

Moreover, individual unions within the one craft often opposed one another with a bitterness which horrified outsiders committed to the formation of a broad social movement.[79] Cork trades unionism was closed and inward looking, and this although there had been close connections with English trade unionism since early in the nineteenth century. Perhaps the clearest sign of this lack of social purpose in the ranks of organised labour was the absence of any attempt by labour to enter local government until 1898. In the mid-1880s were seen the first coherent signs of trade union dis-

[77] *CC*, 15 Aug. 1837.
[78] *CE*, 24 Feb. 1890.
[79] Webb Trade Union Collection, section A, vol III, ff 46–7 (London School of Economics).

Maura Murphy

satisfaction with the local town council. But this was due not to class awareness but to resentment at the town council's refusal to promote building works during a period of high unemployment in the building trade. And though the trades began at this stage to exert their influence in the municipal elections,[80] they made no attempt to put forward a labour candidate for the council. Under the Local Government Act of 1898 the Cork municipal electorate was increased four-fold, and at length the Cork labour candidates, organised by the local Trades Council under pressure from Dublin, made a good showing. They won seven seats on the 56-strong council.[81] But the successful candidates were representatives of the skilled trades rather than of labour as a whole, for not one of them was an unskilled labourer. Moreover, they entered the town council without any social or political programme whatever. They appear to have made no pre-election pledges, and were obviously more anxious to prove the strength of their nationalism than of their 'labourism'.[82]

If trades unionism and commitment to nationalism did not necessarily go hand in hand, neither did nationalism or trade unionism foster radicalism of a social type. Two influences against the growth of radicalism in Cork came from outside the working classes: from the press and the clergy. The local press, liberal as well as tory, remained adamantly opposed to any movement seeking social change, and successfully blocked the local advance of any such movement by the simple expedient of ignoring its existence. Deprived of publicity, a minority movement was doomed to failure. Thus, the Irish Democratic Association of 1849–50 was ignored by the *Cork Examiner*, the local liberal newspaper, and only the evidence of contemporary police reports and of the association's own mouthpiece, the *Irishman,* testifies to its existence in Cork.[83] But perhaps more powerful than the press in discouraging the development of social radicalism was the influence of the Catholic clergy. The Democrats, the Internationale of 1872, and the Irish Republican and Socialist Party of the early 1900s, all came under the lash of clerical opposition, with a consequent decimation of membership.[84] Neither the influence of the press nor the opposition

[80] *CE,* 21, 28 Oct., 25 Nov. 1886; 5, 6, 13 Feb., 18 Nov. 1892.
[81] The municipal electorate rose from c. 3,000 to c. 13,000. *CC,* 18 Jan. 1899.
[82] *CE,* 1, 5, 12 Dec. 1898.
[83] *Irishman,* 16 Nov. 1849; 2 Mar. 1850; 'Outrage Reports' (S.P.O.I. CSO/RP/), 1850, 6/307, 326.
[84] *Irishman,* 11 May 1850; Letter Book of the Irish Socialist and Republican Party, 11 Sept. 1898, 6 Mar. 1900, 2 Aug., 4 Nov. 1901 (N.L.I. MS 15700 (1)).

of the clergy, however, explain adequately the lack of popular response to such movements in Cork. The Fabian movement which put down roots in Belfast and Dublin in the early 1890s made no converts whatever in Cork, and this without the interference of either press or pulpit.[85] And it must also be remembered that the constant opposition of press and clergy did nothing to check the progress of Fenianism in Cork. Clerical and press opposition succeeded only where the popular will to resist it did not exist, and the reasons for the failure of social radicalism in Cork must be sought elsewhere, within the working classes themselves. Working-men were, as the century passed, attaining a higher standard of living. There was less incentive for social radicalism in the late nineteenth century than there had been in the earlier decades, for though wages rose but slowly, living standards certainly improved, as working hours were cut, housing reform attempted, and provision and fuel prices remained relatively stable.[86]

But the primary reason for the failure of radicalism in nineteenth century Cork was, this writer would contend, the structure of the artisan class; a structure in which the small master, the mini-capitalist, remained predominant, even into the twentieth century.[87]

[85] *Fabian News,* Jan. 1892; Feb. 1897; Webb Trade Union Collection, op. cit., Sec. A, Vol III, ff 46-7.
[86] Maura Murphy, 'Nineteenth-century Cork: the working classes', forthcoming in *Cork. Hist. Soc. Jn.* (1979-80).
[87] *CE, 1, 5 Dec. 1898.*

Industrialisation and Health in Belfast in the Early Nineteenth Century

Peter Froggatt

There is small doubt as to which act of the Irish parliament of 1800 is the more memorable, the act for the union of Great Britain and Ireland or the more prosaic 'An Act for paving, cleaning and lighting and improving the several Streets, Squares, Lanes and Passages within the town of Belfast, in the County of Antrim, and for removing and preventing all Encroachments, Obstructions, and Annoyances therein . . .'[1] Yet this second act was sorely needed, whatever might have been the case for the first. Behind the elegant gardens with the gentlemen's houses in Donegall Place unsullied by 'a single shop, hotel or place of business of any kind'[2] and with 'Cromack woods' a mere quarter mile away, lay a more sordid world seen by a correspondent ('Propete') in the *News-Letter* as a

. . . long string of falling cabbins and tattered houses, all tumbling down, with an horrid aspect . . . [and] Oh, cleanliness, celestial maid, what was my surprise at beholding piles of dunghills made up through the middle of the whole town, from one end to the other.[3]

Fifty years later pulses quickened more to the opening of the Queen's College, the royal visit, and the tangible results on all sides of the Belfast *Wirtschaftswünder* than by the preamble to 13 & 14 Victoria, cap. cviii: 'Whereas it is necessary that Provision should be

[1] 40 Geo. III, ch. 37 (Ireland).
[2] George Benn, *A history of the town of Belfast from the earliest times to the close of the eighteenth century* (London, 1877), p. 550.
[3] *Belfast News-Letter*, 19 December 1780.

155

made for the more speedy Removal of certain Nuisances and for the preventing contagious and epidemic Diseases within the said Borough [of Belfast] etc., etc.' This act was needed also: filth, ordure, crowding, squalor, and privation, and their shadows—microbial diseases—linked together the Belfasts of 1800 and 1850 as tightly as they linked together the other burgeoning industrial towns of Europe and north America though screened in 1850 from sight and mind as effectively by factory and commercial building as previously by residence, glade and garden. To Mr and Mrs Hall

it was something new to perceive rising above the houses, numerous tall and thin chimneys, indicative of industry, occupation, commerce and prosperity . . . and full employment. The pleasant and cheery impression we received was increased as we trod the streets; there was so much bustle; such an 'aspect' of business . . . making us for the moment believe we were in a clean Manchester;[4]

but to the clinical eye and lyrical pen of Dr Andrew Malcolm this acceptable face of the Victorian beehive hid

1800 houses . . . in stinking unpaved courts . . . so that it would *seem* to be an understood law of nature that the indigent do not actually require as much fresh air as the wealthy . . . Upwards of 3,000 houses are without yards of any description . . . The great majority of the poorer class of houses . . . consist of four rooms . . . each of seven to ten feet square . . . in two storeys . . . [and] we have known, and not infrequently, so many as eighteen or even twenty persons sleeping [within them] . . . in Bally-macarrett the rain from the clouds and the sewage from the dwellings are at liberty to make their own intersections and channels without any interference on the part of man . . . The great number of open ditch-sewers, the vast extent of damp, undrained common, the repeated 'running up' of . . . tenements . . . must at once attract the attention even of the most careless visitor . . . .[5]

The unsanitariness of urban living for the poor had little changed over most of the fifty years; nowhere were there the traditional objectives of 'air for his health, light for his profit, prospect for his pleasure'. Sanitary amenities for the rich had hardly changed either: Lyon Playfair's report on the sanitation of Buckingham Palace lay long unpublished, an awesome catalogue! Only in medical knowledge, in lighting, paving and policing streets, and in the extent of

[4] S. C. and A. M. Hall, *Ireland: its scenery, character, etc.* (London, 1841–43), iii, pp 52–3.
[5] A. G. Malcolm, *The sanitary state of Belfast with suggestions for its improvement* (Belfast, 1852), pp 5–10 (hereafter cited as Malcolm, *Sanitary state of Belfast*).

public outrage and response at sanitary indecencies, had there been progress, and it was small enough until the eighteen-forties. In sanitary engineering there was progress also but not advance: ironically, by discharging sewage into rivers and then piping the river water from lower down to drinking stand-pipe and house, it facilitated the spread of water-borne diseases, notably cholera. Belfast grew as a British nineteenth century industrial city and for much the same reasons and with much the same problems and it is the effect on health of this industrialisation and urbanisation which this paper examines. I say 'industrialisation' *and* 'urbanisation' because the effects of the two are confounded; in many statistics the effects of occupation on health are subsumed in the effects ascribed to urban dwelling, and anyhow it is impossible to attribute ill-health or fitness unquestionably to one or to the other. In byssinosis in textile operatives, for example, lungs were damaged by flax or cotton fibres inhaled at work but death was due to superimposed lung infection contracted from squalid domestic conditions. None of this is simple, nor is reliance on statistics in favour of anecdote or account conducive to sparkling narrative. To further the discomfiture of the reader, the first half of the nineteenth century, though seminal of medical theories and statistical practice, produced much better dialectic and polemic; while the economic, social, and demographic parameters of population growth, movements of wages, supply and distribution of food, the level of housing and rents, and the many other correlates and determinants of urban health are either imperfectly known or, when known, seem not to have inspired a ready consensus in their interpretation or importance. Moreover, many crucial data are sparse or non-existent or when present are unreliable. The civil registration of births and deaths was neither universal nor compulsory in Ireland until 1864;[6] many of the studies and enquiries into factory conditions and labour either did not apply at all to Ireland or, if so, then only nominally; Friendly Societies were few, those making returns fewer still; the first two decennial censuses in Britain of 1801 and 1811 had no counterparts in Ireland (if we discount the incomplete and unpublished census between 1813 and 1815);[7] the apocalypse of the 1840s with its vast migrations and mortality was not visited on the rest of the kingdom across the seas. I will therefore have to augment direct evidence with analogy from the more extensively documented

[6] 26 Vict., ch. 11.
[7] Peter Froggatt, 'The census in Ireland of 1813–15' in *I.H.S.*, xiv, no. 55 (March 1965), pp 227–235.

British scene—a methodological outrage in the case of Ireland as a whole but perhaps permissible if confined to the rather particular case of Belfast.

THE CONTEMPORARY MEDICAL SCENE

Robert Southey had a lively career. Expelled from Westminster School for criticising flogging, refused entry at Christ Church, a dilettante at Balliol, he later became a companion of Coleridge and Lovell, the husband of a sister of their wives, and planned *en famille* the 'pantisocracy' of a new Utopia on the banks of the Susquehanna. But then as his fortunes prospered he found a new accommodation with constitutional practice and as Poet Laureate alternated indifferent verses and noble prose with obscurantist commentaries in the *Quarterly Review* opposing such platforms as parliamentary reform, Catholic emancipation, and free trade, and died with a country house, a state pension of £300 a year, and a fortune of £12,000. But throughout his political conversion he maintained his basic compassion. 'Moloch,' he wrote of factory children, 'is more merciful than Mammon':[8] the god of the Phoenicians who was fed live children as sacrifices was less rapacious than the god who swallowed everything in pursuit of industrial progress, not just children but morality, honour, and christian principle. These sentiments, now more generalised, found ready echo; and today there is a conventional wisdom that the outrages of the factory system and the attendant horrors of squalid, rapid, and unplanned growth of urban conurbations with their social and physiological disruptions of society must have been destructive to health and not just that of children, as it was to much else. Many looked back to some rural Arcadia more imagined than real. Contemporaries longed for the delights of the countryside: in Milton's words:

> As one who long in populous city pent
> Where houses thick and sewers annoy the air
> Forth issuing on a summer's morn, to breathe
> Among the pleasant villages and farms
> Adjoined, from each thing met conceives delight.[9]

[8] Lucy Taylor, *The children's champion and the victories he won: pictures from the life of . . . Lord Shaftesbury* (London, 1889), p. 53.
[9] John Milton, *Paradise Lost* (London, 1667), Bk. 9, l. 445–49.

But degrading or not, industrial occupations and environments had their hazardous pre-industrial counterparts: drummer-boy and powder-monkey were no less dangerous pursuits than pit-boy or chimney-sweep; soldier, serf, or parish apprentice no safer than urban servant or factory hand; rural hovels were as harsh as urban ones; domestic industry was as remorseless a master as factory discipline (Francis Place as a journeyman outworker on piece-rates often 'worked full sixteen, and sometimes eighteen, hours a day. Sundays and all. I never went out of the house for many weeks, and could not find time for a month to shave myself'[10]): only in the discontinuous nature of domestic piece-working was there an important difference though it was more in attitude, status and social organisation than in health. The great epidemics up to the end of the seventeenth century cheapened life also. The Victorian hymns palliating early death merely echoed earlier, cruder lines derived from folk *mores* of rural plague.

Ring-a-ring-a-rosies
A pocketful of posies
Atishoo, atishoo,
We all fall down,

now a cheerful nursery rhyme was in fact a grimmer verse than ever Cecil Frances Alexander wrote. The 'ring-a-rosies' is the ritual *Metzersprüng* or *Schefflertanz* of the plague apocalypse; the 'posies' the bundles of fragrant herbs to counter the 'epidemic miasmata'; 'atishoo' heralds the deadly respiratory form of bubonic plague; 'we all fall down' is the most easily interpretable line of all. If the heavy child mortality of the early years of the last century is much cited it is as much a sign of changing attitudes to the outrage and its perpetration as it is to any increased prevalence real or supposed. Before the first cart-load of pauper children made its long journey north to the servitude of the new textile mills a house of commons' committee could report that in St-Martin-in-the-Fields, reputedly the parish

most free from frauds and abuses . . . a great many poor infants and exposed bastard children are inhumanly suffered to die by the barbarity of parish nurses who are a sort of people void of commiseration or religion; hired by the Churchwardens to take off a burden free from the parish at the cheapest and easiest rates they can,[11]

[10] M. D. George, *England in transition* (London, 1953), p. 60.
[11] *Commons' Jn.*, xviii, 392, 396 (8 March 1715).

and a broadsheet of 1738 lamented that 'The master may be a Tiger in cruelty, he may beat, strip naked, or starve or do what he will to the poor innocent lad, few people take much notice, and the [parish] officers who put him out the least of anybody'.[12] As is much remarked, the job of children in the eighteenth century was a-dying!, and it was the job of adults also. Strong emotions have been generated by industrialisation and can be the enemy of truth and this makes the evidence of data rather than that of anecdote more vital than for most periods in history. Oddly, it makes it most resisted: perhaps it's human not to wish to have one's prejudices distorted by fact.

If I am to use indices of health I must briefly describe them. An impressive battery is available. These relate in the main either to death ('mortality') or to sickness ('morbidity') or more accurately to *proxies* of morbidity such as visits to a doctor, claims on a sickness fund, hospital admissions, or absence from work, none of which, be it noted, is the exclusive prerogative of the sick! Measurement of true health is something different, nearer an art form rather than a science, and the word 'health' itself is a pawn of professional semantics and definition, the ultimate being the World Health Organisation's somewhat extravagant concept of 'positive health', that is 'health' defined in terms redolent of Nurse Cavell—'Absence of disease and infirmity is not enough: I must be in a state of complete physical, mental and social well-being', an estate, incidently, only admitted to be inhabited by the mentally aberrant and the feeble-minded! Mortality though a crude measure of health has two special advantages: death can be diagnosed without benefit of medical diploma, and secondly, whereas it is an ineluctable fact that those who are alive may be in indifferent health it has never been convincingly argued that those who are dead may be in anything else. Morbidity, on the other hand, while a more sensitive measure of health, sacrifices something of this advantage through the deficiencies of the proxies it uses. In the first half of the nineteenth century these are, in the main, data from hospitals, dispensaries, and from factory and work place surveys, all of which for various reasons are unhelpful, and claims on sickness funds, most particularly on Friendly Societies, which can be comparatively reliable and informative. Apart, however, from their innate limitations both mortality and morbidity indices suffer also from technical deficiencies in the data which generate them. There were no national statistics at this time (civil registration of deaths did not start until

12 M. D. George, *London life in the eighteenth century* (London, 1925), p. 227.

Peter Froggatt

1838) and to be accounted even in sickness-fund statistics one had to be a subscriber to the fund and few of the non-artisan proletariat and even fewer of the *lumpenproletariat* were that, let alone the rich, the self-employed, and women and children. Furthermore, contemporary mortality and morbidity-proxy statistics, such as they were, were collected for purposes other than the measurement of health, a fact too often overlooked. Bills of mortality were initially a barometer of plague so that those who could fly, flew, or those who could delay arrival did so, as did James VI on his way to coronation, dallying several weeks *en route* until the London bills improved. Later the bills became more detailed but less reliable as other diagnoses were added to that of 'plague', and generally it was actuaries more than doctors who exploited mortality data required to calculate annuities, death benefits, and legacy duties, and in tontine operations; not until the work of the creative John Finlaison, actuary to the National Debt Office (and in 1848 first president of the Institute of Actuaries) in the 1820s,[13] were medical objectives *per se* established and still principally as a by-product of the actuaries' search for some generalised statistical law governing average age at death. The actuarial purpose of the Friendly Society morbidity returns was even less equivocal. They were first exploited by the polymath the Rev. Richard Price[14] to compile, at the request of government in 1789, tables of monetary rates for adequate insurance against sickness[15] and although they obtained no official *imprimatur* they became extensively used.[16] Price, however, widened his brief and assiduously and ingeniously generalised the results into his 'law of sickness'—that 'sickness and mortality bear the relation to each other of cause and effect'—a durable 'law' which allowed him to deduce from mortality returns the average number of benefit society subscribers in each group expected to be incapacitated at any time, and whose refutation exercised many commentators no less assiduous and ingenious over the next 60 years. As late as 1845 the energetic actuary to the Medical, Invalid, and General Life Office, F. G. P. Neison, was more than ritually discrediting it[17] and in 1853 John Finlaison's son, Alexander Glen

---

[13] *Laws respecting friendly societies,* H.C. 1825 (522), iv, 321; 1826–27 (558), iii, 869.

[14] Richard Price, *Observations on reversionary payments; on schemes for providing annuities for widows . . . and on the national debt* (7th ed., London, 1807), ii, p. 475.

[15] *Report from the select committee appointed to consider the poor laws,* appendix F, H.C. 1817 (462), vi, 1.

[16] *Laws respecting friendly societies,* p. 6, H.C. 1825 (522), iv, 321.

[17] F. G. P. Neison, 'Contributions to vital statistics, especially designed to elucidate the rate of mortality, the laws of sickness, and the influences of trade and locality on health, derived from

161

Finlaison, also actuary to the National Debt Office, finally laid it to rest though it took the national Friendly Society quinquennial returns of 1846–50 to do it.[18] But this controversy on Price's 'law of sickness', intriguing as it may be, was strictly a by-product of the main actuarial business and was little stressed by the actuaries themselves; it was the rates of benefit and the uncertainties of the data that worried Finlaison *fils,* not primarily the medical *rationale* or importance of Price's law: 'The present existing data,' he wrote, 'have been found imperfect and inefficient . . . and [quinquennial returns] would lead to an exact knowledge of the value of the benefits usually guaranteed, and therefore to a reduction of the contributions to the lowest point compatible with safety'.[19] No mention here of doctors or sickness *qua* sickness: medico-statistical purposes ran a poor second to actuarial ones, though they did run as we shall see.

Medically, two facts of the period stand out. First, equivocal in its results on health is the increase in the skill of doctors and improvement in medical facilities and knowledge; and second, unequivocal except to a small band of obscurantists, is a growing awareness as the period progresses of the role of crowding, dirt, impure water and unwholesome food and unsanitary living in disease causation, particularly in the prevalent 'fevers'. In 1800 there were in Belfast less than 20 'doctors' (physicians, surgeons, or apothecaries) and only some six beds in the newly formed Belfast Dispensary and Fever Hospital, an intake of 50 patients per year in the Lying-In Hospital,[20] and perhaps ten beds for indigent sick at the Belfast Charitable Society's Clifton House.[21] By 1850 there were over 80 'doctors' (physicians, surgeons, apothecaries, or general practitioners), 128 beds in the General Hospital admitting over 800 non-fever patients per year, the (Poor Law) Union fever hospital which in 1847 admitted 3,536 patients, the District Hospital for the

an extensive collection of original data, supplied by Friendly Societies, and proving their too frequent instability' in *R. Stat. Soc. Jn.,* viii, no. 3 (December 1845), pp 290–343; ix, no. 1 (March 1846), pp 50–76 (hereafter respectively cited as Neison, 'Contributions to vital statistics', viii and ix).

[18] *Report and tables prepared under the direction of the lords of the treasury, by the actuary at the national debt office . . . under the provisions of the act 9 & 10 Vict., c, 27,* H.C. 1852–53 (955), c, 295 (hereafter cited as Finlaison, *Report and Tables*).

[19] *Abstract of returns respecting friendly societies in England and Wales,* pp 2–4, H.C. 1852–53 (31), c, 109.

[20] A. G. Malcolm, *The history of the general hospital, Belfast, and the other institutions of the town . . .* (Belfast, 1851), pp 43–5, 49–52 (hereafter cited as Malcolm, *History*).

[21] R. W. M. Strain, *Belfast and its charitable society: a story of urban social development* (London, 1961), pp 54–6, 73.

Insane with an average point occupancy in 1850 of 267 patients,[22] the Lying-In Hospital had some 20 beds,[23] while at times of excessive 'fevers' 200 or more overflow patients were housed in the so-called College Hospital in Barrack Street.[24] During the 1847 epidemic there were allegedly 'as many as 4,000 patients in the various hospitals and the sheds and canvas tents erected in all available spots in their vicinity'.[25] In addition, in 1850, the Belfast General Dispensary medical and allied staff treated over 22,000 patients and filled 45,000 prescriptions as against at the most 700 patients in 1793.[26] From 1807,[27] grand juries were empowered to give limited aid to 'fever hospitals' (£100 at each assize), a requirement liberally interpreted so that much of the money was used for general medical purposes until a stricter enforcement after the 1837-8 'fever' epidemic. The medical school at the Royal Belfast Academical Institution (RBAI), in its 14 years turned out some 500 holders of its general medical certificate qualified in all but minor hospital attendance requirements to sit the final examinations of the main licensing bodies and available, during their training, as skilled and educated clerks and dressers in the hospital wards in place of the Sarah Gamps and motley orderlies disparate in many things but uniform in their ignorance: 'the poor patients,' wrote James Lawson Drummond, the first dean of the medical faculty at RBAI, 'would certainly be in better hands [with the students] than in those of our midwives who are universally ignorant and untaught'.[28] With the Apothecaries' Act of 1815 as a stimulus and the new provincial training schools in England as examples, and with the Irishman, Robert Graves, enunciating the principles of the erroneously but widely termed 'English clinical system' of instruction,[29] all the

[22] Facts in Malcolm, *History,* appendix, pp iv, xxii, xxvi, xxix, xxxi.

[23] C. H. G. Macafee, 'The history of the Belfast school of obstetrics' in *Ulster Medical Journal,* xi, no. 1 (April 1942), pp 20–50.

[24] Peter Froggatt, 'The foundation of the "Inst" medical department and its association with the Belfast Fever Hospital' in *Ulster Medical Journal,* xlv, no. 2 (September 1976), pp 107–145; 'The first medical school in Belfast' in *Medical History,* xxii, no. 3 (July 1978), pp 237–266.

[25] S. Prenter, *Life and labours of the Reverend William Johnston, DD, Belfast* (London, 1895), p. 52.

[26] Malcolm, *History,* p. 41, appendix, p. xxviii.

[27] 47 Geo. III, ch. 44.

[28] *News-Letter,* 7 November 1826. Drummond's letter is also reproduced in full in the 'Minutes of the Fever Hospital Committee', p. 234 (17 December 1826). These minutes have only recently been uncovered and are lodged in the archivist's room of the Royal Victoria Hospital, Belfast.

[29] R. J. Graves, 'On clinical instruction: with a comparative estimate of the mode in which it is conducted in the British and continental schools' in *London Medical Gazette,* x, no. 239 (30

non-Oxbridge universities and licensing bodies greatly improved their curricula in the 1820s and 1830s.[30] Belfast was therefore substantially better equipped with medical resources of manpower, fabric, and knowledge in 1850 than in 1800, though whether this meant better health care or ultimately better health is another question. I have always supposed that it would; it certainly meant more of something for more people. Tom McKeown and his colleagues, however, doubt that it did in Britain, at least for the earlier part of the period,[31] and paint instead a picture of lethal surgery, institutional fevers, dangerous cross-infections in hospital ward, out-patient and dispensary, and no new medical therapeutic technique or regimen which would on balance save life other than smallpox vaccination: 'The chief indictment of hospital work,' they repeatedly allege, 'is not that it did no good, but that it positively did harm'.[32] This is a much challenged though fashionable view: it seems to me based at least partly on the fact that medical men, by claiming too much for specifics in disease causation and treatment in the post-Pasteur period, are tempted to admit too little for non-specifics before it. Contemporary Belfast hospital design, practices, and diets, and dispensary attention and advice,[33] though stuffed with much that was useless, offered on a temporary basis for the denizen of the foetid and stinking slums a degree of cleanliness, fresh air, advice and nourishment he would not otherwise have known. Certainly, contemporaries considered medical facilities a very present help in trouble—not entirely a triumph of hope over reason—and the doctors, as we would suppose, agreed. J. P. Kay (Kay-Shuttleworth) echoed the consensus in 1834:

The condition of the working class has been much ameliorated by the promptitude with which medical assistance has been afforded to them. The mortality of large towns has diminished and considerable subtractions have been made from the great sum of misery which is the inheritance of man.[34]

June 1832), pp 401–6. Graves introduced his revolutionary clinical teaching methods at the Meath Hospital, Dublin, in 1821, thus ensuring the dominance, though short-lived, of the Irish (more specifically Dublin) medical school.
[30] S. T. Anning, 'Provincial medical schools in the nineteenth century' in F. N. L. Poynter (ed.), *The evolution of medical education in Britain* (London, 1966), pp 121–134.
[31] Much of McKeown's earlier work is brought together in Thomas McKeown, *The modern rise of population* (London, 1976).
[32] Thomas McKeown and R. G. Brown, 'Medical evidence related to English population change in the eighteenth century' in *Population Studies*, ix, no. 2 (November 1955), pp 119–141.
[33] Malcolm, *History*, appendix pp i–xxi.
[34] J. P. Kay-Shuttleworth, *Defects in the constitution of dispensaries* (Manchester, 1834), p.

This is not the last word on the subject, but it is my last one in this chapter.

The second fact is the role of the environment. Here we are on firmer though empirical ground based in part on the well-known association between typhus, dirt and crowding and in part on the success of cleanliness regimens in the navy[35] and elsewhere[36] and the experience of individual doctors;[37] hardly at all was it based on theory and that usually incorrect. Somewhere from the jumble of evidence, idea, observation, prejudice, theory, guess, hunch and fact, and the intellectual by-products of anti-contagionism—that strange mixture of liberal politics, commercial self-interest, mercantilism, chauvinism, and medical observation—there emerged by the 1830s the 'sanitary idea', the concept that an unwholesome and noxious environment is damaging to health, the concept which supplied the main thrust to public health legislation after the failure of international quarantine, such as it was, to prevent the European cholera pandemic of 1830–32, which left no port untouched from Istanbul to Belfast. What matters here is not the genesis of the 'sanitary idea' but the fact of its espousal by officialdom in the shape of Edwin Chadwick, because it was Chadwick's reports, Chadwick's drive and ardour, Chadwick's conclusions, and Chadwick's rugged determination which turned the unorganised, leaderless and aimless public health movement into a movement of effective action with legislation as the objective. On this smaller canvas the detail is clearer: though Chadwick was later to claim an early prescience of the roles of preventable ill-health on poverty and poverty on ill-health and boast of his early conversion to sanitary concepts, we should accept some exaggeration and will not go far wrong if we accept 1837 or 1838, rather than say 1833 or 1834, as the date of his journey on the Damascus road with the sponsoring, by the Poor Law Commissioners, of their historic enquiries in London into the relationship between urban poverty and disease with which the names Neil Arnott, J. P. Kay, and Southwood-Smith are forever

5, cited in Edwin Chadwick, *Report on the sanitary condition of the labouring population of Great Britain* (reprint with introduction by M. W. Flinn, Edinburgh, 1965, of original report, 1842), p. 19.
[35] Sir Gilbert Blane, *A brief statement of the progressive improvement of the health of the Royal Navy at the end of the eighteenth and beginning of the nineteenth century* (London, 1830), p. 11.
[36] John Pringle, *Observations on the diseases of the army in camp and garrison ... containing some papers of experiments* (London, 1753), pp 84 *et seq.*, 102 *et seq.*
[37] John Haygarth, *A letter to Dr Percival on the prevention of infectious fever* (London, 1801), pp 73 *et seq.*; John Heysham, *An account of the jail fever or typhus carcerum as it appeared at Carlisle in the year 1781* (London, 1782), pp 24, 31.

remembered.[38] Nor will we go far wrong if we take the 1842 *Report on the sanitary condition of the labouring population,*[39] as the mustering point from which the march was straight, if difficult, to the Public Health Act of 1848,[40] the act which put the sanitary concept into effective practice and started the search for competent local and central authorities to enforce it. Malcolm summarises the contemporary view as well as any in a report of 1848:

1. The chief agents in the generation and propagation of epidemic, endemic and contagious fabrile diseases [responsible for 45 per cent of deaths] consist in local causes capable of removal or at least of material abatement.
2. These causes are embodied in a vitiated atmosphere, produced by deficient drainage, cleansing and ventilation, circumstances over which we have a large control.[41]

The three points to note are: first, that in a general sense the statements are correct; second, that doctors accepted that such diseases could be prevented by simple improvements within man's power to make, all that was needed was 'enlightened self-interest' or, more realistically, effective legislative powers; and third, that epidemics could be controlled or eradicated by man himself without supernatural assistance or recourse to the atavisms of the *cordon sanitaire* or international quarantine. This was a Rubicon in medical thinking: never again would western society look beyond natural forces for the spread of pandemic disease, a faith justified by the medical discoveries in the 1850s of the role of micro-organisms. For most of my period, therefore, crowding, filth, and poverty were considered intuitively by those who suffered them to be damaging to health as to much else but were equally considered, most especially by those who avoided or furthered them, to be inevitable concomitants of urbanisation and industrialisation in a free society commited to the creation of wealth. Only in the 1830s was their effect on health *officially* as distinct from *intuitively*, accepted and effective legislation made a goal; only in the late 1840s was the

[38] *Fourth annual report of the poor law commissioners for England and Wales,* appendix A, no. 1, suppls,1,2,3, pp 67–83, 83–88, 88–96, [C 147], H.C. 1837–38, xxviii, 145; *Fifth report . . .* appendix C, no. 2, pp 100–106, [C 239], H.C. 1839, xx, 1.
[39] *Report . . . from the poor law commissioners on an inquiry into the sanitary condition of the labouring population of Great Britain . . .,* H.L. 1842, xxvi, 1.
[40] 11 & 12 Vict., ch. 63.
[41] A. G. Malcolm, *The sanitary state of Belfast with suggestions for its improvement,* cited in H. G. Calwell, *Andrew Malcolm of Belfast, 1818–56: physician and historian* (Belfast, 1977), p. 103 (hereafter cited as Calwell, *Andrew Malcolm*).

achievement of this goal politically possible. This goes some way to explain the channelling throughout the kingdom during the 1840s of much philanthropic activity into environmental as well as personal and moral improvement. The Belfast Society for the Amelioration of the Condition of the Working Classes was formed in 1845 and built the public baths and washhouses which opened in May 1847 on the corner of Townsend Street and Divis Street, one of Sir Charles Lanyon's lesser-known commissions; the Belfast Working Classes Association for the Promotion of General Improvement was founded in 1846, and its associated but short-lived (14 monthly numbers, January 1847–February 1848) *The Belfast People's Magazine* was first published on 2 January 1847, all local parallels of British, European and North American enterprises. It is a source of pride to a medical man and a wonder to all that they were founded and run by the remarkable Dr Andrew Malcolm.[42]

DATA AND METHOD

I turn now to the data and will present them in four parts. First, I will discuss mortality and morbidity statistics for Britain; second, I will theorise from them what the position in Belfast might have been; third, I will examine the Irish material, as far as it goes; and fourth, I will consider the special role of certain common diseases of occupation. Statistics will dominate: description and anecdote of the squalor and sanitary horror of urban slum dwelling can be found in the 'many ponderous volumes' (as Malcolm called them, see note 41) of contemporary reports and the lighter pages of the novelist and commentator.

The death rate in Britain was falling in the late eighteenth and early nineteenth centuries, a fact once in doubt now generally conceded. From perhaps the second decade of the nineteenth century, however, the trend was arrested, perhaps even reversed, or rather 'seemingly' reversed because without reliable statistics we must rely on the judgement of shrewd men. Finlaison *père,*[43] the 1831 census commissioners,[44] and Cowan in Glasgow,[45] amongst

---

[42] Calwell, *Andrew Malcolm*, ch. 10–12.

[43] *Report of John Finlaison, Actuary of the national debt, on the evidence and elementary facts on which the tables of life annuities are founded*, pp 16, 66–7, H.C. 1829 (122), iii, 287.

[44] *Comparative account of the population of Great Britain, in the years 1801, 1811, 1821, 1831 . . . as required by the population act of 1830*, p. 15, H.C. 1831 (348), xviii, 1.

[45] Robert Cowan, *Statistics of fever and smallpox in Glasgow* (Glasgow, 1837), p. 7.

others, noted the reversal, and that impeccable commentator William Farr, compiler of abstracts to the registrar-general, wrote in 1849 'since 1816 the returns indicate a retrograde movement. The mortality has apparently increased'.[46] The reason seemed beyond doubt: some factor or factors of urbanisation increased infectious disease prevalence and this was compounded by the presence of an indigent and itinerant *lumpenproletariat,* usually Irish: 'The Irish in Birmingham are the very pests of Society,' said a witness before the Poor Inquiry (Ireland) Commission, 'they generate contagion',[47] a view upheld by the commissioners themselves:

from the filthy conditions of the bedding, the want of the commonest articles of furniture, the uncleanly habits of the inmates themselves, and the numbers which without distinction of age or sex, are closely crowded together, they [the Irish] are frequently the means of generating and communicating infectious disease.[48]

As late as 1859 the president of the Manchester Statistical Society could hold that the typhus epidemic of 1846–7 in its 'dissemination and virulence' was related 'not with the prevalence of nuisances, but rather with the current of Irish immigration so remarkable in that year'.[49] Rather hard on the destitute Irish immigrant even if the allegations contain some truth.

With or without friendly Irish help, urban mortality certainly seemed high to many contemporaries: the problem was to show it through reliable national statistics. There was some confirmation in the early returns of the registrar-general after 1838;[50] much more, however, was expected from the first quinquennial returns of the Friendly Societies for 1836–40, both for mortality and sickness proxies. In the event they served little. As already remarked they were deployed actuarily with that caution without which no calculator of annuities is complete. Their analyst, F. G. P. Neison, was able to show a higher life expectancy in rural compared with

[46] William Farr, *Vital statistics: a memorial volume of selections from the . . . writings of W. Farr . . .* (London, 1885), p. 150.

[47] *Report of the poor inquiry (Ireland) commission*; appendix G, 'Report of the state of the Irish poor in Great Britain', p. 6 (evidence John Mouchet Baynham, surgeon of the general dispensary and the town infirmary, Birmingham), H.C. 1836 (40), xxxiv, 427.

[48] Ibid., p. xi.

[49] T. S. Ashton, *Economic and social investigations in Manchester, 1833–1933: A centenary history of the Manchester Statistical Society . . .* (London, 1934), pp 52–53.

[50] See particularly *Fifth annual report of the registrar-general of births, deaths and marriages in England,* pp 194 *et seq.,* [C 516], H.C. 1843, xxi, 341 (hereafter cited as *Fifth report of the registrar-general*).

168

urban areas though he published only a few of the unconfounded
results from no less than 400 trades since 'the examination of each
under the various combinations described would involve the
consideration of so immense a number of Tables as would evidently
perplex the present enquiry'.[51] Government thought they would
evidently perplex the public also since the next quinquennial
returns, for 1841–45, were never published and this allowed William
Guy, professor of forensic medicine at King's College, London,
later co-secretary (with Southwood-Smith) of the Health of Towns
Association, and whose name the gold, silver, and bronze medals of
the Royal Statistical Society perpetuate, to up-stage the actuaries
by showing, in a series of papers in the 1840s,[52] that agricultural
labourers were among the longest-lived (Arcadia exists in England
and is doing well) but that, perversely, the upper classes were the
shortest-lived. His judgements were moral rather than medical:

We can scarcely fail to arrive at the conclusion that the possession of ample
means of self-indulgence is unfavourable to longevity. Luxurious habits,
an absence of the chief motives which stir other men to exertion, and . . .
dissipation combine to impair the health and shorten the lives of those
favoured children of fortune . . . It is impossible to escape the conviction
that temperance, mental occupation, and bodily exercise, are the three
principal elements of health,[53]

useful material for the Methodists and arcadians if not for the
seekers of patents of nobility.

But by now heavier and more reliable metal was on the way. In
one of the great pioneer works of record linkage and data
processing, Finlaison *fils* analysed the 1846–50 Friendly Society
returns, 'over one million person-years' experience [recorded] in
forty large folio volumes each 6″–7″ thick',[54] and there emerged

[51] Neison, 'Contributions to vital statistics', viii, pp 298–9.
[52] Between 1843 and 1881 Guy wrote 13 articles on employment and duration of life in the *Journal of the Royal Statistical Society* alone. The first is W. A. Guy, 'Contributions to a knowledge of the influence of employments upon health' (vi, no. 3 (August 1843), pp 197–211); the last is 'On temperature and its relation to mortality: an illustration of the application of the numerical method to the discovery of truth' (xliv, no. 2 (June 1881), pp 235–268).
[53] W. A. Guy, 'On the duration of life among the English gentry, with additional observations on the duration of life among the aristocracy' in *R. Stat. Soc. Jn.*, ix, no. 1 (March 1846), pp 37–49.
[54] *Report and Tables*, Finlaison, . . . p. iv. The quinquennial returns for 1836–40 were started by Neison (Neison, 'Contributions to vital statistics', viii and ix, and other publications). I have been unable to trace those for 1841–45. Those for 1851–55 were 'lent to an actuary who has long been dead . . . the results . . . were, partially at all events, made known some years ago,

confirmation of previous results and the first clear picture of increased age-specific mortality in cities compared to towns and rural areas (Table I). In the stratified analysis 'weather' and 'the physical demands of labour', those contemporary war-horses, were exonerated; the cause must therefore lie in the city environment itself either of domestic circumstance *per se*, hazards of the urban industries, the physical environment, the soil, food or lack of it, or in one or more of the many other factors plausible and implausible discussed by many, most notably William Farr.[55]

A similar picture emerges from studies of sickness proxies which crowd the pages of contemporary medical and statistical journals, special enquiries, and parliamentary papers: disease—epidemic, infectious, and even so-called 'sporadic'—was most common among the city poor. But as with mortality many of the early results were uncontrolled: the reports containing them survive as important social documents but the data are of descriptive value rather than material for rigorous analysis and interpretation. All that was known with certainty by the 1830s was that after infancy sickness proxies increased with age.[56] Even the Friendly Society quinquennial returns were treated warily. Cautious Neison who had feared being 'perplexed' by occupational mortality tables shrank almost completely from morbidity ones: 'What constitutes sickness in one case is often a very different thing from that in another. The standard seems too indefinite and capricious; and . . . a careful inquiry will shew [the results'] vague nature for medical and other scientific purposes'.[57] His 1836-40 data, however, *do* suggest higher morbidity in the cities (Table II) and an effect due to trade or occupation, though unquantified; as with mortality, however, it was left to Finlaison *fils* and the 1846-50 returns to present the full picture.

Unlike Neison, Finlaison presented very extensive data on sickness proxies covering no less than 856 occupations.[58] Some pertinent results are summarised in Tables III-VII, and when these are

although in his private capacity' (*Special report on sickness and mortality experiences in registered friendly societies, together with certain monetary tables based thereon, by the actuary to the friendly societies (central office)*, p. vi, H.C. 1896 (303), lxxix, 1). Those for 1856-80 were analysed by William Sutton and the series then discontinued (see also note 77).

[55] William Farr, in *Fifth report of the registrar-general*, pp 200 *et seq.*

[56] Much of the work is reviewed in my 'Short-term absence from industry: a statistical and historical study' (Ph.D thesis, the Queen's University, Belfast, 2 vols, 1967, hereafter cited as Froggatt, 'Short-term absence').

[57] Neison, 'Contributions to vital statistics', viii, p. 329.

[58] Finlaison, *Report and Tables, passim.*

Peter Froggatt

interpreted along with other arrangements of the data[59] the picture is one of increasing mortality in the cities in at least the first two decades of the century, highest mortality and morbidity among the poor and the crowded city dweller (though these are not everywhere consistent), sickness proxies generally increasing with age but with no clear effect due to occupation, weather, or geographic location—interpretation of minor trends demonstrated being unwise because of technical differences and limitations of the data used.

We now turn to Belfast. Analogy from British experience, unwise for Ireland as a whole or even Dublin, should be not too outrageous for Belfast. The city grew coevally with many British industrial city-ports and for much the same reasons and at much the same rate; it was under much the same social and economic system, laws and bye-laws; its age structure in 1841 was not grossly disparate from such British cities as Bristol, Liverpool, Edinburgh and Glasgow;[60] it experienced the periodic epidemics of 'fevers' common to industrial towns; it practised vaccination; it shared in the cholera pandemics of 1831–32 and 1848–49; it had much the same range of medical and poor-law services and extent of philanthropic effort. There were differences, some important: in housing for one where Belfast missed the worst of the cellar dwellings; in average weekly earnings in flax and cotton industries where, as against this, sample Belfast age- and sex-related earnings were less than in Scotland and England.[61] I believe on balance that there is basis for legitimate analogy. Unfortunately there is no basis for the validity of direct comparison. To refine the British statistics to a Belfast age/sex base would be possible but an empty labour because the comparators—the actual Belfast data on deaths and sickness proxies—are unreliable or non-existent. The only considerable contemporary mortality statistics collected in Ireland were in the 1841 and 1851 censuses and related to the previous ten years. They were defective for three main reasons: they omitted (i) families and persons who had emigrated during the decade, (ii) deaths which resulted in the extinction of a family, and (iii) deaths not remembered or volunteered. The 1841 census commissioners not surprisingly estimated a deficiency in mortality recording of perhaps twenty-five per cent.[62]

[59] Froggatt, 'Short-term absence' ch. III.
[60] T. A. Larcom, 'Observations on the census of the population of Ireland in 1841' in *R. Stat. Soc. Jn*, vi, no. 4 (December 1843), pp 323–351; *Report of the commissioners appointed to take the census of Ireland for the year 1841*, p. xlviii, [C 504], H.C. 1843, xxiv, 1 (hereafter cited as *Census of Ireland, 1841*).
[61] *Factories inquiry commission: supplementary report of the central board of His Majesty's commissioners . . . hours of their labour*, Part 1, pp 22, 28, 33–35, H.C. 1834 (167), xix, 253.
[62] *Census of Ireland, 1841*, p. xlix.

171

The 1851 census is even less reliable since it covers deaths in the unprecedented migration and mortality of the 1840s (I will not consider the 1851 census further here despite its justified standing as a remarkable *tour de force* and a fitting memorial to the talents of Sir William Wilde).[63] Furthermore, if one did refine the British figures to adopt a life-table approach much favoured by contemporaries we would need to postulate that unrecorded deaths were distributed proportionately as to recorded deaths throughout all age groups, and also that the emigrants from Belfast and from Britain showed the same age-composition—assumptions difficult to accept. Direct comparison of age- and sex-specific death rates is also subject to invalidities but has this advantage: since the Irish and British denominators (i.e. population) are likely to be equally reliable or unreliable for the *de facto* census date and the Irish numerators (i.e. number of deaths) likely to be consistent underestimates especially as the census date and the year of the deaths become more remote, a higher *real* mortality in Irish figures may be deduced if most of the age-specific rates approximate their English comparators and *a fortiori* if they exceed them. Some figures for Liverpool (from a special study) and those calculated for Belfast, are given in Table VIII: as an industrial port, Liverpool is a reasonable comparator for Belfast despite its larger transient and indigent populations. From age 6 to 45 years Belfast mortality *appears* to be heavier: I will return to this result later.

We now for completeness consider the case of an *indirect* as distinct from a direct approach, i.e. compare Belfast mortality with that of other Irish civic and rural districts to see if the order of difference is similar to that between comparable British industrial cities on the one hand and British civic and rural districts on the other. I believe this would be sterile or misleading: the British census and death registration divisions at that time were not coterminus and so the indices would be invalid comparators (Liverpool for the special study in Table VIII is an exception), and moreover would require acceptance of virtually unacceptable assumptions. If we infer anything at all it is that health as measured by age-specific mortality was no better and possibly after infancy actually worse in early nineteenth century Belfast than in one superficially comparable British city; but it might be prudent to follow Connell's rigorous conclusion when he wrote 'We are obliged, it seems, to leave undetermined the relative mortality of Ireland and England in

[63] See my article 'Sir William Wilde, 1815–1876, a centenary appreciation: Wilde's place in medicine' in *R.I.A. Proc.*, lxxvii, sect. C, no. 10 (September 1977), pp 261–78.

Peter Froggatt

the 1840s,'[64] noting however that the purpose of his study was somewhat different to mine.

Mortality comparisons within Ireland present fewer problems. The whole country was subject to the same census (of 1841) at the same time; the commissioners state specifically that 'there is no reason to suspect peculiar inaccuracy in any one part'.[65] On this basis we may make a direct comparison (Table IX), taking deaths recorded for 1840 as likely to be the most reliable in the decade covered by the 1841 enumeration. In every age group except one (46–55 years) the Belfast mortality rates exceed those of other civic districts which in turn everywhere exceed the rural district rates. In the younger groups in fact the Belfast mortality is over twice that for the country as a whole. Unless there was some consistent and substantial bias in recording of deaths or population which was moreover unsuspected by the commissioners the results can be interpreted as showing significantly higher mortality in Belfast than elsewhere in Ireland: since it is most marked in the pre-16-year-old age groups it is likely to be due to living in, rather than working in, Belfast *per se*. Unfortunately we can add no temporal dimension since no reliable previous data exist.

When we turn to sickness proxies the cupboard is nearly bare. Industrial data exist but are unhelpful.[66] Certainly there were appalling mills like Crossan's cotton-spinning-mill in Belfast which a commissioner for the 1833 factory inquiry, James Stuart, said was 'one of the worst specimens of the cotton-mill in point of general arrangement and management I have seen anywhere';[67] but there were bad ones elsewhere and the effect on health of a 'bad' compared to a 'good' mill is problematical in the context of the times. Nor does the rich vein of the Friendly Society returns reach Belfast. Whereas in Britain there were one million members by 1815 in over 10,000 societies[68] and by the 1840s an estimated quarter of a million in the Manchester Unity of Oddfellows alone,[69] in Ireland there were comparatively few. Between 1796[70] and 1831, 281 societies were registered from 26 counties or counties of cities and

[64] K. H. Connell, *The population of Ireland, 1750–1845* (Oxford, 1950), p. 191.
[65] *Census of Ireland, 1841*, p. 1.
[66] I have examined these in detail in my 'Short-term absence', vol. i, pp 60–120.
[67] *First report of the central board of His Majesty's commissioners for enquiring into the employment of children in factories . . .*, A1, p. 127, H.C. 1833 (450), xx, 1 (hereafter cited as *First report on factory children*).
[68] *Laws respecting friendly societies*, p. 6, H.C. 1825 (522), iv, 321.
[69] Neison, 'Contributions to vital statistics', ix, p. 66.
[70] 36 Geo. III, ch. 58 (Ireland).

towns,[71] (exceptions were: Cavan, Clare, Donegal, Fermanagh, Galway, Kerry, King's, Limerick, Longford, Mayo, Monaghan, Queen's, Roscommon, Tyrone), but many were unviable, subsequently wound up, or suffered the amiable fate of many throughout the kingdom where 'the landlord [of public houses] are generally the treasurers, and the members are required . . . to spend a monthly sum in beer for the good of the house, which amount is generally taken from the [subscription] box'.[72] As late as 1870 returns were received from only 223 societies in Ireland covering about 30,000 members—a statistical bagatelle even though an undoubted underestimate of the total[73]—and of these only sixteen had bothered to lodge their rules with the registrar by 1869[74] (and none by the end of my period, 1850[75]) only one, the Belfast Amateur Rowing Club, being in Belfast. Irish societies were legally required[76] to make returns as for societies in England and Wales but because of their sparseness the results were omitted from the 1836–40 and 1846–50 data analysed by Neison and Finlaison respectively (see above) and also from the monumental analysis of the 25-year returns, 1856–80, which took the luckless William Sutton, actuary to the Friendly Societies (central office), 16 years to complete,[77] ended the system,[78] and ended poor Sutton ultimately. The most reliable and relevant proxy index for England has therefore no parallel for Ireland.

We are left then with fag-ends; but one was dropped by Andrew Malcolm and therefore worth picking-up. This was his opinion given at the British Association meeting in Belfast in 1852, that 'the tendency to epidemic visitations and outbreaks is on the increase in this town, *and that such are becoming more fatal*[79] (Malcolm's italics). His evidence for increasing prevalence is the narrowing time-interval between epidemics of what was then called simply

[71] *Return of the number of friendly societies filed by the clerks of the peace . . . so far as relates to Ireland,* pp 3–9, H.C. 1831–32 (259), xxvi, 335.
[72] *Report of the registrar of friendly societies in England,* p. 35, H.C. 1862 (416), xxix, 583.
[73] *Report of the registrar of friendly societies in Ireland for the year 1870,* H.C. 1871 (460), lxii, 413; (460–1), lxii, 415.
[74] *Return of all societies whose rules have been deposited with the registrars of friendly societies in Ireland, under 18 and 19 Vict. C. 63, s. 44, and the date when deposited,* H.C. 1868–69 (359–I), lvi, 205.
[75] Ibid., p. 1.
[76] 2 Will. IV, ch. 37.
[77] *Special report on sickness and mortality experience in registered friendly societies, together with certain monetary tables based thereon, by the actuary to the friendly societies (central office),* H.C. 1896 (303), lxxix, 1.
[78] Ibid., p. vii; 45 & 46 Vict., ch. 35.
[79] Malcolm, *Sanitary state of Belfast,* p. 14.

'fever' (mostly typhus fever), and his evidence for increasing severity is the mortality rate of all cases of 'fever' admitted to the Belfast Fever Hospital (forerunner of the Royal Victoria Hospital) reinforced by the doubling of the mortality rate in the 1848 compared to the 1832 cholera outbreak (Table X). These facts, said Malcolm, 'argue either a deteriorated vitality on the part of the labouring community or a more concentrated animal poison. Either explanation may be due to sanitary influence'.[80] They can of course argue other explanations: we may cautiously say that Belfast was subject to endemic and epidemic contagious diseases, that they seemed to follow epidemiological law as the population and urbanisation increase, that unsanitary influences played a role, and in this respect Belfast was very much a European industrial city.

So far I have considered Belfast citizens as urban dwellers *per se,* not as workers often in hazardous trades. But occupation *does* have an independent effect on health both in the general case where its demands and physiological insults may be injurious, and also in the rarer and more special case of providing specific risks of toxic hazards many of which had by this time been identified even if their mode of action was unknown. We know nothing definite, however, of the *quantifiable* effect on general health of being, for example a 'servant, labourer, or porter' (of whom there were 3,972 listed in the 1841 census),[81] a 'machinemaker' (336), a 'painter or glazier' (253), a 'sailor' (303), a 'boot and shoe maker' (1,198) or perhaps a 'writing-clerk' (689), and although we know that there were specific hazards in being an 'ironfounder' (134), 'stonecutter' (171), or even 'cabinet-maker' (195), we cannot quantify these as the resultant diseases were not then listed as registerable causes of death even when known. We do, however, know something of the specific hazards for some of the 9,811 persons listed in the 1841 census as employed in occupations 'ministering to clothing' not because many contracted its main occupational scourge, byssinosis, due to inhaling cotton or flax dust ('pouce') preparatory to spinning, which they did, but which was not a registerable cause of death, but because the incredible Andrew Malcolm surveyed them.[82] Certainly byssinosis ('hackler's malady'), strangely omitted from the writings of the early nineteenth century observers of Ireland, was by this time prevalent and moreover

[80] Ibid., p. 15.
[81] *Census of Ireland, 1841,* p. 290.
[82] A. G. Malcolm, 'The influence of factory life on the health of the operative, as founded upon the medical statistics of this class at Belfast' in *R. Stat. Soc. Jn.,* xix, no. 2 (June 1856), pp 170–181.

medically recognised.[83] Ramazzini, in 1700, wrote:

. . . those who hackel the flax and hemp to prepare it for being spun and wove, afford frequent instances of the unwholesomeness of their trade; for there flies out of this matter a foul mischievous powder, that entering the lungs by the mouth and throat, causes continual coughs and gradually makes way for an asthma,[84]

and closer to home, Thackrah, in 1831, observed, in the considerable linen trade in Leeds:

Dressers of flax and persons in the dusty rooms of the mills, are generally unhealthy: the early stage of the malady which attacks flax men varies from that of ordinary bronchitis. The cough and difficulty in breathing are not so temporary: one precedes the other sometimes by months, more frequently by years.[85]

In 1807 there were about 20 powered cotton-spinning-mills in Belfast and vicinity; and the trade reached its peak in the late 1820s. By the 1840s it had largely yielded to linen. Flax spinning in factories was introduced later though a domestic trade for many years. Mullholland's Henry Street mill was the first to switch from cotton (after a fire) to flax in 1828 and by the early 1850s some 25 mills with over 200,000 spindles were open in Belfast[86] by which time Malcolm (see note 82) calculated that in the flax spinning industry above, some 1,900 operatives were in the hackling departments, 1,200 in preparing, 4,300 in spinning, 2,000 in reeling, and 2,000 were mechanics and bundlers—some 11,000 in all of which over 3,000, in the dry preparing processes, would have been at a very high risk of byssinosis, a disease haunted by the shadow of tuberculosis and other fatal lung conditions. Malcolm examined 2,078 women flax operatives and found that 12.2 per cent of preparers had 'diseases of the chest' compared with 4.1 per cent of spinners, 0.9 per cent of reelers, and 0.8 per cent of weavers, which confirmed his view of the 'hackler's malady' and many of these would have ultimately appeared in the mortality statistics for 'sporadic diseases of the respiratory and circulatory organs' though under 'consumption', 'inflammation of lungs', 'asthma', and others.

[83] J. A. Smiley, 'Background to byssinosis in Ulster' in *British Journal of Industrial Medicine,* xviii, no. 1 (January 1961), pp 1–9.

[84] Bernardino Ramazzini, *De morbis artificum diatriba . . .,* (2nd ed., Ultrajecti, 1703), p. 214.

[85] C. T. Thackrah, *The effects of arts, trades, and professions, and of civic states and habits of living, on health and longevity, etc.,* (2nd ed., London, 1832), p. 72.

[86] Facts in D. J. Owen, *History of Belfast* (Belfast, 1921), pp 296–99.

Quite apart from this specific hazard there were the effects, hardly beneficial, of the wet spinning room where 'the air is not only very warm but charged with vapour . . . the workers are constantly and sensibly perspiring; and the feet, and a portion of their dress are saturated with the spray from the machinery'[87] though admittedly for not more than 69 hours per week if between 9 and 17 years! The ten-year-old Catherine Macauley, operative in Crossan's cotton spinning mill in Belfast, epitomises our assumptions as to the health of operatives and also the repugnance to our sensibilities of the factory system when she 'depones that she has been about two years working in the mill; that part of her work is in the picking room, and the dust makes her cough and gives her a sore throat; that she gets 1/- a week . . . and that she cannot write'.[88] If she survived until aged twenty it would give her far more than a cough and a sore throat. Ironically, although there was little byssinosis in Belfast in 1800 and a lot in 1850, the quantal effect on the city's health over the half-century was probably very little. Byssinosis was undoubtedly an important precursor of fatal chest diseases (some 200 deaths annually in the 1830s),[89] but these were common for other reasons also, and the whole quantum of chronic disease was in turn dwarfed by the frequent and dramatic epidemics of one sort or another which attacked not hundreds but thousands. Malcolm, no friend of irresponsible factory proprietors though no enemy of free contract either, commented on the high level of 'ailment' in factory operatives and the role of the factory in their production,[90] but significantly he refused to be drawn too far because of the high level of 'ailment' in the population generally, and without unconfounded occupational mortality figures or a lead from Malcolm we can go no further than that.

SUMMARY

To sum up; what picture can we draw from all this and what were the prevalent diseases? I have not dealt with the components of fatal disease or sickness nor how an increase in one component may be balanced numerically by a decrease in another.

In the fifty years 1800 to 1850, Belfast grew from some 20,000 to

[87] See note 82.
[88] *First report on factory children,* A1, p. 128.
[89] *Census of Ireland, 1841: Report upon the tables of death, by William Robert Wilde, Esq.,* pp 114–5, [C 504], H.C. 1843, xxiv, 605.
[90] See note 82.

some 100,000 persons, most sucked-in to man the burgeoning demands of commerce and industry. Housing, the physical environment, and conditions of work, were under virtually no effective control with the consequences well-known in nineteenth century industrial urbanisation: overcrowding, unsanitary conditions, long hours of weary and often dangerous toil, and much ineffective nutrition. Some forty-five per cent of all deaths in the 1830s in Belfast were categorised as due to 'epidemic, endemic and contagious diseases' (6,660 of 16,354 for the decade 6 June 1831 to 6 June 1841)[91] which approximates the forty-six per cent for 'the Metropolis' (London) for deaths registered during 1840–41;[92] and many more were certainly due to infection also. In order of prevalence the 'epidemic, endemic and contagious diseases' were: 'fever' (presumed to be mainly typhus), smallpox, measles, cholera, 'Hooping cough', pemphigus, scarlatina, croup, influenza, diarrhoea, erysipalis, syphilis (rarely entered as a cause of death), and one case each of 'ague' and 'hydrophobia' both in 1835, clearly a bad year![93] Most of these were commonest in infancy and childhood, typhus being an exception, and they wreaked havoc among the young just as they do in many countries today. The other fifty-five per cent, the so-called 'sporadic diseases', were on the other hand commoner among the elderly. Inaccuracy of diagnosis, crudity of nosology, and defects in ascertainment, preclude detailed comment on the data. The 'epidemic' diseases, better recognised and diagnosed, were considered, rightly, to be mainly preventable, and preventable by sanitary reform: and it is the decimation of the young by such 'preventable' diseases coupled with the growing confidence that prevention was possible and moreover the means were at hand, which gave the high mortality in the first half of the nineteenth century something of its emotive force and its reduction, through legislative action, much of the dynamic drive and evangelical fervour lacking previously. It was the harmful effects of factory labour especially on women, young persons, and children which caught the imagination and tugged at the conscience but, paradoxically, they were less harmful than were the crowded courts and alleys. In the last analysis it is unreal to separate urbanisation and industrialisation since they together provided the unhealthy *milieu* and without the industries there would hardly have been the type of urban growth which characterised these decades. It is

[91] *Census of Ireland, 1841: Report etc. by Wilde.*
[92] *Fifth report of the registrar-general,* pp 226–7.
[93] *Census of Ireland, 1841: Report etc. by Wilde.*

equally unreal to covet the *status quo ante*: later in the century industrial wealth was to benefit the whole nation medically and pre-industrial society was not the Arcady some would believe. None of this of course was unique to Belfast: but much of it was unique *in Ireland* certainly on this scale, and the grim harvest in Belfast in human lives was the short-term result, prominent until the rural decimation of the 1840s. The long-term result, however, was very different.

Table I

PERCENTAGE MORTALITY FOR MALES BY DISTRICT OF BENEFIT
SOCIETY REGISTERED OFFICE, BASED ON THE QUINQUENNIAL
RETURNS FROM REGISTERED FRIENDLY SOCIETIES
(ENGLAND AND WALES)
Source: Finlaison, *Report and Tables,* p. 17

| Age (years) | *Percentage mortality* | | |
	rural district[3]	town district[1]	city district[2]
15	0.63	0.40	—
20	0.56	0.93	1.07
25	0.69	0.72	0.84
30	0.72	0.78	0.97
35	0.73	0.86	1.19
40	0.85	1.08	1.63
45	1.00	1.38	1.66
50	1.29	1.71	1.82
55	1.80	2.10	2.72
60	2.27	2.84	3.35
65	3.41	4.05	3.85
70	5.14	6.40	4.94
75	7.52	7.61	7.67
80	12.92	13.67	9.86
84	16.76	20.93	15.15
% withdrawals and exclusions	5.12	2.94	2.59

1. Conurbations with between 3,000 and 65,000 persons.
2. Corporate towns with a population greater than 65,000 and a density of 6 persons or more per house.
3. All those not 1 or 2, or 'excluded'.

Table II

AGE SPECIFIC SICKNESS CLAIM RATES BY DISTRICT OF BENEFIT
SOCIETY REGISTERED OFFICE, BASED ON THE QUINQUENNIAL
RETURNS FROM FRIENDLY SOCIETIES (ENGLAND AND WALES)
1836–40
(*Based on a six-day week*)
Source: Neison, 'Contributions to vital statistics', viii, Table XXII

| Age (years) | *Sickness claim rate (days)[1]* | | |
	rural district[2]	town district[2]	city district[2]
20	5.03	5.14	3.40
25	5.18	5.19	5.79
30	5.25	5.28	6.64
35	5.39	6.07	7.42
40	6.41	7.62	8.80

Table II (*Continued*)

AGE SPECIFIC SICKNESS CLAIM RATES BY DISTRICT OF BENEFIT
SOCIETY REGISTERED OFFICE, BASED ON THE QUINQUENNIAL
RETURNS FROM FRIENDLY SOCIETIES (ENGLAND AND WALES)
1836–40

45	7.52	10.99	10.88
50	9.54	15.36	14.30
55	13.96	19.81	19.82
60	23.12	29.48	26.58
65	45.78	54.83	35.41
70	85.17	93.00	59.77
75	124.71	144.07	134.32
80	146.13	197.90	211.24

1. Defined as the 'average duration of (successful) claims for sickness per annum for every member', i.e. (sum of successful claims in weeks divided by average number of members) × 6.
2. Listed in F. G. P. Neison, *Contributions to vital statistics; being a development of the rate of mortality and the laws of sickness from original and extensive data procured from Friendly Societies* (London, 1845). Appendix, Note II.

Table III

DATA BY AGE FOR MALES BASED ON THE QUINQUENNIAL RETURNS
FROM REGISTERED FRIENDLY SOCIETIES (ENGLAND AND WALES)
1846–50
(*Based on 'adjusted' rates and a six-day week*)
Source: Finlaison, *Report and Tables*, p. 2

Age (years)	Number of members	Sickness claim rate (days)[2]	Claim duration rate (days)[3]	Per cent mortality	Per cent withdrawal and exclusions
15	1,190	5.32	21.33	0.76	6.13
20	9,448	5.90	22.17	0.83	5.04
25	22,154	5.85	24.45	0.70	5.21
30	25,882	5.92	26.25	0.85	4.01
35	24,521	6.12	27.35	0.85	3.29
40	21,296	7.04	30.26	1.14	2.33
45	17,512	8.01	33.21	1.20	1.71
50	13,779	9.85	37.87	1.48	1.11
55	9,653	11.96	42.53	1.98	0.95
60	6,615	16.05	51.68	2.76	1.03
65	3,699	23.45	66.38	3.45	0.89
70	1,934	37.41	89.88	5.54	0.72

Table III (*Continued*)

DATA BY AGE FOR MALES BASED ON THE QUINQUENNIAL RETURNS
FROM REGISTERED FRIENDLY SOCIETIES (ENGLAND AND WALES)
1846-50

75	740	57.27	115.75	7.82	0.67
80	287	83.73	147.07	13.54	0.35
84	62	84.95	151.69	18.75	1.36

TOTAL   158,788

1. 'Effected by taking the sums and averages of every five years, for the middle year of each five . . . to give the results, when thrown into pecuniary shape, greater regularity of measure', (Finlaison, *Report and Table,* pp vii–viii).
2. See Table II, footnote 1.
3. Defined as 'average duration of (successful) claims for sickness for every (successful) claimant', i.e. (sum of successful claims in weeks divided by number of successful claimants) × 6.

Table IV

AGE SPECIFIC SICKNESS CLAIM, AND CLAIM DURATION RATES,
FOR MALES BY DISTRICT OF BENEFIT SOCIETY REGISTERED
OFFICE, BASED ON THE QUINQUENNIAL RETURNS FROM REGIS-
TERED FRIENDLY SOCIETIES (ENGLAND AND WALES) 1846-50
(*Based on 'adjusted' rates and a six-day week*)
Source: Finlaison, *Report and Tables,* p. 17

Age (years)	Sickness claim rate (days)			Claim duration rate (days)		
	rural	town	city	rural	town	city
20	5.90	5.90	5.83	21.78	23.42	21.65
25	5.98	5.81	5.06	24.73	24.73	21.46
30	6.10	5.78	5.53	26.42	26.53	24.66
35	6.24	6.06	5.80	27.46	27.77	25.91
40	7.08	7.04	6.87	30.00	31.39	28.83
45	8.00	7.93	8.21	32.98	33.83	32.69
50	9.48	10.39	9.97	36.91	39.81	36.88
55	11.13	13.31	11.76	41.23	45.89	40.37
60	15.60	17.20	14.77	52.30	51.96	48.28
65	23.74	23.82	21.13	69.01	65.54	57.97
70	38.48	38.54	29.63	93.19	91.03	72.16
75	60.38	58.37	37.69	121.58	114.21	84.84
80	83.53	101.21	46.71	144.11	179.53	92.06
84	87.81	90.52	38.77	155.61	165.64	66.14
% of subjects	58	31	11			

Peter Froggatt

Table V

AGE SPECIFIC SICKNESS CLAIM RATES FOR MALES IN CERTAIN
OCCUPATIONS, BASED ON THE QUINQUENNIAL RETURNS FROM
REGISTERED FRIENDLY SOCIETIES (ENGLAND AND WALES) 1846–50
(*Based on 'adjusted' rates and a six-day week*)
Source: Finlaison, *Report and Tables,* pp xxvi, 18 *et seq.*

		Sickness claim rate (days)			
Age (years)	mariners	miners and colliers	police	railway employees	all others
20	4.49	7.58	6.36	7.41	5.90
25	4.46	7.64	4.83	7.91	5.85
30	5.65	8.25	7.26	8.50	5.92
35	7.73	8.84	7.00	7.62	6.12
40	6.67	9.90	8.55	9.35	7.04
45	9.78	12.78	17.00	10.41	8.00
50	11.49	18.45	23.91	13.05	9.85
60	21.04	24.42	—	13.20	16.91

Table VI

AGE SPECIFIC CLAIM DURATION RATES FOR MALES IN CERTAIN
OCCUPATIONS, BASED ON THE QUINQUENNIAL RETURNS FROM
REGISTERED FRIENDLY SOCIETIES (ENGLAND AND WALES) 1846–50
(*Based on 'adjusted' rates and a six-day week*)
Source: Finlaison, *Report and Tables,* pp xxvi, 18 *et seq.*

		Claim duration rate (days)			
Age (years)	mariners	miners and colliers	police	railway employee	all others
20	26.58	20.83	26.60	23.29	22.16
25	28.61	21.90	19.71	23.93	24.45
30	31.61	23.58	23.25	25.04	26.25
35	41.00	24.96	24.05	22.34	27.35
40	38.30	28.06	27.91	29.01	30.26
45	47.67	32.79	47.47	32.43	33.20
50	51.58	47.55	65.49	42.89	37.86
60	75.14	44.94	—	31.61	51.68

Table VII

SICKNESS DATA BY REGION OF BENEFIT SOCIETY REGISTERED
OFFICE, DERIVED FROM THE QUINQUENNIAL RETURNS FROM
REGISTERED FRIENDLY SOCIETIES (ENGLAND AND WALES)
1846–50
(*Based on 'adjusted' rates and a six-day week*)
Source: Finlaison, *Report and Tables*, p. xi

Region	Claim duration rate (days) (a)	Percentage at risk taken sick (b)	(a) × (b)
North	43.18	19.89	8.59
Welsh	39.19	22.14	8.68
Manufacturing	38.58	22.34	8.62
South-west	33.98	27.77	9.44
East	32.04	26.42	8.46
Metropolitan	32.00	25.31	8.10
South-east	31.90	25.88	8.26
Midlands	31.17	29.29	9.13

Table VIII

AGE SPECIFIC PERCENTAGE MORTALITY USING DEATHS REGIS-
TERED FOR LIVERPOOL IN 1841 AND RECORDED FOR BELFAST FOR
1840 AND POPULATIONS ENUMERATED AT THE 1841 CENSUSES

Age[1] (years)	Liverpool[2]	Belfast[3]
—2	24.154	16.850
2–5	10.449	5.691
6–15	1.156	1.308
16–25	0.869	1.008
26–35	1.278	1.628
36–45	2.050	2.030
46–55	3.206	2.167
56–65	5.083	4.464

Totals	Pop.	223,003
	Deaths	7,556

1. Age groups for Liverpool are cited as: 0–1, 1–2, 5–10, 10–15, etc.
2. *Fifth report of the registrar-general,* pp xxv–xxvi.
3. See Table IX.

Table IX

PERCENTAGE MORTALITY USING DEATHS RECORDED FOR 1840
AND THE POPULATION ENUMERATED IN 1841 IN VARIOUS AGE
GROUPS FOR BELFAST AND OTHER DIVISIONS IN IRELAND

Age (years)	Ireland	Ireland (rural districts)	Ireland (civic districts)[1]	Belfast
—2	8.925	8.135	13.578	16.850
2–5	2.060	1.722	4.046	5.691
6–15	0.513	0.451	0.953	1.308
16–25	0.705	0.656	0.983	1.008
26–35	0.913	0.834	1.308	1.628
36–45	1.260	1.143	1.830	2.030
46–55	1.826	1.716	2.459	2.167
56–65	3.493	3.339	4.130	4.464
66–75	6.521	6.405	7.276	7.453
75+	14.025	14.071	13.557	16.450

Source: *Census of Ireland, 1841,* pp 150–1, 260–1, 288–9, 362–3, 428–9, and *Tables of Deaths* facing pp 65, 105, 116–7, 153, 181, 183.
1. These omit Belfast.

Table X

Reproduced from Malcolm, *Sanitary state of Belfast,* p. 15

Period of 5 years	Cases[1]	Deaths	Mortality %
Ending March 1823	3,278	142	4.4
— March 1828	2,478	145	5.7
— March 1833	2,919	196	6.7
— March 1838	6,794	742	10.9
— March 1843	6,311	696	11.0
— December 1847	10,585	1,112	10.5

1. 'Fever cases treated at the Belfast Fever Hospital.'

Epidemics	Cases	Deaths	Intervals
Fever of 1817–18 (24 mths)	2,706	118	—
— 1826–27 (11 mths)	1,527	81	8 years
— 1831* (12 mths)	1,061	73	4 years
— 1836–7–8 (20 mths)	4,669	530	5 years
— 1839–41(37 mths)	3,764	422	1 year
— 1843–4 (17 mths)	3,961	252	1½ years
— 1847–8 (15 mths)	5,137	680	2½ years

* 'Asiatic cholera broke out in 1832–3 and 1848–9'.

Belfast Urban Government in the Age of Reform

Cornelius O'Leary

I

The setting up by the Whig government in 1833 of a royal commission to enquire into the existing state of municipal corporations in England and Wales and 'to collect information respecting the defects of their constitutions' led to a revolution in British urban government as remarkable as the revolution in parliamentary government set in motion by the Great Reform Act. But it is only in recent years that a handful of scholars have highlighted the differences between the intentions of the reformers and the actual consequences.[1]

At that time, to quote Bryan Keith-Lucas, borough corporations appeared to different people in very different lights: 'as parliamentary constituencies, as organs of local government, as local judiciaries, as a conveyancing device for holding public property, as an essential element in the proper and established order of society, or as part of the system of political and social privilege and corruption damned by Cobbett as "The Thing" '.[2] The young radical barristers on the royal commission, who accumulated the detailed

---

[1] The most complete (though somewhat slanted) account of the municipal reform is still to be found in volume three—*The manor and the borough*—of Sidney and Beatrice Webb, *History of English local government* (reprinted London, 1963). See also G.B.A.M. Finlayson, 'The politics of municipal reform, 1835', in *E.H.R.*, lxxxi (Oct. 1966), pp 673–92, and 'The municipal corporation commission and report, 1833–35' in *I.H.R.Bull.*, xxxvi, (May 1963), pp 36–52; and B. Keith-Lucas, 'Municipal corporations' in *Aspects of government* (Dublin, 1978), pp 74–9.

[2] Keith-Lucas, op. cit., p. 69.

information on the 200 boroughs surveyed, produced in their report a startling indictment of municipal inefficiency and malpractice, summed up in the images of venison feasts and lucrative sinecures as the characteristic features of the old system. The most common and most striking defect of the existing corporations, they reported, was 'that the corporate bodies existed independently of the communities among which they are found. The Corporations look after themselves and are considered by the inhabitants as separate and exclusive bodies . . . in most places all identity of interest between the Corporation and the inhabitants had disappeared'.[3]

The Melbourne government reacted quickly by introducing the Municipal Corporations Bill which became law in the same year (1835) as the royal commission reported. The act tried in four main ways to remedy the defects disclosed by the commissioners.

(1) The mismanagement of corporate property, by long leases or alienation in fee simple to members of the corporations, and the failure to keep adequate municipal accounts were dealt with by the provision of a single borough account, governed by rigorous procedures of compulsory audit, comparable to the single Consolidated Fund established for government accounts in 1787.[4] The principle that all municipal property was held in trust for the people of the town was thereby established.

(2) The failure of borough corporations to perform their statutory judicial duties was met by provisions separating the judicial and administrative functions: borough justices were to be appointed by the crown and also qualified recorders in towns with quarter sessions; only the mayor was to continue as an *ex officio* borough magistrate, an exemption that continued until 1968.[5]

(3) Of lesser importance (in the view of the commissioners) than their role as trustees and judicial bodies was what we regard as the characteristic role of municipal corporations: organs of local government. To quote E. P. Hennock, 'municipal reform was primarily meant to change the basis of authority, and only to a very limited extent to change the functions of corporations'.[6] The act provided that the new borough councils be responsible for a small number of public services, mainly police and lighting. Other

[3] *First report of the commissioners appointed to inquire into the municipal corporations in England and Wales,* [116] H.C. 1835, xxiii, 32.
[4] See C. O'Leary, 'Consolidated fund and appropriation bills' in *N.I. Legal Quart.,* xvi (Mar. 1965), pp 67–72.
[5] Keith-Lucas, op-cit., pp 80, 129.
[6] E. P. Hennock, *Fit and proper persons. Ideal and reality in nineteenth-century urban government* (London, 1973), p. 186.

functions then performed by separate boards (improvements and paving) might be transferred to the new councils, but there was no compulsory process of acquisition.

(4) As might be expected from its provenance, the act embodied the principle of the wider franchise already established for parliamentary elections in 1832, the great whig panacea for urban ills. In theory at least, the act established a wider electorate than for parliamentary elections: *all* ratepaying male householders, as compared to £10 householders. But this wider franchise was illusory: since holdings valued at less than £10 were not in practice rated at all, at least until the Small Tenements Rating Act of 1850, and, since the resident freemen retained their parliamentary, but not their municipal, vote, the electorate for parliamentary elections was paradoxically slightly larger than the municipal.[7]

The Municipal Corporations Act of 1835 applied to 178 existing boroughs in England and Wales, but it also provided that previously unincorporated towns (of which Birmingham was the most notable) might acquire a corporation through petition of the inhabitants. The new borough councils elected in the late 1830s and early 1840s were generally liberal-dominated (Liverpool, the only major exception, will be discussed later) and it was these councils, manned by 'fit and proper' persons of sufficient wealth to meet the property qualification (owning real or personal property worth £1000 or occupying property of a rateable value of £30) and sufficient leisure to spend hours of unpaid labour at their municipal duties, that had to deal with the problems of rapid urbanization, especially in the north and midlands, in the succeeding decades. The prototype of the new councillor might well be the fictitious Gideon Bagsworth, described as follows by a Birmingham newspaper:

Here is Bagsworth, with every qualification requisite for a Town Councillor, shrewd, honest, liberal, energetic, and persevering, ready in word and deed, with a decent balance at his bankers and sufficient leisure on his hands.[8]

The story of how England became the most urbanized country in the world is well-known and may be briefly summarised. In 1801 (the year of the first census) only 17% of the population of England and Wales lived in towns of more than 20,000 and only London exceeded 100,000 people. By 1911 the number of towns with a

---

[7] B. Keith-Lucas, *The English local government franchise* (Oxford, 1952), chap. 3.
[8] Hennock, op. cit., p. 78.

population in excess of 100,000 was 44, and the proportion of the population living in towns of over 20,000 was 61%; in the rest of the world only the United States, the states of Prussia and Saxony in the German Empire, and the Netherlands could claim more than 10%.[9] In 1831, outside of London, only Dublin, until 1800 the capital of a separate kingdom, had a population exceeding 250,000 and the growing industrial conurbations of Liverpool, Manchester, Birmingham and Leeds lay between 120,000 and 210,000. However, in the census of 1901, while Dublin with suburbs had expanded merely to 375,000, the other four cities had grown to between 500,000 and 750,000.[10] The corporations of these urban growth centres had to face the complex problems involved in very large numbers of people living together, for the solution of which there were no successful precedents for, as Professor Hennock so delicately puts it: 'Europeans had never yet lived in large towns without poisoning themselves with their own waste products'.[11]

This lengthy preamble was necessary in order to set the stage for the discussion of a particular borough, Belfast, in the period after reform.

II

Similar royal commissions were set up for Scotland and Ireland in the same year as the English commission was established. The report of the Scottish commissioners did not lead to a single great reformist measure, but to a series of statutes dealing with different aspects of the question. Ireland, however, followed a very similar course to England.

The Irish commission appointed in 1833 comprised one serjeant at law (Louis Perrin), and 12 barristers, one of whom later became lord chancellor (Maziere Brady) and another a high court judge (D. R. Pigot). They surveyed the 60 corporations then existing (another 30 had become extinct in the decades following the Union) and delivered their report in tones of scarcely qualified pessimism very similar to that of their counterparts in England and Wales:

The Corporations have long become unpopular, and objects of suspicion. As at present constituted they are, in many instances, of no service to the

[9] See E. E. Lampard, 'The urbanizing world' in H. J. Dyos and M. Wolff, *The Victorian city. Images and realities* (London, 1973), i, 3–57.
[10] B. R. Mitchell and P. Deane, *Abstract of British historical statistics* (Cambridge, 1962), pp 24–5.
[11] Hennock, op. cit., p. 2.

community; in others, injurious; in all, insufficient and inadequate to the proper purposes and ends of such institutions. The public distrust in them attaches on their officers and nominees; and the result is a failure of that respect for, and confidence in, the ministers of justice and police, which ought to subsist in well-regulated communities, which, where they do exist, conduce so much to the peace and good order of society, and without which the authority of the law may be dreaded, but cannot be respected or effective.[12]

The commissioners 'respectfully' urged a 'general, complete and speedy' reform. Although the English report had been followed by legislation passed in the same year, a five-year delay ensued in the case of Ireland, due mainly to persistent Conservative opposition in the Lords to the various bills introduced by the whig government. Eventually, in 1840, a bill became law[13] which abolished 58 corporations, some in very small towns, but including the sizeable town of Galway (population, 30,000) which had to wait almost a full century for its corporate status to be restored. Only 10 corporations were preserved (Dublin, Cork, Limerick, Belfast, Derry, Drogheda, Kilkenny, Sligo, Waterford, Clonmel), although, as in England and Wales, non-incorporated towns were entitled to petition for incorporation. The franchise was to be narrower than in England, the same £10 household qualification as for parliamentary elections, and the powers of the new borough councils would also be slightly narrower, e.g. not including control of police.

Belfast was then a town of 53,000 people (according to the census of 1831) just on the brink of its great industrial break-through. By 1835, the year of the report, over half the total exports from Belfast were linen, and already the town was the first port in Ireland in value of trade: £7.9 million per year to Dublin's £6.9 million.[14] By its charter, granted in 1613, the corporation was of the closest type then existing: merely the lord of the castle (then the second Marquis of Donegall, lineal descendant of Sir Arthur Chichester, the founder of the town), the sovereign and twelve burgesses, all of whom were nominated by the lord and several related to him. The commissioners reported that the corporation had 'ceased to be an object of interest to the inhabitants'[15] and was in fact so distrusted by parliament that various local acts had already transferred certain municipal functions to elected bodies: the police comissioners,

---

[12] *First report . . . municipal corporations in Ireland,* H.C. 1835, xxvii, 45–6.
[13] 3 and 4 Vict. c. 108.
[14] See I. Budge and C. O'Leary, *Belfast: approach to crisis. A study of Belfast politics, 1613–1970* (London, 1973), pp 19–22.
[15] *First report . . . municipal corporations in Ireland,* H.C. 1835, xxviii, 288.

established by an act of 1800 and elected on a very narrow franchise, were given responsibility for paving, lighting and cleaning the streets, for providing a fire service and a night watch; the development of the port had been entrusted to the Ballast Board (originally set up in 1785, and by an act of 1831 comprising elected members); and, most remarkable of all, the Belfast Charitable Society, established in 1752 to provide material relief and hospital-isation for the destitute poor, not only had its own poorhouse but was empowered by the Belfast Police Act of 1800 to levy a rate for providing piped water to the town and was also responsible for a public graveyard.[16]

According to all the criteria applied in the English report and followed in the Irish report, the Belfast Corporation was found wanting. Its natural functions had been superseded by the establish-ment of local boards; it had dissipated corporate funds, and it had even failed to provide a judicial body for the town. (The sovereign, although enjoying an annual income of £500 from the market tolls, had refused to try people arrested by the night watch, established by the act of 1800, and the unpaid justices of the peace had followed suit; so the police commissioners had been obliged to employ a stipendiary magistrate, Mr C. M. Skinner, who was succeeded by his son, both of whom distinguished themselves by charging and appropriating to their own use fees for which no statutory authority could be found.)[17]

III

The Irish Reform Act of 1833 had allocated Belfast two members of parliament; by the Irish Municipal Corporations Act 1840 it was given a corporation (one-third of whom retired annually) of 30 councillors and 10 aldermen elected by the £10 male householders. So, in a matter of ten years, the town was transformed from one of the closest of close boroughs, with members of parliament and corporation all creatures of the lord of the castle, to a status similar to that of the great towns of the north of England. (Before 1832 Liverpool had both members of parliament and corporation; Leeds had a corporation, but no members; Birmingham with neither corporation nor parliamentary representation had a very effective

---

[16] For a succinct account of the diverse activities of the Charitable Society see R. W. M. Strain, *Belfast and its Charitable Society* (Oxford, 1961).

[17] *First report . . . municipal corporations in Ireland*, H.C. 1835, xxviii, 258–61.

pressure group, the radical Political Union, which in effect became the Liberal organization in the town.)

In Belfast organized party politics virtually started in 1832. The beginning of the Liberal party can be traced to a town meeting of November 1830 during the campaign for parliamentary reform; the beginning of a Conservative organization to the setting up of a Constitutional Club during the general election of 1832.[18] The result of the 1832 election was two Conservative MPs; in 1835 one Conservative, one Liberal; in 1837, two Liberals (for the only time) and in 1841 two Conservatives again. After 1841 that pattern continued for the rest of the century, with the solitary exception of a Liberal elected in 1868. The Conservative party was also successful in winning all forty seats at the first election to the reformed corporation in 1842.

What was the reason for the decisive defeat of a party which had at its outset the support of some of the leading families in commerce and industry (Sinclair, Grimshaw, Tennent) and one of the two daily newspapers, the *Northern Whig*? Any answer must obviously be tentative, but in all probability the Conservative hegemony was attributable to the gradual but definite alignment of politics and religion that later came to characterise Belfast: Catholics and Anglicans being consistent in their allegiance to Liberals and Conservatives respectively, while the Presbyterians were divided. The religious distribution given by the *Report of the Commissioners on Public Instruction, 1835* (Ireland's first religious census) was Presbyterian, 25,939; Roman Catholic, 22,078; and Church of Ireland, 17,942.[19]

The second probable cause was that the Belfast Conservatives had the good fortune to have a permanent agent who was endowed with all the qualities of the modern machine politician, the solicitor John Bates,[20] who became in 1842 the first town clerk of the reformed corporation and displayed a skill equal to that of Coppock or any of the celebrated English election agents in manipulating the intricacies of the new registration system, i.e. objecting to potential opponents, or ensuring that potential supporters were placed on the register. By 1842, when a Commons select committee, under O'Connell's chairmanship, enquired into an election compromise of 1841, they reported that not only had

[18] The 1832 general election is treated extensively in S. E. Baker (Mrs Sybil Gribbon), 'Orange and Green. Belfast, 1832–1912' in Dyos and Wolff, op. cit., ii, 790–3, and in Budge and O'Leary, op. cit., pp 41–4.
[19] *First report of the commissioners on public instruction,* [45] [46] H.C. 1835, xxxiii, 268.
[20] See Budge and O'Leary, op. cit., chap. 2 ('The age of John Bates'), pp 41–65.

that election been marked by 'gross corruption and personation' but that there were only 1,800 actual electors out of 6,000 names on the register.

This Conservative monopoly of the government of a rising industrial town went quite against the trend of the times. Birmingham, Manchester, Sheffield, Leeds, and in Scotland, Glasgow, all had Liberal-dominated corporations elected under the Municipal Corporations Act 1835, and also returned Liberal members to parliament. The only exception was Liverpool,[21] where the pattern of development was similar to Belfast's, a struggle between Liberals and Conservatives in the 1830s, ending in Conservative control of the town council and Conservative monopoly of parliamentary representation. But this was also due to peculiar circumstances. Before 1835 the Liverpool Corporation was virtually an arm of the Established Church, maintaining schools and church property and paying the clergy. The cause of reform united Catholics (then over 50% of the population, a much larger share than in the other large English towns) with Nonconformists against Anglican privilege; but in return an Anglican clergyman, the Reverend Hugh McNeile (from Donegal), with considerable demagogic skill organized a Protestant Association, which quickly became allied to the Conservative party and won the support of working class Protestants. The religious struggle continued to dominate Liverpool politics right down to our time: for many years the main issue centred on the interdenominational schools, which the Liberal-controlled corporation set up in the 1830s and which were fiercely opposed by the Protestant Association. (As is well known, Liverpool and Glasgow were the only British cities where the Orange Order flourished.) Even in 1903, when religious controversies were waning elsewhere, Archibald Salvidge (possibly the most famous Liverpool Conservative) wrote that:

the fidelity of the Conservative workingmen of Liverpool to Conservative principles (exists) because they recognize that the first and fundamental principle of Conservatism is the maintenance of Church and State.[22]

The main legislative instrument in the hands of the reformed corporations anxious to cope with the problems of industrialization and urbanization was the Private Act, which until 1847 had to be

---

[21] The best study of Liverpool politics is C. A. Collins, 'Politics and elections in nineteenth century Liverpool' (M.A. thesis, University of Liverpool, 1974). See also D. Fraser, *Urban politics in Victorian England* (Leicester, 1976), pp 116–7, 133–42, 160–6.
[22] S. Salvidge, *Salvidge of Liverpool* (London, 1934), p. 44, cited in Collins, op. cit., p. 340.

promoted entirely at the expense of the town concerned.[23] Each town dealt with its own specific problems. Leeds promoted an improvement act which became the prototype for similar legislation, a comprehensive measure granting powers for paving and drainage, setting minimal standards for housing and providing for the suppression of vice. Manchester promoted an act which became the basis for all subsequent schemes of slum clearance, prescribing that houses deemed unfit for human habitation could be closed without compensation. Liverpool, the first town to appoint a medical officer of health, put through a sanitary act which became the model for the Public Health Act, 1875. Birmingham, an inland town unable to discharge sewage into a large river or an estuary, pioneered sewage farming.

Having mentioned Liverpool as a town characterised by politico-religious tensions, it is revelant here to note that one very disputatious issue cut clean across the existing divisions: the issue of a water supply. The adoption by the council of a scheme to build a reservoir at Rivington Pike at a staggering cost precipitated a major battle, and for years councillors (prompted by engineers) exchanged insults over such technical questions as whether local sources could yield three, eight or twelve million gallons daily, and whether more bore holes would yield more water or merely deprive existing wells of supplies.[24]

IV

Belfast Corporation, untroubled by party dissension and spurred on by the energetic town clerk, promoted three improvement acts in the succeeding years 1845, 1846 and 1847.[25] These acts involved the expenditure of hitherto unheard-of sums, exceeding £200,000. (To get this into perspective, one must remember that the total public service of the United Kingdom in 1845 was just under £10.9 millions,[26] so Belfast Corporation was borrowing a sum equivalent to 2% of the total British budget on the security of the Belfast rates. But this expenditure was exceeded by other large towns. The total cost of the Rivington Pike scheme was nearly £2 millions.) The

[23] Hennock, op. cit., pp 4–5.
[24] See Fraser, op. cit., pp 160–6; Collins, op. cit., pp 75–84.
[25] See Budge and O'Leary, op. cit., pp 54–65. Belfast municipal records (which may be consulted by courtesy of the town clerk) go back to 1842—e.g. minute books of the town council—but there are considerable gaps and the collection has never been catalogued. At the time of writing a city archivist is about to be appointed.
[26] See Appropriation Act 1845 (8 and 9 Vict. c. 130).

money was to be spent in widening existing streets, building new ones, buying-out the privately-owned gasworks and draining the evil-smelling Blackstaff river. The act of 1847 also laid down minimum standards for houses, each with at least a small yard with lavatory or ashpit, and prescribed a maximum ten-hour day for women and children working in the textile factories. However, to their later embarrassment the corporation acted *ultra vires*. Instead of buying out the gasworks, they bought a site for a new central market, and because of opposition from millowners to losing their water supply, the Blackstaff remained undrained. In 1852 the corporation secured the passage of another private act, extending the boundary so as to increase the town area by seven times, but shortly afterwards they were sued in the Irish Chancery Court by a radical solicitor, John Rea, on the grounds of over-spending and *ultra vires*.

In his judgement (June 1855),[27] the Lord Chancellor of Ireland, Maziere Brady (who twenty years previously had been a member of the Irish Royal Commission on Municipal Corporations), firmly asserted one of the governing principles of the English Municipal Corporations Act. He referred to the case *Attorney-General v. Wilson* (1840), arising out of the sale by certain members of the old Leeds Corporation of property belonging to the corporation on the ground that they were free to dispose of it as individuals. The English Lord Chancellor, Lord Cottenham, however, insisted that the property held by the corporation was held in trust in a strict and enforceable sense for the people of the town. Following this precedent, Lord Chancellor Brady held that while before the reform corporations had in fact dealt with corporate property after the manner of private individuals, that was no longer permissible.

But all that is changed and gone since the passing of *3 and 4 Vic., c. 108* (the act of 1840); and now Municipal Corporations are bodies entrusted by their fellow-citizens, the burgesses at large, with the management of their common affairs, with the care and supervision of them . . . such Corporations are at present mere trustees of the public funds placed in their keeping; and they are liable, as trustees, to be called to account in this Court, in like manner as the trustees of any charitable fund previously were, and still are.[28]

The Lord Chancellor found all the allegations against the corporation proved; it had borrowed in excess of the funds allowed,

---

[27] *Irish Chancery Reports*, iv (1856), pp 141–72.
[28] Ibid., pp 142–3.

had misapplied the funds so borrowed, and had also borrowed illegally. The special respondents, the ten longest serving members of the corporation, were held personally responsible for a sum of £273,000.

In the immediate aftermath of the chancery suit, John Bates resigned all his offices (he was town solicitor also) and was dead within three months—of a broken heart, according to his obituary notice in the *Belfast News-Letter*.[29] At the annual election for one-third of the council in 1855, six Liberals (including a Catholic) were returned, and the Conservatives tried to secure their approval for another private bill—this time indemnifying the special respondents; but the Liberals refused on the ground that the ratepayers should not be saddled with the cost of Conservative mismanagement, and the dispute dragged on in an undignified manner for several years, eventually being submitted to an arbitrator, who in effect recommended that each side should pay its own costs (1861). In the meantime the Conservative majority had done a deal with the Liberals by allowing them 17 unopposed returns to the council, and they elected in 1861 the only Liberal mayor (Sir Edward Coey), who was also the only non-Conservative, or non-Unionist, civic head of Belfast until the election of Alderman David Cook, 116 years later.

The chancery suit with its consequences caused a great deal of ill-feeling between the two parties in the town and was followed by a quarter century during which the corporation maintained what is nowadays called a low profile. It also earned for Belfast urban politics the corrupt reputation which was long to remain. But there are some factors more favourable to the Belfast Conservatives, which have rarely been stressed: the trustee doctrine was quite new and had previously been adumbrated only in one or two judicial decisions; and although the sums spent were not applied to the purposes specified in the acts, they were undeniably used to improve the town, demolishing old streets and building new ones (Victoria Street and Corporation Street), and the provision of a new central market, as a royal commission reported in 1859, was a more urgent need for the rapidly expanding town than a new gasworks.

The most remarkable feature of this episode, however, is the way in which the Belfast political parties seem to have acted out of character. While the Liberals became advocates of cheese-paring and municipal meanness, the Conservatives seemed to have adopted the general attitude of the Liberals in the developing towns of

[29] *Belfast News-Letter*, 29 Sept. 1855.

England, summed up in the term, 'the politics of improvement'. This common philosophy of urban reformers was expressed grandiloquently by the famous Baptist minister, George Dawson:

A town is a solemn organism through which should flow, and in which should be shaped all the highest, loftiest and truest ends of man's moral nature.[30]

Or, more specifically, by the wood-screw manufacturer (also from Birmingham) Joseph Chamberlain, who was to become one of the greatest of municipal reformers:

A paternal Government provides for our criminals in gaol 1000 cu. ft. of air as a minimum; and those criminals, after their confinement is terminated, go back to their homes in which 300, 200 and 100 cubic feet of air is the maximum. Hardly a gleam of sunshine ever comes into the dark and dreary courts, which exist in the centre of all large cities.[31]

The message in both statements is clear: those who control expanding towns have an imperative duty to ensure decent living conditions for the people within their jurisdiction. Now let us look at the speech delivered by Andrew Mulholland, one of Belfast's first captains of industry, after his election as mayor at the beginning of 1845—the year in which the first Belfast improvement bill was promoted. His aim, said Mulholland, would be to ameliorate the condition of the operatives and he went on:

The rapid increase of the population of this town has from the causes which led to the increase, necessarily consisted in an overwhelming proportion of those classes; and the growth has been so sudden, that arrangements necessary for their physical and moral well-being have not kept pace with it. In this we do but resemble the large manufacturing towns of England; but during the past year great efforts have been made in them to remedy the want. I am sure, when properly brought forward, we will not here be behind in following their example; and in admitting the obligation of providing for the wants of that portion of the community who, in this respect, are not in a position to do so for themselves. The object is, of course, generally to promote their health and cleanliness and to give them better habits and higher tastes.[32]

There the gospel of improvement is preached as definitely as in any of the utterances of George Dawson or R. W. Dale.

[30] Hennock, op. cit., p. 75.
[31] C. W. Boyd, *Speeches of Joseph Chamberlain* i, 63–4, cited by Hennock, op. cit., pp 140–1.
[32] *Belfast News-Letter,* 3 Jan. 1845.

V

As will be remembered, one of the criteria of municipal competence adopted by the English royal commission was the efficient administration of justice by impartial and qualified magistrates. This was ensured by having borough justices and (where necessary) recorders appointed by the crown.

In Ireland this reform meant in practice appointment by the under-secretary and, as is well-known, the most famous of all under-secretaries, Thomas Drummond, removed more than one-third of the existing justices: mainly clergymen, small landowners (or 'squireens') and land agents. Drummond also secured in 1836 the passage of a major piece of legislation amalgamating the existing county and peace preservation corps (the original Peelers, established in 1814) into a single national police force, the Constabualary of Ireland (after 1867 the Royal Irish Constabulary), centralised, professional, well-paid and quasi-military, the only remaining exceptions being the local police in Dublin (afterwards the Dublin Metropolitan Police), Belfast and Derry.[33]

The Belfast police force (supported by the police rate) continued until 1865, but there were widespread complaints that during the riots of 1857 and 1864 they (and the ten local magistrates) were too partial to the Protestants. In 1857 only 6 or 7 of the 160 police were Catholics,[34] and in 1864 only 5 out of 160, while the superintendent of police was the former master of an Orange Lodge.[35] The committee of inquiry into the riots of 1864 recommended as an 'absolute necessity' a new police force of over 450 men, under a commissioner appointed by the government, and two resident magistrates, one Catholic, one Protestant.

However, an act passed in 1865 abolished the Belfast police and transferred 450 of the Irish Constabulary (mainly Catholics) into the town. During the next serious rioting, in 1886, there was a widespread belief among Belfast Protestants that the Gladstone government was packing the town with Catholic policemen from the south and the resulting animus against the RIC continued right up to its disbandment in 1922.[36] In 1866 Belfast was given a separate court of quarter sessions with a recorder.

[33] See R. B. McDowell, *The Irish administration, 1801–1914* (London, 1964), pp 135–45.
[34] *Report of the commissioners of inquiry into the origin and character of the riots in Belfast in July and September 1857,* [2309] H.C. 1857–8, xxvi, 4.
[35] *Report of the commissioners of inquiry 1864, respecting the magisterial and police jurisdiction, arrangements and establishment of the borough of Belfast,* [3466], H.C. 1865, xxviii, 5–7.
[36] S. E. Baker in Dyos and Wolff, op. cit., pp 805–9.

At this point it may be convenient to sketch the structure of local government in Belfast in the year 1865, when the private act was passed consolidating the existing rates into a single general rate and abolishing the local police force.

(1) The poor law guardians of Belfast and district (including parts of Antrim and Down), elected by the £10 householders (under the Irish Poor Law Act of 1838), levied the poor rate, built workhouses, and were also entrusted with responsibility for out-door relief, for fever and other state-aided hospitals, and the peculiarly Irish institution of dispensaries. They were the nearest approximation to an urban sanitary authority.

(2) The town council was concerned with roads, public buildings, baths and washhouses, libraries, museums, bridges and lunatic asylums. The council subsisted on police rate and washhouses rate (under the Improvement Act of 1845).

(3) The Water Board, established by a private act of 1840, which transferred the provision of a water supply and the power to levy a water rate from the Charitable Society, built several reservoirs, but was continually falling behind demand until the purchase of the Silent Valley in south Down in 1893. In 1865, for example, daily water consumption in Belfast was a mere two million gallons, at a time when Manchester (with nearly three times the population) and Glasgow (nearly four times as populous) were constructing water-works supplying thirty and fifty million gallons respectively.[37]

(4) The Harbour Commissioners, elected from occupiers rated at not less than £20 and supported by the ever-increasing harbour dues (which quadrupled in twenty years), so successfully developed the harbour that (unlike Dublin) the largest passenger and cargo liners could dock.[38]

This system, involving a plethora of *ad hoc* authorities was, however, gradually moving towards the more modern type of a single (or all-purpose) urban authority. In 1875 the Irish Public Health Act applied the principles of the English Public Health Act of 1875 in constituting the borough councils as the main sanitary authorities, and in 1898 the Irish Local Government Act transferred to the borough councils from the poor law guardians the power to levy the poor rate. The other measures affecting Belfast were the Belfast Main Drainage Act (1887), which established a modern

[37] The celebrated journalist Jack Loudan has written quite a lively history of the Belfast Water Board. See J. Loudan, *In search of water* (Belfast, 1940).
[38] See J. C. Beckett and R. E. Glassock, *Belfast. The origin and growth of an industrial city* (London, 1967), pp 98–108.

sewage system, and the Belfast Corporation Act (1896), which trebled the area of the borough and created fifteen wards, which survived to our own day.[39] With the municipalisation of gas, electricity and public transport, the structure of urban government was complete, excepting the services of housing and education which largely belong to the twentieth century.

VI

Detailed studies of the urban politics of the major English cities by Fraser, Hennock, Keith-Lucas and others have revealed the extent to which the modest designs of the Royal Commission on Municipal Corporations were within less than fifty years transformed into a set of obligations accepted by urban governments to provide minimal living conditions for all the inhabitants within their care, at an aggregate expenditure far in excess of the national budget. In the mid-nineteenth century the corporations, not the government, were the big spenders. Although the underlying philosophy was utilitarianism, the characteristic liberal creed, Conservative politicians also helped to realise these goals. The Conservative-dominated corporation of Liverpool was just as committed to the gospel of improvement as the Liberal corporations of Birmingham and Manchester.

With these cities Belfast, under almost continuous Conservative rule, must also be classified. Belfast in the middle and later nineteenth century took its standards from the developing English cities, not from Ireland. 'We Belfast people,' wrote the *Belfast News-Letter* at the very end of the century,

are proud of our city and its many activities. We are in the very front in the race of civic development and industrial progress, and we have a laudable ambition to keep there. (12 September 1899)

This boast was substantially justified. If Belfast's record in public health,[40] much affected by typhoid and tuberculosis, was inferior to Birmingham's, in housing it was superior to Glasgow's. The desire to emulate and even outstrip the great English cities was best illustrated by the extravagant scheme to build a city hall, which in scale and magnificence would rival any British civic temple, and

[39] For the details of the act see Budge and O'Leary, op. cit., pp 116-9.
[40] For public health see an interesting article by Sir Ian Fraser, 'Father and son—a tale of two cities' in *Ulster Medical Journal,* xxxvii (Winter 1968), 1–12, and the contribution by Dr Peter Froggatt to this volume, pp 155–185.

incidentally leave Dublin's modest city hall far behind. The eventual cost of £320,000 caused an outcry at the time.[41]

To these aims of urban improvement both parties in varying degrees subscribed, as can be seen in the history of the three institutions on which the party balance varied. The Water Commissioners were less Conservative than the corporation and the Harbour Commissioners were mostly Liberal-dominated; but all three subscribed to the gospel of improvement. Nor should too much be made of the town council's reputation for corruption. It is perfectly true that in the '40s, '50s and '60s the great industrial and commercial families (Sinclairs, Dunvilles etc.) tended to shun the corporation and to seek seats (if anywhere) on the Harbour Board. But by the 1880s a seat on the council and representation of the town in parliament were sought by the greatest captains of industry. For example, the first four members for Belfast North (created in 1885), who also served in the mayoralty, were Sir William Ewart (1885-89), Sir Edward Harland (1889-95), Sir James Haslett (1895-1905) and Sir Daniel Dixon (1905-07). Dixon's successor as lord major (the title was conferred in 1892, and the rank of 'city' in 1888) was the Earl of Shaftesbury, one of the last aristocrats to serve as the civic head of any city in the United Kingdom.

In the foregoing pages I have presented a perspective, perhaps unfamiliar to those who regard Belfast as merely notorious for sectarian bigotry, rioting and corruption. All those elements were certainly there, but they were not the whole story.

[41] Budge and O'Leary, op. cit., pp 121-2.

An Irish City: Belfast 1911

Sybil Gribbon

In urban history we are inclined to follow two methods: to deal in impressions or to rely on statistics; at best perhaps both—the 'image' and 'reality' which the late Professor H. J. Dyos had perceived.[1] It is fitting that the conference upon which this book is based with its theme 'the town in Ireland' should have been held in the week in which his first memorial lecture has been given. It is proposed to use here some of both image and reality, but warning is given that the cards are merely being reshuffled. Many readers will be familiar with them, and many more skilled than the present writer to play them. The apology for such revisionism is that once she thought to write a history *of* Belfast; but the times were out of joint, and in the long run the death toll clarifies the mind wonderfully. Nevertheless, it has taken much heartsearching to reach the conclusion that one day she might understand enough to write a history *for* Belfast.

The image of Belfast is by no means consistent. Its citizens and outsiders have reacted to it with affection and antipathy. 'Neglect you?' wrote William Drennan to Mrs McTier from Edinburgh in the 1770s, 'Why I declare I cannot read two pages without thinking of Belfast . . . I dream of Belfast'.[2] In 1794 another champion of the town, the *Northern Star,* squared up to its detractors: 'Who then is it that dislikes Belfast?'[3] Alas, some of its native-born did. 'Belfast,'

[1] H. J. Dyos and Michael Wolff (eds), *The Victorian city: images and realities* (2 vols, London, 1973), i, xxviii, and ii, 907.
[2] Letter no. 3, William Drennan to Mrs McTier, D. A. Chart (ed.), *The Drennan Letters* (Belfast, 1931), p. 1.
[3] Quoted in D. J. Owen, *History of Belfast* (Belfast, 1921), p. 128.

wrote Sam Allen on a home visit in 1910, 'looks more Belfasty than ever. What an unattractive place it is!'[4] The city was frequently the butt of the visitor or journalist, especially from the end of the nineteenth century. Jack Yeats, according to Beatrice Webb, epitomised its religion as 'the man who sells his cow too cheap goes to hell',[5] and that formidable lady on her honeymoon in 1892 had time to observe and disapprove of the town's 'hard-fisted employers and groups of closely organised skilled craftsmen'.[6] The London correspondent of a local Nationalist newspaper claimed in 1900 that political circles in England thought of Belfast as divided into two classes, 'well-to-do bigots and bigoted rowdies'.[7] The *Daily Mail* in 1903 called it 'a commercial cockpit where sordid little struggles are continuously in process'.[8] It was said that San Francisco in 1910 had declined to have a street named Belfast because of its association with bigotry, riots and bloodshed.[9] Indeed, even some of our own history colleagues have not taken to us. 'Belfast,' Emmet Larkin has written of the Edwardian period, 'was not only a seething political volcano in these years, but more than that, a volcano spewing religious bigotry'.[10] And yet within a few years of that era there was Richard Rowley (it will be granted, not in quite the same poetic category as 'Wee Wullie' Yeats) walking the Belfast streets afire with their beauty. We who love Belfast will have to rest our wounded vanity, perhaps a bit uncomfortably since Rowley's eloquence at times does not quite fit our local tongue, upon his reassurance to his mother city:

> Not that thou lackest beauty, but their mind
> Is dull, and their unloving eyes are blind.[11]

Divided reactions to Belfast are not in themselves a good reason for questioning whether it was an Irish city. They might, however, at least suggest that Belfast struck some people as peculiar. Was it peculiar in Ireland? There are cities whose image is not associated fully with the age or the land in which they existed. Carthage was neither African nor Roman. What worlds apart were Philadelphia and New Orleans! Some visitors certainly regarded Belfast as un-

[4] W. E. D. Allen, *David Allen's: the history of a family firm, 1857–1957* (London, 1957), p. 195.
[5] Beatrice Webb, *My apprenticeship* (Penguin ed., 1971), p. 40.
[6] Beatrice Webb, *Our partnership,* ed. Barbara Drake and M. I. Cole (London, 1948), p. 31.
[7] Cited by *Belfast News-Letter,* 19 April 1900.
[8] *Daily Mail,* 16 July 1903.
[9] *Nomad's Weekly,* 8 Jan. 1910.
[10] Emmet Larkin, *James Larkin, 1876–1947, Irish Labour leader* (London, 1965), p. 316.
[11] Richard Rowley, *The city of refuge and other poems* (Dublin, 1917).

Irish. Paul-Dubois was quite clear in 1907: '. . . with its red-bricked and smoke-blackened buildings after the American pattern, its factories and palaces, this workers' city resembles Liverpool or Glasgow rather than an Irish town'.[12] Stephen Gwynn, in a sense the founding father of Irish comparative urban historiography, wrote his *Famous cities of Ireland* between 1914 and 1915. The political tenor of the time may have influenced his conclusion that, 'Belfast and the Ulster which is coming increasingly to centre about Belfast. is nearer to Scotland and more related to it than to southern Ireland'.[13]

Yet there were so many ways in which Belfast could not escape its Irish setting. One third of Ireland's declining population was living in *some* form of town. All Irish towns in some part had shared the problems of urban density common throughout the United Kingdom but which by 1911 science, technology and legislation had gone a fair way to remove. It was possible to provide a reasonable infrastructure and to improve housing and health. Primary education was a right, indeed an obligation, rather than a privilege or a choice. Other towns in Ireland as well as Belfast found causes of poverty reduced by the humanitarian legislation which had been applied progressively from Victorian and Edwardian Westminster. On the other side of the coin the slowing down of entrepreneurial impetus, changes in the empire, and the growing competition from other agricultural and manufacturing countries meant for Irish towns besides Belfast a variety of economic adjustments. Finally, demands by the working classes and by women for more political power-sharing were also voiced elsewhere in Ireland, often in urban political climates markedly distinct from those in Britain. It was not so much that Irish urban activity was different, as that it had an additional dimension. Although legislation from Westminster might be applied to any part of it, town life was the concern not only of locally elected councils, but of specificially Irish Boards such as Local Government, Education and Works. Whatever their diversities and particular bye-laws all Irish towns were to some extent obliged to meet, or to be confined by, both national regulations and United Kingdom standards. Most of them were affected, if in varying degree, by Ireland's declining population which provided for all a source of cheap unskilled labour, but which reduced the size of the surrounding market for some while it improved residual agriculture and raised consumers' purchasing power for others. Ireland's dependent economy involved them all, but particularly the

---

[12] L. Paul-Dubois, *Contemporary Ireland* (ed. Dublin, 1911), pp 102–3.
[13] Stephen Gwynn, *The famous cities of Ireland* (Dublin, 1915), p. 311.

east-coast ports. Retail trading was becoming more specialised and even multiple stores, many of them based in Great Britain, were not peculiar to Belfast.

This is simply to state the obvious, and illustrations need not concern us long. Inspectors from Dublin were seldom very welcome anywhere in Ireland, although Belfast and the northern towns were regarded by Sir Henry Robinson, perhaps a partial observer, as more malleable than some.[14] The city threatened on at least half-a-dozen issues between 1911 and 1914 to go its own way: to raise its own education rate;[15] to refuse to build municipal housing;[16] not to pay the additional police levy imposed upon it by the Castle;[17] to grant more out-relief than the Local Government Board approved.[18] In effect the reality was more conformist than the image. The new primary syllabus was introduced as in the rest of Ireland in 1913; despite a fiery confrontation between the L.G.B. Inspector and the town solicitor an initial housing project was agreed in 1914;[19] the Royal Irish Constabulary continued to patrol the streets; and the city did not refuse to accept advice whenever it chose, nor funds whenever they were provided from central government.[20] That seems like a *very* Irish city.

Like much of Ireland the urban infrastructure had met delay and resistance before completion. It was not until 1906 that a municipal electrified tramway system replaced the horse trams, an outmoded transport of which the citizens by then quite rightly felt ashamed. The installation of coin meters for gas in 26,000 homes had only just made it possible for the working class to abandon their oil lamps when the new tramway consumption reduced the price of electricity so dramatically (fourth cheapest in the United Kingdom) that gas, too, was outdated.[21] Tramlines radiating to the extended boundaries of 1896 shaped the final infill of the city, with speculative builders busy on the white-collar suburbs, owner-occupier houses in Osborne, *bijou* villas in the garden estate of Cliftonville, rented

[14] Sir Henry Robinson, *Memories wise and otherwise* (London, 1923), pp 131–2.
[15] Phenix to Birrell, 19 May 1911 (S.P.O., C.S.O. Regd papers, 2801/1913); *Belfast Telegraph*, 29 Oct. 1912; *Northern Whig*, 2 May 1913.
[16] Minutes of the joint meeting of the improvement and public health committees, 25 November 1909 (City Hall, Belfast, Local government board inquiry records (C.H.B., L.G.B.I.), 30).
[17] *Irish News*, 3 Dec. 1912; *Northern Whig*, 22 Aug. 1913.
[18] Minutes of the Belfast Board of Guardians, 1911 (P.R.O.N.I., BG VII/A/87, p. 199).
[19] Minutes 4–5 Dec. 1913, 10–13 Feb. and 9–13 Mar. 1914 (C.H.B., L.G.B.I., 46, 47 and 49).
[20] Belfast Corporation, *The Belfast book: local government in the city and county borough of Belfast* (Belfast, 1929), p. 156.
[21] *Belfast News-Letter*, 1 Jan. 1910; Electric light undertaking, 3 Oct. 1911 (C.H.B., L.G.B.I., 38).

Sybil Gribbon

semi-detacheds in Bloomfield. Not until much later did the
Corporation appreciate the consequences of the Edwardian failure
to extend the boundary further, before it became confined by a
growing ring of independent commuting urban district councils.[22]
  Improvements in public health had been steady, but always just a
little more tardy than in Great Britain. By 1911, for that very
admirable reason to which Dr O'Leary adverts in chapter nine, that
a Queen's University Professor had finished his ten-year research,
Belfast had solved its sewage disposal problem through sedimenta-
tion tanks and pumping station,[23] and the water closet was installed
in almost every house.[24] Nevertheless Belfast was still a bit
malodorous, for in Irish fashion the power in the 1911 local act to
compel landlords to provide bins left thirty-two per cent of the
households with ashpits even in 1914, and these were emptied every
seven or eight weeks.[25] (Glasgow had abolished ashpits in 1899)[26]
The National Insurance Act of 1911 gave unemployment provision
to considerable numbers of the city's workers; but its medical
benefits were weakened in Ireland by the attempt to apply it through
the old dispensary system.[27] Nonetheless between them, Westminster and Belfast had begun to reduce the dangers of poverty and
disease. By 1914 annual death rates per thousand in Belfast, Dublin
and Cork were down to 21.6, 22.7 and 21.8, very similar to Glasgow,
Manchester and Liverpool, although these were no shining examples of the pure and healthy life.[28]
  Belfast shoppers were well supplied, not simply with five palatial
department stores, four of which had been built by local residents,
but with new chain stores like Duffin's seven downtown shops for
men's wear, or fourteen Co-operative grocery branches. Tyler's had
twelve shoe shops, and Mr Allingham from Sligo five 'Hustler shoe
stores' for cheap American boots. Competition came from further
afield than Sligo, for example Lipton's had established four
groceries and the Home and Colonial Stores six. The two major
frozen-meat retailers in Great Britain, James Nelson and Sons and
the River Plate Company, had eighteen and twelve branches

[22] For this appraisal I am grateful to Mr John Dunlop, C.B.E., town clerk of Belfast, 1943–68.
[23] Minutes 16 Nov. 1910 (C.H.B., L.G.B.I., 33, pp 15–18).
[24] H. W. Bailie, *Annual report of the medical superintendent officer of health for Belfast, 1911* (Belfast, 1912), p. 39.
[25] Ibid., 1914, p. 105.
[26] Glasgow Corporation, *Municipal Glasgow 1911–14* (Glasgow, 1914), p. 153.
[27] *Irish Citizen*, 24 Jan. 1914; *Report of the Irish public health council on public health and medical services in Ireland, 1920*, pp 6–17 [Cmd 761], H.C. 1920, xvii, 1075.
[28] Sir C. A. Cameron, *Report upon the state of public health and the sanitary work etc. performed in Dublin during the year 1914* (Dublin, 1915), p. 35.

respectively. Scottish firms like Sawyer's (butchers), Thornton's (waterproofs) and Lizar's (opticians) had opened premises in Belfast.

Nevertheless it would be wrong to see expansion as one-way. Robinson and Cleaver had three shops in London and one in Liverpool; and Anderson and McAuley had set up in Brighton and Bournemouth. Lipton, himself, was the son of emigrants from County Monaghan. Retail advertising was off-setting the decline in theatrical posters for the sons of David Allen, whose London offices now dwarfed the original Belfast works. H. and J. Martin Ltd, who had built very many of Belfast's finest Victorian and Ewardian buildings as well as some 300 acres of housing, had enterprises in other parts of Ireland; and one son managed a branch in Dublin. Cantrell had been a Belfast doctor, but Cochrane from Cavan was a Dublin alderman, while their trade was worldwide. Although Ireland as a whole produced only about six per cent of the United Kingdom's mineral waters, one would not have guessed this from their advertisements:

The popping of Cantrell and Cochrane's corks is heard in the bungalows of the British cantonment in the great dependency in the Far East, and its sparkle is familiar to the Vice-Regal entourage up in the hot season refuge of the Anglo-Indians at Simla. Dons and seignorinas quaff this liquid boon in the tropical climes of South America; the West Indies welcome it as a treasure; Afric's 'sunny fountains' are out-rivalled in their very habitat by its gleam; the Antipodes have taken this gift of the Mother Empire with gratitude.

Turning from that irresistible gem to the more serious matter of trade-union organisation and political activity, one need not dwell on that most obvious fact that Larkin and Connolly looked first to Belfast and then to Dublin to organise Ireland's more poorly-paid workers; and that they met stiff resistance in both cities; or that in both cases, although less successfully in Belfast, the tramways were one of their targets for organisation. Andrew Nance, for all that he was merely the manager for the Belfast Corporation and not the owner, as William Murphy was in Dublin, had an even more forthright method than Murphy of disposing of the challenge:

I now invite every Motorman and Conductor who intends to have nothing to do with the strike, to be true to his self, and to remain at his duty, and thereby retain his situation instead of permanently losing it, to write to me, addressed Tramway Office, Sandy Row, stating that he intends to

[29] Papers in the possession of Messrs Cantrell and Cochrane Ltd, Mineral Water Manufacturers, Castlereagh Road, Belfast.

Sybil Gribbon

maintain his free right to work. The correspondence will be treated by me as strictly confidential.[30]

It was mainly in the towns, and again especially in the two large cities, that Irish women found education and the political and social experience to press for extended suffrage. Groups in Belfast and Dublin consciously exploited their unusual political situtations to their advantage, though it was the Belfast women who first won municipal concessions because of the exceptional electoral tension (and therefore of their own value as electoral assistants) in the northern city.[31] In Belfast also, the nonconformist ethos allowed women of strong personality to come to the fore.[32] But in the Edwardian era the campaign north and south remained distinctly Irish and its newspaper, published in Dublin, regularly contained articles from both cities and from all political shades.[33] Belfast suffragists may have been shocked when Asquith barely escaped bruising by a toffee-hammer in Dublin, or when Mrs Sheehy Skeffington knocked off Birrell's hat at Greystones, but they had their own tribulations with extremists, as when a home-made bomb was found in the gas oven of the W.S.P.U.'s house in University Street.[34] Envious southern feelings ran high, however, when the unionist section of the northern women succeeded in winning the promise that the Provisional Government would be elected on the municipal and not on the parliamentary franchise.[35] Nevertheless they were Irish feelings, directed towards each other and not to Westminster.

So far the case has been argued for the Irish aspect of Belfast. Not everyone might agree. Professor Beckett in his concluding survey in *Belfast: the origin and growth of an industrial city* noted and re-emphasised the Halls' remark of the 1840s that it was 'the only manufacturing town in Ireland'.[36]

[30] Reported by Nance 18 Dec. 1911 (Belfast Corporation Transport Department, Minutes of the tramway and electricity committee 1911, p. 286).
[31] Report of meeting of the Belfast Women's Suffrage Society, *Northern Whig,* 23 Sep. 1885; *Municipal Corporations (Ireland) Act, 1887;* Isabella Tod(d), 'Women's Suffrage',*Victoria College Magazine* (Belfast, 1890), pp 481–5.
[32] Miss Tod(d) above was only one of such women, whose middle and upper-class Unionism may account for their present relative neglect in Irish feminist historiography. Anne Good, *Breaking barriers: pioneering Irish women 1840-1940* (Dublin, 1979) has recognised the wide span of the northern contribution and has included within it Mrs Byers of Victoria College.
[33] Belfast contributors to the *Irish Citizen* ranged from Mrs Margaret McCoubrey, wife of a Scots engineer employed by Harland and Wolff, through Dr Elizabeth Bell of the Belfast child-care clinics, to Miss L. A. Walkington of Edenvale, Strandtown who engaged in philanthropic works.
[34] S.P.O., C.S.O. Regd papers, 13437/1914.
[35] *Irish Citizen,* 20 and 27 Sep. 1913; 13 June 1914.
[36] J. C. Beckett and R. E. Glasscock (eds), *Belfast: the origin and growth of an industrial city*

In 1911 that impression remained strong. It would be impossible to discuss here the difficulties in reaching accurate figures for each branch of manufacture in 1911, but one may list some of the main manufactures' workers as approximately 30,000 in linen; 20,000 in shipbuilding; 13,000 in making-up; 6,000 in tobacco; 5,000 in engineering or foundries; 1,000 in paper and printing. For all its faults *Class V, Industrial* of the Census provides the best comparison for the present purpose. Its greatest drawbacks, of course, are that it included those concerned in building and in food and lodgings, and that many of its unspecified labourers were not necessarily in manufacturing. At any rate, the flaws apply in something the same way to all the towns with which we may wish for the moment to be concerned. In 1911 Class V, male and female, was 33.4 per cent of Belfast in contrast to Dublin's 24.0 per cent. That is a disparity very well known. But a look at some of the Ulster linen towns shows Lisburn, Newtownards and Portadown also had about one third in Class V even if that is a very imprecise measurement. Yet, turning with some suspicion to one of them, Portadown (and who has not at some point of his life looked dubiously at Portadown?), to examine its occupations in detail, the pattern, for such a small town expanding rapidly and being a railway centre, did not seem so very unlike Belfast, save that linen employed a higher proportion of male workers than it would have done in the larger city. So one might claim that Belfast's manufacturing was not peculiar in Ireland: only the much larger total number engaged in it.

Was the size of Belfast, itself then, peculiar? Not if we remember that Dublin and Belfast in 1911 were the eighth and ninth cities of the United Kingdom outside London and had about equal populations of some 400,000.

Was the pace of Belfast's growth unique in Ireland? Using Vaughan and Fitzpatrick's 1821–1911 terminals (admittedly not a true reflection of the points between which each town's growth changed), Belfast had multiplied roughly by 10; so had Kingstown and Portrush; Lurgan, Ballyclare and Ballymena by 4 to 5; good old Portadown again by 50.[37] While many Irish towns had stagnated or declined in the nineteenth century, it is clear that there were a number of others which shared the buoyancy of rapid growth. It is

(London, 1967), p. 184. This aspect was only one of many perceptive and considered judgements in Professor Beckett's concluding survey.
[37] W. E. Vaughan and A. J. Fitzpatrick, *Irish historical statistics: population 1821–1971* (Dublin, 1978), pp 28–41. This is intentionally a provocative argument. The addition of some 2,000 people to Portrush could not be compared seriously with the addition of over 300,000 to Belfast.

true that Belfast, like Liverpool or Glasgow, had a high death rate[38] so that replacement turnover was considerable, but this was, as it always had been, a characteristic of urbanisation, and those Irish towns which were burgeoning were no exception.[39] Steep death rates were equally a feature of Portadown, Lurgan, Ballymena and Dublin;[40] and of these Portadown had no Union workhouse to weight the figure. One can observe, too, the high birth rate of early urban marriages and youngish populations not only in Belfast and in Dublin's inner city, but in Portadown, Lurgan and Ballymena.[41]

What *was* unique about Belfast? Dr O'Leary in the previous chapter has described the 'humanitarian conservatism' of Belfast's Victorian Corporation, common to many British cities: but not so uncommon in Ireland either, where a combination of landed gentry and commercial gentlemen retained, outside Dublin Castle, so much control of local government until the end of the nineteenth century.

Was Belfast's reputation for sectarianism at the root of the matter: a wee bit different from the tolerance of eighteenth-century Armagh city? What do we mean by sectarianism? Its definition appears to have expanded since Commonwealth times, and we now use it pejoritively to represent positive discrimination against another sect, in employment or in business, by political mal-practices, by violent speech, by segregation, by outright aggression; or negative discrimination through ignoring the needs of, or dragging one's feet on, reforms which disproportionately benefit other religious groups. It is not proposed here to look at details of Belfast's particular forms of discrimination, for we are presently concerned to consider how prevalent sectarianism might be in Ireland. In 1912 after the shipyard pogrom the Board of Erin and the Ancient Order of Hibernians:

compiled a list of tradesmen in Belfast who had anti-Home Rule tendencies, and distributed them throughout the south and west of Ireland with a view to boycotting such firms, and in many instances considerable injury was done to the trade of these firms.[42]

Railway returns early in 1913 showed 'a great falling off in goods out

[38] *Belfast health commission: report to the local government board for Ireland,* pp 14–15 (Cd 4128), H.C. 1908, xxxi, 699–700.
[39] *Irish News,* 7 July 1909; *Northern Whig,* 7 May 1913.
[40] H. W. Bailie, *Annual report of the medical superintendent officer of health for Belfast, 1900* (Belfast, 1901), p. 19.
[41] Ibid., 1906, p. 20.
[42] Monthly report of the Police Commissioner for Belfast to Inspector General, Dublin Castle, 8 Nov. 1912 (P.R.O., C.O. 904/88).

of Belfast'.[43] Of course the Unionist clubs responded by boycotting
Catholic publicans until the situation calmed down.[44] It would be
very difficult in that extended chain of reprisals to decide where
provocation and retaliation were first initiated. One might recall
other instances, too, where 'sectarianism' could be applied to one or
other side's position in Ireland's chequered history. Perhaps, for
example, there may have been something of that blend of religion,
passion and economic interest in both parties to the Tithe War, a
violent and sectarian issue in which one might reasonably claim that
Belfast for once played little part? Nor was it difficult to find
malpractice at personal or municipal level elsewhere in Ireland. A
Belfast foundry wrote to a gentleman in Harold's Cross in 1913:

In reply to your favour of the 13th inst. we regret that since the passing of the
Corrupt Practices Act a few years ago, we have been obliged to discontinue
the practice of giving Christmas presents . . .[45]

Birrell commented in his memoirs that,

Mr Cosgrave has abolished the Corporation of Dublin by a stroke of his pen.
Any English Chief Secretary who had attempted to do the same piece of
good work would have been compelled to resign by a combination of
Unionists and Nationalists in the House of Commons. I had to be content
with the abolition of the Corporation of Sligo.[46]

Was Belfast unique in Ireland in accepting or promoting physical
segregation between its antipathetic working classes? Ireland had a
long tradition of an English and an Irish town conjoined, and not
only in Ulster. The Pound, like the Tunnel in Portadown and the
Bogside in Derry, had many parallels of which Limerick was a
particularly fine example.

Were Belfast rioters alone among the urban Irish in their
recurrent fights? Other linen towns sustained their workers' riots.
The faction fighting in an agricultural market town has been
described by Carleton.[47] Emigrants took the fighting habit with
them to Great Britain. They fought the Welsh in the Bute-
Merthyr colliery with stones and guns in 1857.[48] They were just as

---

[43] Ibid., 1 Jan. 1913.
[44] Ibid., 1 Mar. 1913.
[45] Letters and accounts outwards 1910–16, no. 4, 15 Dec. 1913 (P.R.O.N.I., Fairbairn,
Lawson, Combe, Barbour papers, D 769/32).
[46] Augustine Birrell, *Things past redress* (London, 1937), p. 219.
[47] William Carleton, *Traits and stories of the Irish peasantry: first series* (London,
1877), pp 110–139. Note Carleton's distinction between the 'deadly' party fight and the good-
humoured cudgelling in the faction fight, pp 128–9. It is with the latter that P. D. O'Donnell,
The Irish faction fighters of the nineteenth century (Dublin, 1975) is concerned.
[48] J. V. Hickey, *Urban catholics: urban catholicism in England and Wales from 1829 to the
present day* (London, 1967), pp 54–5. The Celtic affinity between, for example, the Scotch

212

ready to fight each other. Charles Booth recorded of Limehouse at the turn of the century, 'Amongst themselves they fight terribly, and no one not Irish would be tolerated at all'.[49]

Did Belfast's peculiarity lie in its growing rivalry with the capital, Dublin? It is true that it took a delight in gibing at the southern city, from which the principal exports were porter and politicians, and where careers were open to verbal talent.[50] It was pleased to see from the Registrar General's statistics that a man now lived three years longer in Belfast than Dublin. Dubliners responded that no one would want to live another three years in Belfast.[51] Belfast, however, was not alone in being both jealous of, and somewhat awed by the capital. Dublin jackeens were metropolitan and polyglot, and they laughed at, and were resented by their country cousins.[52]

Was Belfast's peculiarity the retention of a high protestant ratio, three quarters of the city in a province where protestants were little over a half, and in a country where they were one quarter? Its adjacent territory of South Antrim, North Down and North Armagh, of course was itself overwhelmingly protestant, but one would not wish to claim for one minute that methods had not been applied in nineteenth-century Belfast to preserve those proportions. Nonetheless, again it would suggest that a *balance* in religion can be seen in many Irish towns. In Ballyclare and Newtownards catholics were a little less than one tenth; in Banbridge, Ballymena and Coleraine one sixth; in Portadown about one quarter; and in Lurgan a little over one third.[53] That might be, indeed, just the same old linen-conurbation factor. Yet looking again at the Vaughan and Fitzpatrick statistics, one is struck by those small towns in the other provinces where Protestants were frequently much less than one tenth of the citizens. Undoubtedly there were good reasons, historical, cultural and economic for their isolated sparsity; and some may have had considerable social status or economic influence. After all in 1911 why should more than 65 have chosen to continue

Cattle of the Welsh coalfields and the Ribbonmen, or between the followers of Rebecca in South Wales and the Molly Maguires in north-west Ireland and in the anthracite mines of Pennsylvania deserves further exploration. W. J. Broehl Jr, *The Molly Maguires* (Camb. Mass., 1964) drew upon sources on both sides of the Atlantic to stimulate interest in these mining communities to which dispossessed Celtic tenantry were attracted.

[49] Charles Booth, *Life and labour of the people in London: third series, religious influences* (7 vol. London, 1902), i, 47.

[50] J. H. Stirling, Address to annual meeting of Linen Merchants' Association, *Belfast News-Letter*, 1 Feb. 1908.

[51] F. Frankfort Moore, *The truth about Ulster* (London, 1914), p. 276.

[52] Christine Pakenham, Countess of Longford, *Biography of Dublin* (London, 1936), p. 6.

[53] *Census of Ireland, 1911, pt ii, General report, with tables and appendix,* table 125, 222–4 [Cd 663], H.C. 1912–13, cxviii, 222.

to live in Dingle or 101 in Roscommon?[54] But why were there
declining ratios in the most prosperous towns of the East: only 228
in Navan's total population of 3,706; or 500 in Wexford's 11,500.[55]
As a Northerner it is an uncomfortable experience to look, not at
the retreating figures of the landlords, but at the cold columns of
those diminishing small communities.

They *were* abandoned, even though later they met a tolerance
they need not have been shown. Does that abandonment in 1911
mean that Belfast was not an Irish city, but at best an *Ulster* city,
where 89 per cent of its population had been born either in Belfast or
in Ulster? Much more detailed work is now in progress on the
Edwardian Census,[56] but on earlier examination the individual
households of Hamill Street, showed that while 43 per cent of the
adults had been born outside the city, only three out of 173 *in toto*
had come from the south or west of Ireland.[57] Hamill Street was a
fairly poor labouring and catholic street, where immigration replacement would be high. A cursory survey of the suburbs showed
many more second-generation and native-Belfast families. The
Ulster affinity cannot be dismissed. No one entering the North and
Belfast can doubt the common culture (be it only the commonality
of our incompatibility), which centuries of living together has bred.
There are few experiences we have not shared. As we know, Captain
Tom Gaffikin of Queen's Elms died at the Somme, leading his
company of the 36th Ulster Division with an orange handkerchief
waving in his hand. But the catholic 7th Leinsters and the 6th
Connaught Rangers were 'almost to a man followers of Mr Devlin
from Belfast'.[58] In either case they were far from the first Irishmen to
fight for Britain. Do you recall Kipling's story, 'With the Main
Guard'? In a pass held by the Pathans on the Afghan border the
Black Tyrones 'saw their dead' and went in hand-to-hand, while a
sergeant sat on the head of their 'little orfcer bhoy' to keep him safe
because, 'His father howlds my mother's cow feed in Clonmel'. Yet
it was from their garrison service in Dublin that they renamed the

[54] Ibid.
[55] Ibid.
[56] Dr A. C.. Hepburn, New University of Ulster, is engaged on a sociological study, and Dr A.
F. Boal, Queen's University, Belfast, has been examining the geographical distribution in
Belfast.
[57] Householders' returns for Hamill Street (P.R.O.I., 1901 Census).
[58] F. J. Whitford, 'Joseph Devlin, Ulsterman and Irishman', p. 98 (London University,
unpublished M.A. thesis). I am grateful to the late Mr Whitford for his permission to read and
use his thesis; George Berkeley's papers, ch. ix (National Library of Ireland, MS 10,923); T. J.
Campbell, *Fifty years of Ulster, 1890–1940* (Belfast, 1941), p. 82; D. McCullough, 'The events
in Belfast', *Capuchin Annual,* 1966, p. 381.

bloody gorge 'Silver's Theatre', coined by a 'Dublin dock-rat . . . wan av the bhoys that made the leesee av Silver's Theatre gray before his time wid tearin' out the bowils av the benches and t'rowin thim into the pit'.[59] That account, fictional though it may be, seems to illustrate as much the rich diffusion of urban Ireland as the heterogeneity of an Ulster battalion.

Ulster, be that as it may, requires some more attention in relation to Belfast. The sheer numbers of Belfast catholics, 100,000 of them, gave confidence, scope for social advance, political representation, their own press and cathedral. It was the late Tommy Henderson who said that Devlin, the 'wee bottle washer', and James Craig would blast at each other in the College Green Chamber and then be found sitting amicably on the steps outside, chatting and smoking together. In 1930 Craig was rumoured to be gravely ill, and Devlin wrote a confidential letter to a Dublin member of the Dail:

> I hear Jimmy Craig is in a bad way. I'd be sorry to see him go. He and I have had many a tough fight, but he's an Ulsterman like myself, and I know where I am with him. Dear God, that's the trouble with them all. We can't abide them, but we feel at home with them . . . Now don't you be telling your fellows down there that.[60]

Belfast was not only the capital, but the pass of the North. When Gwynn surveyed the city from the top of the Cave Hill in 1914 (on what must have been a remarkably clear day) he looked from Slieve Donard to the Donegal Hills across Strangford and Lough Neagh. He wrote that '. . . the Ulster problem lies there under your feet, centering in, and radiating from that great city of Belfast'.[61] He had recognised an aspect of Belfast which was sometimes overlooked, for Belfast was above all a port. Between 1860 and 1914 the port's tonnage multiplied by five.[62] The small mixed farms of Ulster were the backbone of Belfast's trade. Through the 136 acres of Edwardian docks and basins poured out the farm produce to help feed Britain's northern industrial population; and back through the port came the hardware, the agricultural machinery, the groceries, timber and the livestock feeding stuffs to the Ulster farms. In 1906 harbour receipts were one-and-a-half times those of Dublin and five-and-a-half times those of Cork,[63] the combination of regional agriculture and regional manufacture. Sir James Haslett, 'Oily

---

[59] Rudyard Kipling, *Soldiers three and other stories* (Uniform ed. London, 1899), pp 66–9.
[60] MSS, papers, letters and recollections passed to the author in 1967 by the late Mrs Marie A. Johnston, Clontarf, Dublin, who gave generously of these in her 93rd year.
[61] Gwynn, *Famous cities*, p. 340.
[62] Annual accounts of the Belfast Harbour Commissioners (Harbour Office, Belfast).
[63] *Thom's Irish almanac and official directory, 1908* (Dublin, 1908), p. 769.

Jemmy', had made his fortune importing paraffin oil for Ulster's farm lamps.[64] On one typical day in January 1910 Grattan's, the Belfast chemist, made up prescriptions for Fivemiletown, Cookstown, Newtownbutler and Downpatrick.[65] Several bakeries sent bread and biscuits throughout the north.[66] Half-a-dozen of Belfast's large drapery stores combined retail, whosesale and manufacturing operations in one concern, like B. and E. McHugh of Rosemary Street, where each floor was given over to one branch of the business, and several hundred girls sewed shirts on the fourth.[67] Robertson, Ledlie and Ferguson with a similar business sent travellers throughout Ireland and as well as their top-floor manufacture employed another 750 domestic rural workers on linen and damask for export.[68] Lindsey Brothers had been one of the early United Kingdom firms to appreciate the mail order business and they exported through the world.[69] Sinclair and Coey, the main curers, had met the American challenge by allying with companies in Kansas, Iowa and Indiana, so that they imported cheaper American bacon for the Irish market and exported the more expensive Irish product to the London and Yorkshire middle class.[70] Gracey Brothers had established an egg warehouse, begun to export eggs to the Argentine, and bought a fruit-preserving factory in County Armagh.[71] There was a continuous intermeshing between shippers, merchants and manufacturers, not only of capital, but of individual expertise. They sat on each others' Boards and, if they could not find a West Hartlepool shipping heiress,[73] married each others' sisters.

In 1796 Richardson had reported to the government that 'the disposition to rebellion is more or less in proportion to the distance

[64] *Belfast Telegraph*, 18 Aug. 1905.
[65] Prescription book, 5 Jan. 1910 (P.R.O.N.I., Grattan and Co. Ltd, D 1072/3/171).
[66] *Industries of Ireland: Part I, Belfast and towns of the North* (Historical Publishing Co., London, 1891), pp 67, 89 and 138.
[67] Ibid., p. 100.
[68] Ibid., p. 102.
[69] Ibid., p. 64.
[70] Ibid., pp 91 and 108; W. P. Coyne (ed.), *Ireland, industrial and agricultural* (2nd ed., Dublin, 1902), p. 244.
[71] Letter from Gracey Bros Ltd, 29 July 1955 (P.R.O.N.I., Business records files).
[72] For example, Sir Robert Anderson, co-founder of the departmental store of Anderson and McAuley, was also chairman or director of Belfast firms concerned with the manufacture of vulcanite, brick-making, property development, the spinning, weaving, finishing and printing of linen, timber importing and insurance. R. M. Young, *Belfast and the province of Ulster in the twentieth century* (Belfast, 1909); see also company directors listed in *Henderson's Belfast directories*, 1911–14.
[73] The wife of R. J. McMordie, lord mayor, and a member of parliament for Belfast 1910–14, was the daughter of Sir William Gray, shipbuilder, of Greathem and West Hartlepool.

from that seat of mischief—Belfast'.[74] By 1911 the provincial connexions were even clearer. Whether they were about to form 'an embryonic nationalism'[75] or simply 'a regional identity'[76] two of Belfast's sons have not been able to agree, despite attending its Academical Institution and its university, and together helping to reform Irish historiography across the divide between Ireland's major cities. We owe them a debt, not merely for that reformation, but for their agreement to express their difference, for it has kept open the problem of the Belfast identity. The majority in Belfast in 1911 appeared to have no doubt that it intended to remain British. Yet when the Unionist and Grand Lodge delegates met in Rosemary Street to pledge their opposition to a Dublin parliament and its decrees, it would seem that they had set their feet upon a path which made them finally and irredeemably Irish.

Once Ulster Protestants spoke and wrote of their feelings as religious. Then it became fashionable to deride the role of religion; to describe it as ethnicity; to look only for economic motives in the selfish nature of man or in a capitalist plot which blinded the working classes. Dr A. T. Q. Stewart was bold enough a little time ago to write a book, which in its opening chapter declared decisively that with the Ulster Plantation 'the sharp line of division was one of religion, not of race'.[77] It is a fine book, that opened with religion and ended with politics, but in between, those who are not presbyterian might begin to wonder what had happened to the strength of those beliefs of the other protestant groups and of the catholics who made up a somewhat greater share of later nineteenth and twentieth-century Ulster.[78] In 1911 Belfast to some extent had put behind it many of the older doctrinal issues which bothered the seventeenth and eighteenth centuries, although certain vestiges of these remained.[79] It had not forgotten, however, indeed it had revived, the basic religious issue which cleft Europe at the Reformation: salvation by faith alone, and the independent line which linked a man directly to his God.[80] In consequence, can one write the

---

[74] J. Richardson to government, 15 Oct. 1796 (S.P.O., Rebellion papers, 620/125/171).

[75] J. C. Beckett, 'Northern Ireland', *The Ulster debate: report of a study group of the Institute for the Study of Conflict* (London, 1972), p. 20.

[76] T. W. Moody, *The Ulster question, 1603–1973* (Cork, 1974), p. 99.

[77] A. T. Q. Stewart, *The narrow ground: aspects of Ulster, 1609–1969* (London, 1977), p. 25.

[78] Presbyterians were 33.74 per cent of Belfast and 26.3 per cent of Ulster in 1911. *Census of Ireland, 1911, Province of Ulster, City of Belfast*, p. 36 [Cd 6051 I], H.C. 1912–13, cxvi, 1.

[79] A. T. Q. Stewart, op. cit., p. 80.

[80] D. W. Miller, *Queen's rebels: Ulster loyalism in historical perspective* (Dublin, 1978), p. 82. Dr Miller has focused attention again on the 'evangelical' change and its effects in nineteenth-century Ulster episcopalianism and presbyterianism with his American term 'conversionist'.

history of Ulster or Belfast between 1870 and 1911 without noting the divisive effect of the proclamation of Papal Infallibility in 1870 and the application to Ireland of the *Ne Temere* decree at Easter 1908?[81]

For a substantial section of Belfast's protestants in 1911 religion was a deeply held conviction,[82] and its idiom in familiar use. That redoubtable tramcar manager, Andrew Nance, in his annual report in 1912 declared, 'My friends, God has abundantly blessed those who have been engaged in working Belfast Tramways'.[83] Such an expression would have been totally foreign in an English context.

One cannot blame onlookers for underrating religion as a source of division when catholics and protestants stoned each other, for they might well have doubted the nature of their Christianity. Such rioters rarely or only partly understood their doctrinal differences, and at best in simplistic terms. It was amongst the section which did not go on the streets that the beliefs were formulated or accepted, not I think just as lightly as Dr Stewart suggests.[84] In that much smaller, but highly important section of Belfast which in 1911 not only went to church, chapel or gospel hall, but attended Bible classes,[85] prayer meetings,[86] catholic fraternities and retreats,[87] men

[81] The McCann marriage case or 'the Belfast kidnapping', which caused such a storm in the city did credit to none of its participants; but it raised issues of liberty of person and of conscience (and, indeed, of women's rights) as well as the vital issues of tolerance and proselytism, which the old and happier Irish compromise of 'boys follow father, girls follow mother' had avoided. The great meeting of 5 Jan. 1911 which filled the Assembly and Grosvenor Halls, when resolutions against 'papal pretensions' were moved by protestant clergy of all denominations, was more than a political exercise. Miss L. A. Walkington, LL.D., on 'man-made law', *Belfast News-Letter* 6 Dec. 1910; *Belfast Telegraph*, 11 Jan. 1911; *Hansard 5* (Commons), xxi, 7 Feb. 1911, 176–193 and xxii, 27 Feb. 1911, 161 and 1378; for a more objective account see 'The Belfast mixed marriage case', 1911 (P.R.O., Intelligence notes, judicial division, C.O. 903/16, pp 44–6).

[82] Men and women were still alive who remembered not only the Moody and Sankey missions of 1867–92, but also the '59 Revival. In 1903 the two renowned American preachers, Dr R. A. Torrey and Mr Charles Alexander had filled the Ulster Hall for a month.

[83] *Belfast News-Letter,* 26 Oct. 1912.

[84] A. T. Q. Stewart, op. cit. p. 180.

[85] In the Church of Ireland the evangelical disposition of the Belfast laity was reflected in their enthusiasm for the building of new parish churches and mission halls in contrast to their dislike of new High Church ritualism and their lukewarm response to the proposal to build a cathedral. J. F. McNeice, *Some northern churchmen and some notes on the church in Belfast* (Belfast, 1934), p. 31; L. M. Ewart, *Handbook of the united diocese of Down, Connor and Dromore* (Belfast, 1886), pp 32–4; *Belfast News-Letter,* 20–27 May, 7 Sep. 1899 and 6 June 1904; reminiscences to the author by Commander Philip Smiles, son-in-law of Sir William Quartus Ewart, leading layman of Belfast's episcopalians.

[86] The presbyterian magazine, significantly named *The Witness,* was so popular that it became a bi-weekly in the Edwardian period. The Rt. Hon. Thomas Sinclair, like Sir William Ewart, put his religious duties as an elder before those of business or politics. Sir Robert Anderson (footnote 72) who had come from Monaghan in 1852 to serve as a draper's

218

and women understood the convictions they held. It was their misfortune that these convictions were so often so very badly expressed to each other,[88] and that the very extent of the gulf between their religious practices or organisations made it the more difficult for men of good will to attempt to explain to each other that conflict of faith. These were the people who, in any other community, would have healed the social wounds and gone out of their way to show concern.

To have dwelt on this may help reverse our tendency to make too little of the religious element,[89] which deserves reconsideration[90] if we are to understand the emotive strength in Belfast in 1911. We give weight, overall, to the allegiance the Irish catholic had to the Old Faith, but perhaps we have been inclined to undervalue the attachment of the Irish protestant to the Reformed. It was an attachment which had been appreciated in the earlier campaigns in Ulster, but by 1911 Great Britain (and even White Anglo Saxon Protestant America[91]) was losing its Victorian fear of Roman Catholicism. Just as missionary work was no longer an acceptable reason for imperialism, fighting for religion was out of date. Only in Germany did the State, unwilling to re-rouse the Protestant/ Catholic hostilities of its southern provinces, refuse to accept the *Ne Temere* decree. Protestant Belfast by declaring its intention to defend protestantism within a protectable barrier in Ireland, as well as to preserve its British caste, paradoxically broke the latter. It had stepped beyond the British understanding. Only in Ulster could the code be interpreted.[92] Only in Ireland could that mixture of religion and politics be fully understood. Belfast was no longer a British, but an Irish city.

apprentice, devoted much of his later leisure and wealth to the Young Men's Christian Association, and as High Sheriff in 1902 had obliged his guests to toast the judges in non-alcoholic wines!

[87] Between 1898 and 1907 the Belfast Catholic laity supported a monthly confraternity magazine, *Sancta Maria*, from which the Catholic Truth Society of Ireland grew in 1900. J. J. Campbell, 'Great catholic organisations in the North', *Irish News centenary, 1855–1955* (Belfast, 1955), p. 52.

[88] Only on a very few humanitarian bodies such as the N.S.P.C.C., was there opportunity for even social dialogue between catholic and protestant clergy. *Northern Whig,* 6 Dec. 1901; *Belfast Health Journal,* Dec. 1904, p. 40.

[89] I am indebted to Mr G. Slater, P.R.O.N.I., and Professor R. F. G. Holmes, Assembly's College, amongst others for discussion of this point: the conclusions, of course, must be my own.

[90] A notable exception is *Problems of a growing city: Belfast, 1780–1870* (P.R.O.N.I., 1973), p. xi.

[91] F. M. Carrol, *American opinion and the Irish question, 1910–23: a study of opinion and policy* (Dublin, 1978), p. ii.

[92] The application of 'code' is but one of the many illuminating perceptions in Stewart, *The narrow ground,* p. 70.

Belfast was a Plantation town, designed for settlement and for seige. Essex in 1575 hoped to build it to command the plains of Clandeboy, to hold open the pass between Carrickfergus and Newry, to keep those of Kilruth, Kilmartin and the Dufferin in obedience, while being victualled at pleasure by the sea.[93] In 1911 it prepared again to hold its region, protect its settlers, and retain its trade. Three and a half centuries after Essex had made his plans it remained an Irish Plantation city.

[93] Owen, *History of Belfast*, p. 15.

Late Nineteenth and Early Twentieth Century Dublin

Mary Daly

This essay examines varied aspects of the history of Dublin from the second half of the nineteenth century to the year 1914. A deliberately broad approach has been chosen to highlight the interaction between the city's economy and politics and its social problems and also to avoid excessive concentration on local detail. It is hoped that such an approach will reveal aspects of the city's history which contrast with or reflect the experience of other Irish cities.

A key to an understanding of nineteenth-century Dublin is the continuing sense of the loss of her native parliament. The Act of Union proved a severe psychological blow to the city's self-esteem and many elements of her population, particularly the skilled trades and the city council, were constantly preoccupied by this loss. The final decades of the parliament in College Green had coincided with a period of general expansion, whereas its departure was followed by economic decline. Many sections of the city's population assumed that a resident parliament was synonymous with prosperity.[1] There is little doubt that the history of Dublin during the nineteenth century would have proved different if the Irish parliament had survived, though whether this would have guaranteed greater prosperity is doubtful.

The consciousness of the loss of its parliament was undoubtedly increased by the city's singularly unspectacular expansion during the second half of the nineteenth century. In 1798 it was estimated

[1] Fergus D'Arcy, 'Dublin artisan activity, opinion and organisation 1820–60' (M.A. thesis, National University of Ireland (U.C.D.), 1968), ch. 3.

that the population stood at 170,000.[2] By 1841 it had risen to 232,000 and reached 258,000 in 1851. Forty years later the population had fallen to 245,000. In 1851 Dublin was still the second largest city in the United Kingdom. By 1871 she had declined to sixth place and in 1891 had suffered the final indignity of losing her position as Ireland's largest city to the upstart Belfast, whose population had numbered a mere 20,000 in 1800.[3] The realisation that Belfast had a larger population than Dublin provoked near-hysteria in nationalist circles. The subsequent extension of Belfast's boundaries further increased the latter's population advantage and prompted urgent efforts to extend Dublin's boundaries to regain her position as the largest city. One nationalist M.P., pleading the case at Westminster, stated 'Dublin should be in reality, as it is in name the first city of Ireland in all respects'.[4]

Yet even if we allow for the movement of population to the suburbs, the city's expansion remains extremely sedate. Greater Dublin grew from 317,000 in 1851 to 347,000 in 1891 and 404,000 in 1911.[5] In a country whose overall population had fallen by almost four million this was perhaps a reasonable performance, yet contrasted with Belfast, or with English or Scottish cities, or indeed in a European context it was insignificant.

The key to the slow growth of Dublin's population lies in the local economy, which was in turn closely related to that of the country as a whole. Until the 1880s deaths exceeded births, a not unique experience at the time.[6] However migration into the city was extremely low. As few as 6,500 may have moved there between 1881 and 1891, while four times that number emigrated from Dublin to the United Kingdom or North America. Although the level of net migration was considerably higher, at 47,000 in the following decade, it remained an inconsiderable movement relative to total Irish emigration.[7] There is little doubt that had employment opportunities proved more satisfactory migration and population

[2] J. Warburton, J. Whitelaw and R. Walsh, *History of the city of Dublin* (2 vols, London, 1818), i, ix.
[3] Geoffery Best, 'Another part of the island' in H. J. Dyos and Michael Wolff, *The Victorian city, image and reality* (2 vols, London, 1973), i, 391.
The population of Belfast was 255,950 in 1891.
[4] *Irish Times* (hereafter *I.T.*), 6 June 1899.
[5] For detailed figures, see Table I.
[6] Eric Lampard, 'The urbanising world' in Dyos and Wolff, op. cit., i, 13–4.
[7] These calculations are based on the figures relating to the birth-places of Dublin residents in *Census of Ireland*, I, 1911, Dublin City Tab. XXV, and the net inflow of migrants is calculated using a method devised by M. A. Shannon in 'Migration and the growth of London: a statistical note, 1841–91' in *Econ. Hist. Rev.*, v, no. 21, (April 1935), pp 79–86.

growth would have been considerably higher. Throughout the century the traditional industries (poplin, carriage making, cabinet making and other luxury trades) declined, while alternative industries failed to emerge on any significant scale. The decline of traditional craft industries should not occasion surprise, this was an experience common to cities such as London at the same time.[8] However few sources of alternative industrial employment emerged. The most significant industry, brewing, proved extremely capital intensive and failed to generate a level of employment commensurate with its output. In 1886, Guinness's brewery, the largest firm in the sector, was capitalised at a value of £5m but only employed 2,000 wage-earners.[9] In 1893, York Street spinning company in Belfast with a capital value of £500,000, one-tenth that amount, employed 4–5,000 workers.[10] The shipbuilding industry also provided much greater employment relative to its output.[11] Other industrial concerns do not merit individual attention. A number of isolated firms existed, such as Jacob's biscuit factory or Goulding's fertiliser plant plus several distilleries and large flour mills, but their contribution to the city's employment was limited. More surprising perhaps, given the city's population and its role as the centre of the Irish distribution trade, was the failure to develop a substantial dressmaking trade, even of the much maligned sweated variety. By 1911 there were a mere 7,000 female dressmakers and seamstresses and the number had fallen steadily from the 1860s.

Transport and distribution provided a possible alternative source of employment. Dublin was the centre of the Irish railway network and the country's principal port. During the early decades of the nineteenth century the port expanded at a steady pace, more than doubling in tonnage handled between 1792 and 1841 and doubling yet again by 1860 and once more by 1878.[12] By the late seventies however the period of rapid expansion had ended and the 1880s brought a phase of temporary decline, at a time when many of the city's smaller industrial firms were experiencing economic diffi-

---

[8] Gareth Stedman-Jones, *Outcast London* (London, 1971).

[9] Patrick Lynch and John Vaizey, *Guinness's brewery in the Irish economy 1759–1856* (Cambridge, 1968), p. 186.

[10] *Irish Daily Independent,* 17 Aug. 1893.

[11] In 1907 the gross output of iron and steel, shipbuilding and engineering in Ireland totalled £5.8m. and employment was 37,811. Gross output of brewing and milling was £5.9m. but employment only 6,595 (*Census of production 1907. Final report* [Cd 6320] H.C. 1912–13, xix).

[12] Anthony Marmion, *The ancient and modern history of the maritime ports of Ireland* (4th ed., London, 1860), p. 242 and Dublin port and docks board report and accounts 1915, appendix D, (N.L.I.).

culties. Expansion subsequently resumed though at a slower pace. While port employment and jobs in related activities certainly rose during the nineteenth century they did little more than compensate for employment losses in other industries.

The building industry, another substantial employer, was marked by increased employment from 1851 until 1881, but the depression of that decade led to a drop in the number of craftsmen employed and, by implication, in the number of labouring jobs. Although employment had risen by 1911, if we allow for the extension of the city's boundaries and the greater overall population, building craftsmen had declined as a percentage of the city's workforce. This reflects the comparatively slow expansion in the Dublin housing stock and the lack of significant industrial or commercial development. The port of Dublin undertook a certain level of capital development from the 1830s until the early 1870s,[13] but thereafter falling revenue and the slow expansion in port activity meant that no major investments took place until the early twentieth century. As a result of the stagnant economy the number of occupied male workers in the city was somewhat lower in 1891 than in 1861.

Yet even if the port and related trades had generated a substantial increase in employment, the jobs provided were predominantly unskilled, while those disappearing had been in skilled trades. The city's artisan population fell from 1851 to 1891 and though it had increased by 1911 (mainly due to boundary extension), the percentage of artisans in the workforce had fallen from approximately 35% in 1851 to a mere 22% in 1911.[14] The gulf between skilled and unskilled workers was considerable in terms of wages, social status and general outlook. In the 1860s an unskilled labourer earned an average of 10–12 shillings per week, his skilled counterpart as much as 30 shillings, with some exceptional trades such as carriage manufacture paying their craftsmen as much as 60 shillings.[15] By 1914, although this gap had narrowed a skilled worker earned from 35 to 40 shillings, almost twice the £1 to 22 shillings[16] which was the average unskilled wage. Although the income of the average unskilled worker had improved by 1914 the fact that a higher

---

[13] Dublin port and docks board report and accounts 1868–1915.

[14] All statistics relating to occupations unless otherwise stated come from *Census of Ireland, 1851*, VI, Tab. V; 1861, V, Tab. VI; 1871, I Tabs XVIII, XVIIIa; 1881, I, Tabs XVIII, XVIIIa; 1891, I, Tabs XVIII, XVIIIa; 1901, I Tab. XIX; 1911, I Tab. XIX.

[15] *Returns of wages published between 1830 and 1886,* [C 5172], H.C. 1887, lxxix, 273.

[16] *Report of the departmental committee appointed to inquire into the housing conditions of the working class in Dublin. Evidence and appendices.* Appendices xxiii and xxvi [Cd 7317], H.C. 1914, xix, 107.

proportion of the city's population had fallen to the unskilled category meant that the advance in living standards among the working class as a whole was slight. For some families who had slipped from skilled to unskilled status it was non-existent.

Family income is however a more important concept than individual income. Opportunities for female employment were few, except as laundry women. Live-in domestic servants were traditionally recruited from the more docile country girls,[17] while few firms employed women. In 1891 only 34% of the Dublin female population was classified as occupied, compared with 39% in Belfast. If we restrict our calculations to women aged twenty or more the contrast is more dramatic with only 43% of Dublin women occupied, compared with 53% in Belfast. The possibilities for supplementing family income by children's earnings were also limited. Opportunities except as newspaper boys and messengers were few. A witness to the inter-departmental committee on street-trading children stated, 'In Dublin you will not find cases of excessive child labour—there is so much unemployment'.[18] The problem of children of school-age working long hours was much less common than in British cities, but on the other hand families derived little extra income from this source.

An examination of working class employment reveals a predominance of unskilled workers attached to various jobs in transport and distribution. The numbers of factory-type employment were slight. The emphasis on commercial rather than industrial occupations is also reflected at a higher social level. Over the years the city of Dublin produced many successful industrialists, men such as the shoe manufacturer, Joseph Winstanley, but the majority of city businessmen in the late nineteenth century were engaged in non-manufacturing activities. The Dublin Chamber of Commerce, the principal representative of the city's businessmen was dominated by commercial rather than industrial interests. Of the twenty-six council members in 1911, only three had manufacturing interests.[19] A total of eight members were engaged in businesses closely related to agriculture such as corn merchants or cattle salesmen and these formed the largest identifiable block, indicating how closely Dublin's trading and commercial fortunes

---

[17] Only 27% of domestic servants in Palmerstown Road and Palmerstown Park, Rathmines were Dublin-born in 1911. Calculated from Census enumerators forms 1911 (P.R.O.I.).
[18] *Report of the inter-departmental committee on the employment of children during school age, especially in street-trading in the large centres of population in Ireland, with evidence and appendices.* Para. 1219 [Cd 1144], H.C. 1902, xlix, 209.
[19] *Thom's Directory*, 1911 (Dublin, 1911).

related to those of Irish agriculture. However the distinction between industrial and commercial interests is a rather artificial one in the case of the Dublin business community. Many firms combined manufacture and trade, particularly an importing business with some domestic manufacturing and the transition from manufacturer to trader was easily accomplished.

The city's business community, particularly the city's larger businesses was a closely integrated group bound together by common economic, and not infrequently political interests and on the whole by a common religious background. The majority of leading businessmen were Protestants who gradually found themselves alienated from what was becoming a Catholic-dominated city. In common with their counterparts throughout the United Kingdom, Dublin's business and professional families moved from the city to the suburbs, and in the process curtailed their involvement in city politics.

This suburban migration was concentrated in the decades from the 1840s to the mid-1870s. At this point suburban growth slowed and when it revived the migrants tended to be the lower middle classes. The socially acceptable Dublin suburbs developed to the south of the city, along the line of the Dublin-Kingstown-Bray railway line, or adjacent to the city in the townships of Rathmines and Pembroke. In numerical terms Rathmines and Pembroke were the most important suburbs. By 1881 Rathmines had a population of 24,000, Pembroke was slightly smaller. At this stage both housed predominantly business and professional familes: professional men accounted for 34.6% of occupied males in Pembroke in 1881, and 34.89% in Rathmines, compared with a mere 12.6% in the city.[20] A further indication of their social composition is the high proportion of domestic servants. These accounted for 34% of the total occupied population of Pembroke and 33.5% in the case of Rathmines, but a mere 20.4% in the city. Pembroke and Rathmines together, with a total population of less than 50,000 contained more professional men than the city which had a population five times that level.

The suburban residents were not merely professional; they tended to be Protestant. Catholics comprised a minority of the Rathmines population until 1901 by which stage the working class and lower middle class housing of Harold's Cross had been built. Pembroke had a significantly greater Catholic population, primarily because it contained the old working class villages of Ringsend and Irishtown. Among the more distant suburbs the Monkstown Ward of Black-

[20] *Census of Ireland*, 1881, I Tabs XIX, XIXa.

rock Urban District Council still retained a Protestant majority as late as 1911. This was also the area with the highest proportion of male servants, whose numbers continued to increase until 1911 though by this stage they were declining in other areas. The major suburb on the north side of the city, Drumcondra, was a later creation which provided relatively modest housing for those on clerical incomes. Consequently from the outset it was an area with a predominantly Catholic population.

With the flight of the prosperous to the suburbs, the city became increasingly the home of working class and lower middle class. Some areas of prestige housing remained, notably Fitzwilliam Square and surrounding streets, but there was no major building scheme of first class houses within the city boundaries during the latter half of the nineteenth century. Such houses as were built catered for those on modest incomes. As a consequence of the loss of middle class residents the city's population became more Catholic. The 1861 census revealed that Catholics comprised 77.1% of the city's population and from that date the proportion gradually increased. In the decade 1861–71 the number of Church of Ireland city residents fell by 10,000 and by 1911 over 83% of the city's population was Catholic.[21]

The diverging social and religious patterns between the city and the suburbs, particularly Rathmines and Pembroke had various consequences.While it was not uncommon for businessmen in English cities to move houses beyond the city boundaries they frequently retained an active involvement in local city politics. They remained eligible to vote and to stand for election and in their capacity as ratepayers were concerned with the development of the city. In Dublin the move to the suburbs apparently caused a psychological break. Certainly throughout the second half of the nineteenth century Dublin Corporation became an increasingly Catholic and nationalist body which contained few representatives of the leading city businesses.

Until 1840 the corporation was controlled by a small body of hereditary freemen. However as a result of municipal reform legislation this was replaced by an assembly elected by ratepayers.[22] The electorate included all those on the ratepayers list who had resided at the same address for approximately three years. However tenants of properties rated at less than £8 and those in monthly tenancies had their rates paid by the landlord and were effectively

21 Ibid., 1911, I, Tabs XXIX, XXIXa.
22 3 & 4 Vict. ch. 108 *Municipal Corporations (Ireland) Act.*

disenfranchised. Until 1898 the municipal electorate was a relatively restricted one.[23] In 1895 it amounted to a mere 8,000 voters in contrast to the 37,000 parliamentary electors.[24] Candidates for election had to reside within seven miles of the city and own property valued at £1,000 or occupy a house rated at £25. The qualifications for both electors and candidates were therefore propertied, but the requirements were relatively modest.

In its early years the reformed corporation contained a significant proportion of the city's business elite. In 1851 a total of fourteen members of the corporation were either bank or railway directors or members of the chamber of commerce.[25] Eight members of the council of the chamber of commerce were also members of the corporation and councillors and aldermen included four brewers (Benjamin Lee Guinness, John D'Arcy and two members of the Sweetman family), two distillers (George Roe and John Jameson), Thomas Hutton, the city's largest carriage maker, plus an impressive number of leading merchants. The lord mayor was Benjamin Lee Guinness whose brother was president of the chamber of commerce.[26] By 1876 there were only two chamber of commerce members in the corporation and no bank directors and this, broadly speaking, remained the pattern in subsequent years. Conscious of the changing representation the chamber of commerce petitioned in 1875 in favour of an amended electorate which would give greater representation to property owners by means of plural voting.[27] In evidence to the committee on local government and taxation of towns in 1876, Joseph Todhunter Pim, a leading businessman, emphasised that

Men who would make more suitable members of the corporation cannot be induced to come forward—absenteeism from participation in municipal office is now in fact just as much the rule in Dublin amongst the more extensive mercantile men as in the United States.[28]

The departure of leading businessmen was not total. There was however a distinct lowering of the wealth and social class of the average member, though this is difficult to document with precision and the majority of members still had business connections. However by 1860 one pawnbroker had appeared; by the 1870s the

[23] *Report from select committee on local government and taxation of towns (Ireland)* p. 13, H.C. 1878, (262) xvi, 1.
[24] *I.T.,* 6 Nov. 1895.
[25] *Select committee local government etc.,* para. 2361.
[26] *Thom's Directory,* 1851 (Dublin, 1851).
[27] *I.T.,* 19 Mar. 1875.
[28] *Select committee local government etc.,* para. 2301.

228

publicans and small grocers were in the ascendant; and by 1890 twenty members, one third of the total, were either grocers or publicans, the majority combining both trades. This is a proportion far in excess of any English city, the city of Exeter recording the peak English figure in 1871 when 22% of its councillors were publicans.[29] The changing status of Dublin Corporation members was gradual. While many deplored the declining quality of members in the 1870s, the transition was one from old wealth to new and perhaps lesser wealth. In 1876 the rateable property of members had an average value of £167,[30] a substantial sum of money, though members included men such as Peter Paul McSwiney, owner of a large drapery business which was rated at £755 and J. P. O'Reilly, a poultry salesman with property valued at £28, barely exceeding the minimum membership qualifications. By 1911 however the property holdings of members had significantly declined. A mere seven of the eighty members had property rated in excess of £100 and twenty members, one in four, had property rated at less than £25 and would have been excluded from membership of the corporation prior to 1898.[31]

The change in membership was not merely social; it was also political and many of the criticisms levelled against the declining status of members are indirect comments on the political loyalties of the new members. In general the large businessmen who were displaced had belonged to the Conservative party, while the small business and publican element were generally nationalists. The corporation chamber was a forum not merely for issues of immediate concern to the city, such as water, housing and sanitation, but for topics of wider political concern. This use of the corporation as a substitute for the absent Irish parliament began in 1842 when Daniel O'Connell took advantage of his position as lord mayor to press for repeal of the Act of Union.[32] The political activities of the corporation waned and increased in relation to the degree of national political excitement but during the 1860s it became a leading platform for the National Association and matters such as disestablishment of the Church of Ireland and university education for Catholics were debated at meetings.[33] These issues proved highly contentious to the city's Protestant population and to the Conservative councillors, so much so that polite con-

[29] E. P. Hennock, *Fit and proper persons* (London, 1973), p. 35.
[30] *Select committee local government etc.,* para. 3307.
[31] *Thom's Directory,* 1911 (Dublin, 1911).
[32] Beckett, *Mod. Ire.,* p. 322.
[33] Norman, *Cath. Ch. & Irl.,* pp 80, 158, 181, 320.

ventions which had hitherto prevailed in city politics temporarily lapsed. The practice of alternating a Conservative (generally Protestant) and Liberal (generally Catholic) lord mayor broke down for a number of years, while the unanimous vote of thanks to the retiring lord mayor was not given in 1865.[34] This highly charged political atmosphere resulted in corporation seats which had hitherto fallen to the Conservatives without challenge being contested and these elections, combined with a dwindling Protestant population meant a gradual increase in nationalist strength. In the late 1850s both sides had been evenly balanced; by the late 1870s Conservative representation had fallen to one-third[35] and was further eroded by strong Parnellite gains in the early 1880s. The last Conservative lord mayor was elected in 1881.[36] In 1896 there were only eleven Conservative members in a total of sixty and this was further reduced as a result of the increased electorate in 1899.[37] From the early 1880s nationalist supremacy in the corporation and its offices was assured and though subsequent years brought a number of splits and the emergence of opposition groupings such as Sinn Féin during the early years of the twentieth century, the dominance of the mainstream nationalist councillors was never seriously challenged.

The pattern of local representation in the more prosperous suburbs of Rathmines and Pembroke contrasted strongly with that in the city, reflecting the composition of the population. Although qualifications for candidates and electors differed little from those in the city the elected members were more strongly representative of property. This was particularly so in Rathmines, where in early years elections were rare and vacancies among the commissioners were generally filled by co-opting property developers who were not already members.[38] In 1870, of twenty commissioners, twelve owned property valued at £59,000.[39] Turnover among commissioners was infrequent and one man, Frederick Stokes, a major property developer both in the township and in the city, remained chairman for thirty years.[40] The position was somewhat different in

[34] Ibid., p. 156.
[35] *I.T.*, 2 July 1878.
[36] T. D. Sullivan, *Recollections of troubled times in Irish politics* (London, 1905), p. 225.
[37] *I.T.*, 18 Jan. 1899.
[38] *Report of Royal Commission appointed to inquire into the boundaries and municipal areas of certain cities and towns in Ireland. Evidence* paras. 4151 and 6613, [C 2827], H.C. 1881, 1, 65.
[39] *Return of owners of land, of one acre and upwards in the several counties, counties of cities, and counties of towns in Ireland.* [C 1492], H.C. 1876, lxxx, 61.
[40] *I.T.*, 7 Dec. 1877.

Pembroke. The dominant landlord was the earl of Pembroke and through his agent he largely controlled the commissioners. Pembroke was run in the manner of a private estate rather than a municipal township. The Pembroke commissioners, like their Rathmines counterparts, tended to be property owners. In 1870, seven out of fifteen owned property in County Dublin with a rateable valuation of almost £7,000, though some of this lay outside the township.[41] While there is thus a greater concentration of property in one commissioner (the earl, through his agent), like Rathmines, and unlike the city, local politics were controlled by propertied interests. The representation in Rathmines showed no major change over time. On occasions, notably in the 1880s, an abortive ratepayers party emerged to run candidates at local elections. Even the swelling numbers of lower middle class residents and the reform of the electorate in 1898 failed to bring a significant change and Rathmines politics continued to be dominated by property-owning Conservatives. This was achieved by an informal zoning of housing within the township which concentrated most of the smaller houses in the Harolds Cross area. In municipal elections the more socially exclusive East Ward had twelve seats, while the West Ward which contained the smaller houses had only nine seats. As a result, as late as 1903 twelve of the twenty-one councillors still lived in the premier Palmerston Park area and Catholics remained significantly under-represented in local politics. Eight of the council members had business interests directly related to property or the building industry, while in contrast to the corporation, only one, a wholesale wine merchant, was involved in the drink trade.[42]

Pembroke local politics were more evenly balanced, due to a relatively large indigenous working class population which gained the franchise in 1898. Prior to this date Pembroke commissioners had been largely composed of professional or business men with local property interests. As in Rathmines a ratepayers association emerged, but it made only a slight impact.[43] In 1898 however the local electoral register was increased from 1,800 to 4,750, mostly working class voters, though 800 of the new voters were women.[44] By 1911 the composition of Pembroke Council differed considerably from that of Rathmines. Four of the fifteen members were shopkeepers, two of them grocers-cum-publicans, one fruiterer and

[41] *Return of owners of land,* op. cit.
[42] *I.T.,* 13 Nov. 1903 and 27 May 1904.
[43] *Evening Telegraph,* 10 Nov. 1891.
[44] *I.T.,* 17 Jan. 1899.

one butcher—men who would not have been out of place in Dublin Corporation. By this date, the earl, who had underwritten many municipal expenses in earlier years and had guaranteed the township debts, was lessening his involvement in local politics, while his agent was no longer a councillor.[45]

Politically there were subtle differences between Pembroke and Rathmines. Both were stongly Conservative until the end of the nineteenth century, though Rathmines tended to proclaim its politics with greater insistence and was more outspoken in its criticism of the corporation. In 1885, at a time when Home Rule was a dominant political issue and the corporation had refused an address of welcome to the Prince of Wales on his visit to Ireland,[46] Rathmines invoked its unionist loyalties as an argument against annexation by the city. In a letter to the lord lieutenant, the township commissioners stated:

It would be neither just nor politic that the Government should take up and lend their powerful assistance to pass a bill of compulsory annexation which necessarily would prove an act of spoliation and subversion of a township which has always been loyal and law-abiding, and thus assist in furthering the designs of a body such as the Corporation of Dublin, the majority of whose members have so recently done all they could or dare venture, to parade their disloyalty to Crown and Constitution.[47]

Subsequent efforts by the corporation to extend the city boundaries in the years 1898–1900 were countered by similar political arguments. Opposition to boundary extension in the Commons was led by Sir Edward Carson (whose father held property in both Rathmines and Pembroke and was for many years a Pembroke commissioner, and also a member of Dublin Corporation) and by Colonel Saunderson, the latter admitting that 'the objections raised by the townships to becoming incorporated into the corporation had undoubtedly to a considerable extent been affected by political considerations'.[48] The ultimate defender of the interests of Rathmines and Pembroke was the House of Lords, which on two occasions rejected Commons votes in favour of annexation. On the second occasion one member remarked that if they had reversed their previous decision against annexation 'they would deliver a very serious blow at the independence of their house'.[49]

[45] *I.T.*, 12 Mar. 1903.
[46] Sullivan, op. cit., p. 222.
[47] S.P.O.I., CSO/RP 1885/7695.
[48] *I.T.*, 14 June 1899.
[49] *I.T.*, 4 Aug. 1899.

In 1900 the city boundaries were extended to include the lower middle class nationalist suburb of Drumcondra, the impoverished and unsuccessful though largely unionist suburb of Clontarf and the self-contained industrial township of Kilmainham, but Rathmines and Pembroke were excluded.[50] The city's population and valuation increased, vacant land for working class housing became available and the corporation assumed responsibility for sanitary improvements in Kilmainham and a drainage scheme in the hitherto backward suburb of Clontarf. However the social composition of the city was largely unaltered. The professional class declined slightly as a percentage of the total population, while the commercial class increased slightly. The proportion of general labourers remained virtually unchanged. While Rathmines remained a strong bastion of conservative politics in subsequent years, nationalists gained temporary control of Pembroke in 1902 and from that date Pembroke politics were very evenly balanced.[51]

The city suburban relationships are significant in an understanding of Dublin during the late nineteenth and early twentieth century. Both Pembroke and Rathmines provide examples of local authorities which contrast in social and political composition to that in the city. They may prove of value in our efforts to evaluate the validity of the criticism directed at Dublin Corporation. Much of it was motivated by hostility towards the political viewpoint expressed by the corporation rather than its administrative ability. In 1864 when corporation concern with Catholic rights were in full flood, the *Irish Times* commented:

The Corporation of Dublin is continually engaged in accomplishing the ends of favouritism or faction and compelling the most sincere admirer of municipal institutions to seek in the abolition of the corporation itself the only safety of the city. Instead of discussing in a business spirit the scavenging of our streets the members have formed themselves into a vituperative Parliament where a ridiculous assumption is defended by portenteous clamour.[52]

Later criticisms tended to become more specific, focusing on their financial extravagance, the awarding of positions to political favourites and ultimately on inefficiencies and corruption in the administration of local bye-laws, particularly those concerning health and sanitation. Analogies were frequently made with

[50] 63 and 64 Vict. ch. 214 *An Act to extend the city of Dublin and for other purposes.*
[51] *I.T.*, 18 Jan. 1905.
[52] *I.T.*, 16 June 1864.

Tamanny Hall[53] and much of the criticism rested on the assumption that Irish nationalists were incapable of efficient or honest government. Commenting on the report of the 1914 housing inquiry, Lord Robert Cecil remarked, 'this particular report does furnish a very strong and brilliant lesson of the disadvantages of nationalist rule as compared with unionist rule in Ireland'.[54] For their part neither Pembroke or Rathmines can stand immune from criticism though their administrative tasks were considerably lighter. Rathmines was severely criticised by the royal commission on municipal boundaries for its failure to enforce sanitary regulations. One official nominally employed by the township spent much of his time working for a local developer who was also a commissioner, proving that dishonesty was not a nationalist monopoly.[55] Pembroke can be indicted for financial incompetence and maladministration. In 1891 the township was seriously in debt and the financial situation deteriorated when the township secretary disappeared with a considerable sum of public funds.[56] Further financial problems emerged during the early years of the twentieth century. However Dublin Corporation remains the most important local authority, governing the largest area and with the greatest responsibility for the health and well-being of the city and its inhabitants. The remainder of this essay will assess the efficiency with which it discharged its duties and the validity of the criticisms which were directed at its administration.

Our analysis will concentrate on public health and social policy as these were the matters which involved the greatest increase in the responsibilities of local authorities during the late nineteenth century. Before embarking on a detailed analysis it is advisable to note that Dublin Corporation operated under certain severe handicaps. A very high proportion of the city's population belonged to the unskilled working class and this meant that the city contained an abnormally large percentage of residents who were living in inadequate conditions and vulnerable to disease. The city also suffered long-term financial problems which imposed constraints on municipal expenditure. Unlike many contemporary cities, there were no municipal buildings of note erected in Dublin in the century prior to 1914. This may seem to indicate a lack of municipal pride but is more probably a reflection of financial stringency. The 1849

[53] *I.T.*, 3 Feb. 1898.
[54] *Hansard 5* (Commons), lxi, 16 Apr. 1914, 375.
[55] *Municipal boundaries report* op. cit., p. 22 and *evidence* pp 158, 211, 214.
[56] Pembroke ratepayers association memorial to the Chief Secretary (S.P.O.I., CSO/RP 1892/13946).

234

improvement act had fixed the city's improvement rate, the rate from which general expenses were met, at a maximum of 2 shillings in the £.[57] This was done on the basis of a total valuation for the city of £663,768; however in 1854 Griffith's valuation reduced this to £541,377.[58] From this reduced level the valuation climbed very slowly. The pre-1854 valuation figure was not reached until the late 1880s and by 1913, despite a boundary extension which brought an increase in valuation of approximately £100,000, the city's valuation barely exceeded £1m. This was a remarkably modest increase in contrast with most British cities. As a result the total municipal revenue increased very slowly and borrowing powers, which were limited to twice the total valuation, were seriously constrained. The contrast with the position in England and Wales emerges from a statement by Asa Briggs:

Although the total rate expenditure of England and Wales increased from £10–10.5m in 1868 to £28m in 1890 and £56m by the middle of the first decade of the twentieth century the average rate poundage changed little until the explosion of the 1890s. Rateable valuation rose more rapidly than population and corporations could spend more without increasing their rates. Willingness of cities to spend more was conditioned not only by their 'civic drive' or by their capacity to harness business flair but by the facts of their financial strength.[59]

The lack of growth of Dublin's poundage meant that rates were consistently at a high level, frequently the maximum permissable. In addition to the burden of municipal rates, poor rates fell more heavily on the city than on the neighbouring suburbs. Rates within each poor law union varied between the different electoral divisions as each division was held financially responsible for the paupers coming from its area. The middle class suburbs produced relatively few workhouse inmates and so their burden was low while that of the city was high.[60] As a result total rates in the city were substantially higher than in adjoining suburbs, giving a further incentive for middle class families to move to the suburbs. In 1872, total rates in the North City area totalled 9/3 compared with 4/6 in Clontarf and 4/- in Rathmines[61] and although this gulf narrowed somewhat in later decades, a discrepancy remained. The desire of the corporation to annexe neighbouring suburbs was not merely to

[57] 12 & 13 Vict. ch. 107. This limit was removed in 1878.
[58] Dublin Municipal Council minutes, 14 June 1860.
[59] Asa Briggs, *Victorian cities* (London, 1963), p. 40.
[60] Extension of municipal boundaries (S.P.O.I. CSO/RP 1874/17604).
[61] *I.T.*, 16 June 1874.

record a population greater than that of Belfast. It also stemmed from the need for higher total valuation and consequently greater borrowing powers and from a belief that the suburbs were not bearing their fair share of public expenditure. In this belief the corporation was not alone. Even the *Irish Times* which had considerable sympathy with the political beliefs prevailing in the townships and none with those of the corporation noted in 1880 that the question of city boundaries was

whether a very large number of persons who are to all intents and purposes citizens of the metropolis shall be allowed to evade a great proportion of their responsibilities because they live beyond the municipal boundary.[62]

While making due allowance for the difficulties which the city authorities faced, Dublin's public health record, measured simply by the crude death-rate was extremely poor in decades prior to 1914. The first accurately recorded death statistics relate to the year 1864, but in Dublin these proved initially to be seriously defective respecting deaths.[63] Adjusting these in line with burial records, the city's death rate averaged 31.6 per thousand in the years from 1864 to 1880. The comparable figure for the Dublin Registration District, an area which included the suburbs and part of the county, was 29.6. This was much greater than the figures prevailing in English cities. London's death-rate for the twenty years before 1880 averaged 23.4, Birmingham's was somewhat higher. The closest comparable English city was Liverpool with a death rate of 29.3, marginally lower than the figure for the Dublin Registration District.[64] At the beginning of recorded statistics therefore the Dublin death-rate was relatively high; from this high level it declined much more slowly than the lower English figures. By the decade 1895–1904 the London rate had fallen to 18.2, a decline of 5.2 points or 28.6%. The Dublin Registration District recorded a smaller absolute fall, to 25.3 which was still higher than the London average in the decades prior to 1880 and in percentage terms was a fall of only 14.5%. The performance of the city was even worse. The death rate fell by a mere 3.4 per thousand or 10.75%. In contrast Liverpool, the worst English city achieved a much greater absolute

[62] *I.T.*, 20 May 1879.
[63] *Census of Ireland*, 1871, II, sect- viii. Burials exceeded deaths by an average of 9.7%.
[64] *Registrar-general, decennial summary of the births, deaths, and marriages registered in Ireland, 1871–80*, [C 4153] H.C., 1884, xx, 996; Lampard, op. cit., p. 20; Asa Briggs, *History of Birmingham* (2 vols, Oxford, 1952), ii, 225; Brian D. White, *A history of the corporation of Liverpool, 1835–1914* (Liverpool, 1951), p. 92.

and proportionate decline.[65] By 1905 therefore the gap between Dublin mortality levels and those of major English cities had actually worsened, despite the fact that it should have been easier to effect an improvement given the higher initial death-rate in Dublin. The widening gap becomes more significant when it is recalled that Dublin operated under health and sanitary legislation almost identical to that prevailing in England at the time and it is generally recognised that several English cities were slipshod in implementing public health measures. The higher Dublin death-rate was due either to inadequate enforcement of sanitary measures, or was caused by factors unaffected by such measures.

The major initiatives in public health during the late nineteenth century included improved water supplies, sewerage and drainage schemes, better and cleaner housing and measures to prevent food contamination. The city of Dublin tackled all these matters with varying degrees of enthusiasm. In 1862 Dr Charles Cameron was appointed as public analyst, the third such appointment in the United Kingdom.[66] Two years later Dublin was again a pioneer with the appointment of Dr Edward Dillon Mapother as medical officer of health.[67] However both appointments were part-time and this would suggest that the city's commitment to enforcement of health measures was somewhat limited. The 1860s however were dominated by efforts to provide a new water supply. The city's previous source had been the canals and new supplies had been sought, because this was now inadequate and the canal company would only provide more water at a substantially higher price.[68] The fact that the canal water was polluted was not initially of importance. Following lengthy reports and several acrimonious debates a water scheme taking supplies from the Vartry river was commenced in 1862 and completed nine years later.[69] This was promoted mainly by the liberal and nationalist members of the corporation, in particular by Sir John Gray, editor of the *Freeman's Journal* against the strong opposition of business interests including the chamber of commerce and the Ballast Office, which then controlled the port.[70] The city's Conservative councillors were also hostile, as were the

[65] Lampard, op. cit., p. 21; *Registrar-general, decennial summary 1891-1900* [Cd 2089] H.C. 1904, xiv, 1085 and *1901-10* [Cd 7121] H.C. 1914, xv, 15.
[66] Dublin Municipal Council minutes, 3 Oct. 1862.
[67] Ibid. 20 June 1864.
[68] Parke Neville, *A description of the Dublin corporation waterworks* (Dublin, 1875), pp 7-8.
[69] Dublin Municipal Council, Report of the Waterworks Committee, 21 Nov. 1862 and 18 Feb. 1871.
[70] *Freeman's Journal,* 18 Feb. 1861.

Rathmines commissioners, primarily on the grounds of expense, though the loss of income to canal company shareholders was also a factor. The eighteenth report of the waterworks committee, which triumphantly announced the scheme's completion, declared that the matter had been 'fought out on religious divisions—a battle of the Boyne and Blackwater'.[71] The Vartry supply gave Dublin the cheapest water scheme in the British Isles[72] and provided an adequate supply of unpolluted water. Throughout the city the polluted wells fell into disuse and both the quality and quantity of the city's water improved considerably. However the impact on health was not apparent. Mortality in the city was higher in the 1870s than in the previous decade.

The next major preoccupation, the main drainage of the city, proved a much less successful operation. The obsession with main drainage, or rather with the purifying of the river Liffey, was a by-product of contemporary fallacies concerning the origin and spread of disease. It was commonly believed that contaminated water emitted noxious gases which in turn caused epidemics of cholera and other fevers.[73] The theory was given added credence as a result of the cholera epidemic of 1866 which claimed 1,186 lives,[74] many of them residents of areas close to the Liffey or its tributaries.[75] In fact mortality was high in such areas because they contained over-crowded houses populated by impoverished, ill-nourished people. The common belief in the miasmic theory of disease, coupled with the stench from the river during fine weather meant that main drainage was a favourite topic of leader writers and of letters to the newspapers. The journalist, A. M. Sullivan, explained to the select committee on local government:

Whenever the weather gets hot and as the thermometer rises the cry of 'cleanse the river at all hazards' resounds in Dublin, but whenever the weather gets cold it is most unpopular in the city to propose an additional taxation even for cleaning the Liffey.[76]

It is probable that the condition of the Liffey worsened during the 'sixties. When the corporation took control of sewers from the

[71] Dublin Municipal Council, Report of the Waterworks Committee, 18 Feb. 1871.
[72] Best, op. cit., p. 397.
[73] Royston Lambert, *Sir John Simon, 1816–1904 and English social administration* (London, 1963), pp 48–57.
[74] *Report of the Registrar-general, Third Annual Report,* [C 130] H.C. 1870, xvi, 845.
[75] Thomas W. Grimshaw, *Remarks on the prevalence and distribution of fever in Dublin* (Dublin, 1872), p. 17.
[76] *Report from select committee on local government,* op. cit., para. 4681.

defunct paving commission in 1851 the city was seriously lacking in a systematic scheme for surface drainage or domestic sewerage. During the following years however the problem of surface drainage was tackled and this, coupled with the spread of water closets, increased the volume of waste matter channelled into the Liffey. Rents of properties along the quays fell sharply[77] and the area declined in social status, either because the smell from the river worsened, or because of contemporary beliefs that the river was a health hazard. In 1870 the smell was apparently so bad that the lords justices in the Four Courts sent a memorial to the corporation claiming that they were unable to continue court hearings.[78] The concerted publicity resulted in many efforts to carry out a main drainage scheme. This was a fashionable venture for many cities at this time; London had successfully completed a main drainage scheme some years previously and there was also a belief that main drainage could be made profitable by the development of sewerage farms. In 1864 an enterprising firm of solicitors, Barrington and Jeffars, (they also planned an underground railway through Rathmines) proposed such a scheme.[79] Dublin councillors enthusiastically visited sewerage farms in Croydon and Edinburgh, returning with glowing accounts of luxury villas erected in their vicinity.[80] However the leading expert on the matter, J. W. Bazalgette, dismissed these proposals as not feasible[81] and it was decided to promote a straight-forward scheme. In 1870 government approval was obtained for a loan of £350,000[82] and the corporation introduced a main drainage bill. This measure was delayed by efforts to conciliate local ratepayers and neighbouring suburbs and the resulting delay proved critical. By 1873, when tenders were opened raw material costs had escalated; the price of iron pipes had more than doubled and wages and cement had also risen as a result of the inflationary boom which followed the Franco-Prussian war.[83] The tenders submitted ranged from £775,000 to almost £1m, far in excess of the city's financial resources.[84] Although costs subsequently fell and economies were made in the plans it proved impossible to complete a main drainage scheme within the financial

[77] *Dublin Builder*, 1 Feb. 1866.
[78] *I.T.*, 4 July 1870.
[79] J. W. Bazalgette, *Report on the Dublin sewerage utilisation bill 1868* (Dublin, 1868), p. 10.
[80] John Norwood, T.C., *The purification of the river Liffey* (Dublin, 1866), p. 2.
[81] Bazalgette, op. cit., p. 10.
[82] Dublin Municipal Council, Report of the Main Drainage Committee, 3 Oct. 1870 (Dublin City Hall).
[83] Ibid., 1873, no. 55.
[84] *I.T.*, 18 July 1873.

limits. There is little doubt that some solution to this impasse could have been found, particularly if the suburban townships agreed to shoulder part of the burden. However conciliation, particularly of political enemies was not the corporation's strongest point. Instead they decided to sue the Dublin Port and Docks Board, a body hostile to the corporation, for failure to clean the river.[85] This alienated the suburban townships and the Conservative councillors and only resulted in further postponement.[86] An appeal to the chief secretary for increased borrowing powers and a deferral of repayments caused him to write to the treasury arguing that 'the existing high rate of local taxation in Dublin may not unfairly be urged as a reason for special consideration being shown in this matter towards the ratepayers of that city'.[87] However the treasury felt that there was insufficient security for an increased loan and suggested that the area of taxation be extended to include the area of the Dublin Metropolitan Police and that the government be represented on the main drainage board, a proposal which was rejected out of hand by the corporation.[88] This threat caused the corporation to postpone the main drainage scheme[89] a decision which was strengthened when a ratepayers group led by John McEvoy, a city businessman and Kingstown commissioner obtained an injunction restraining them from pursuing any further main drainage legislation.[90] There the matter rested. The townships of Rathmines and Pembroke rallied to the cry of Frederick Stokes, chairman of Rathmines commissioners, that 'Rathmines will drain alone'.[91] Their limited scheme was completed in 1881, with two-thirds of the costs being borne by Pembroke township, a considerable proportion personally by the earl of Pembroke.[92]

Interest in main drainage waned during the 1880s largely because a report on the city's drainage had concluded 'that upon the evidence placed before us, we cannot hold the Liffey responsible for the high rate of mortality which has prevailed'.[93] The city's tenement

[85] *I.T.*, 27 June 1874.
[86] Letter from Dublin Corporation main drainage committee 23 July 1874 (S.P.O.I., CSO/RP 1874/10666).
[87] Dublin main drainage, confidential memo, T. H. Burke to Chief Secretary, Sir Michael Hicks-Beach (S.P.O.I. CSO/RP 1875/10072).
[88] S.P.O.I., CSO/RP 1875/111000.
[89] Town clerk to CSO 6 Nov. 1875 (S.P.O.I., CSO/RP 1875/17121).
[90] *I.T.*, 19 Nov. 1875 and 27 Nov. 1875.
[91] Rathmines township minutes, letter dated 28 Oct. 1875 (Dublin City Hall).
[92] *I.T.*, 25 June 1882.
[93] *Report of the royal commission appointed to inquire into the sewerage and drainage of the city of Dublin and other matters connected therewith, evidence, appendix.* p. xxx [C 2605], H.C. 1880, xxx, 1, i.

Mary Daly

houses, they concluded, were the prime factor. With this judgement, the preoccupation with the Liffey smell also lapsed. Newspaper comment on this topic was non-existent during the following decade, suggesting that the reassurance of an official report had made nostrils less sensitive, or perhaps more plausibly, that a knowledge of the cost of main drainage had made citizens willing to bear with the smell.

In 1889 the Dublin Corporation Loans Act[94] made it possible to consolidate the municipal debt and as a result main drainage plans were reconsidered in 1891.[95] Work was eventually begun in 1897 and completed in 1906.[96] The delays in completing the city's main drainage contrast with the successful implementation of a water scheme. Financial stringency was a major factor in the delay. Yet whereas in the 1860s the corporation, led by Sir John Gray, was willing to tackle widespread opposition in order successfully to complete the water scheme, there was considerably less commitment to the main drainage effort and the corporation reacted to criticism by displaying more overt hostility to bodies such as the suburban townships and the Irish administration. The chairman of the main drainage committee, Councillor Norwood, was a member of the Conservative minority[97] and this may have reduced his ability to gain widespread support for his scheme. The impact of this delay on the city's death-rate is difficult to establish. It was possibly a factor behind the high incidence of enteric fever (typhoid) in Dublin. Mortality from this disease actually rose during the 1880s and by the end of that decade was higher in Dublin than in any United Kingdom city except Belfast.[98] The relationship between typhoid and inadequate drainage is well-established and the incidence in Dublin does decline after 1900. However another possible cause of typhoid was contaminated milk supplies, and the prevalence of insanitary dairy yards within the city[99] rather than the delay in the city's drainage scheme may have been the key factor.

The next topic for discussion is the city's tenement housing which was viewed as the principal cause of ill-health and excess mortality from 1880 until 1914. Tenement housing, or multi-family occupancy

[94] 52 & 53 Vict. cap. cxxix. *An Act to authorise the Right Honourable the Lord Mayor, aldermen, burgesses of Dublin to consolidate the loans and create corporation stock.*
[95] Dublin Municipal Council minutes, 4 May 1891.
[96] Ibid., 1 Feb. 1897; *I.T.*, 25 Sept. 1906.
[97] *Freeman's Journal*, 21 Sept. 1884.
[98] Dublin Municipal Council Reports, 1893, no. 183. Report of the public health committee on typhoid.
[99] Typhoid inquiry. Report local government board (S.P.O.I., CSO/RP 1896/20950; 1897/1011, 2219, 6084.

of one house, was the city's traditional form of housing and congestion had a long legacy. Rev. Whitelaw's survey of Plunkett Street in the Coombe in 1798 revealed an average of 28.7 occupants per house.[100] In 1851 a total of 28,039 families, slightly less than one half of the city's total, lived in fourth class accommodation (one-roomed dwellings). By 1891 the position had improved so that 19,342 families, or 37% of the population was so housed.

The improvement in the years prior to 1891 was primarily due to the falling population and the flight of the more prosperous citizens to the suburbs which released large houses which were turned into tenements. A 'levelling up' occurred as families who had occupied one room rented two or three rooms. In addition the number of second class houses (those with from five to nine rooms) rose from 9,693 in 1851 to 14,600 by 1891. During these decades a substantial proportion of lower middle class and artisan families improved the quality of their housing. The advance in the quality of the city's housing took place independently of the actions of the corporation or of philantropic bodies and was due primarily to the declining population. In registering an improvement during these decades, Dublin's position contrasts with many English cities where population growth and demolition programmes due to transport schemes or other economic advances, were common. Large-scale demolition was uncommon in Dublin. The railway stations were built on the periphery and the comparative lack of industrial development meant that no large-scale displacement of families took place. The largest private clearance involved the South City Markets Company's development of the George's Street area when 3,570 were displaced.[101]

The 1890s however were a time of population increase and of growing pressure on housing. By 1901 the number of families living in one-room dwellings had risen by 2,000 and though this declined somewhat by 1911 the number was greater than in 1891.

The contribution of Dublin Corporation to the city's housing was not insignificant. By 1914 they had housed a total of 1,385 families, or approximately 7,500 persons, 2.5% of the population, a proportion which, one corporation spokesman claimed, was greater than in any other United Kingdom city.[102] By the same date London County Council had provided a total of 9,746 units, proportionately

---

[100] Warburton, Whitelaw and Walsh, op. cit., i, 243.
[101] *Report of the royal commission appointed to inquire into the housing of the working classes. Third report, evidence.* para. 23053 p. 46, [C 4547], H.C. 1884–5, xxxi, 187.
[102] *Report of the departmental committee appointed to inquire into the housing conditions of the working class in Dublin. Evidence and appendices* [Cd 7273] H.C. 1914, xix, 107.

a much smaller contribution.[103] Even Glasgow, which has been regarded as a pioneer in working class housing[104] had not done more. By 1902 the municipal authority had built a total of 2,488 dwellings,[105] again housing a smaller proportion of the city's population than in Dublin.

In addition to corporation schemes, philanthropic organisations, most notably the Artisans Dwellings Company, and large employers such as the Great Southern and Western Railway Company had provided a total of 5,271 dwellings housing 24,561 people.[106] Some of these were reconditioned tenements rather than new buildings. The combined corporation and other schemes provided 6,656 dwellings, almost one-fifth (18.75%) of the housing stock in 1914. This contrasts quite favourably with London where the local authorities and philanthropic bodies had provided a total of 38,724 dwellings.[107] The quality of housing provided by the Dublin philanthropic agencies tended however to cater for more prosperous workers than its London equivalent. The Dublin agencies concentrated on building three- and four-roomed cottages which were too expensive for the most needy citizens.

Housing built by philanthropic agencies, by number of rooms (percentage)[108]

	1 room	2 rooms	3 rooms	4 rooms or more
Dublin	8.2%	27.1%	38.9%	25.7%
London	17.1%	45.2%	35.4%	2.3%

More than half of the original residents of the Coombe housing scheme were skilled workers or policemen and none of the original residents of the demolished tenements were rehoused there.[109] In 1914 the average rent of Artisans Dwellings Company properties (they were the largest such body) was 5/5 per week, an impossible figure for unskilled workers whose earnings averaged £1. Some of the smaller agencies such as the Association for the Housing of the Very Poor provided renovated tenements at low cost, but they tended to operate on strict principles, disciplining tenants and removing those who were not sober, hygienic and punctual in rent payments.[110]

103 Anthony S. Wohl, *The eternal slum*, (London, 1977), app. iv.
104 Best, op. cit., pp 397–8.
105 C. M. Allen, 'The genesis of British urban redevelopment with special reference to Glasgow' in *Econ. Hist. Rev.* (second ser.), xviii (1965), p. 608.
106 *1914 housing inquiry evidence* p. 22.
107 Wohl, op. cit., appendices, iii and iv.
108 Ibid., appendix iii; *1914 housing inquiry evidence*, p. 182.
109 Spencer Harty, 'The Coombe housing scheme' in *Stat. Soc. Irl. Jnl.*, viii, no. 7 (July, 1884), p. 514.
110 *1914 housing inquiry evidence*, p. 19.

In terms of their contribution to the city's total housing the corporation's record appears favourable. Considerably more housing was needed: the 1914 inquiry estimated that 14,000 were urgently required, however the stringent limits on the city's borrowing powers would have precluded such lavish undertakings. The corporation is however open to the criticism that in their housing, as in that of the Artisans Dwellings Company, they catered for more secure and prosperous workers. A comparatively modest development of eighty three-roomed cottages, built at the rear of Eccles Street were rented at 4/6 per week. However, as in the Coombe, virtually none of the displaced residents lived there as they could not afford such high rents.[111] The average rent of tenements built by the corporation at Bride's Alley was 5/-, while some houses erected on the city outskirts at Inchichore were rented for 11/-.[112] Yet only 28% of tenement residents paid rents in excess of 3/- and a mere one family in eight paid more than 5/-.[113] Despite the predominance of expensive dwellings, corporation housing schemes showed a deficit.[114] Lower rents would have meant greater deficits which would not have been permitted by the local government board auditors.

It is possible that there was some scope for greater efficiency in the corporation's housing operations. The cost of most schemes was greatly in excess of the original estimates, in part due to the heavy costs incurred in compensating the owners of insanitary premises to be demolished. There is little doubt that some payments were excessive. Tenement owners of houses in the Coombe were paid sums amounting to ten years net rental, while weekly tenement keepers, or middlemen, were awarded six months rent.[115] In 1881 the corporation embarked on a clearance of Plunkett Street where no house was regarded as sufficiently sound to be reconstructed. Claims for compensation amounting to over £60,000 were lodged and despite a more stringent policy than that applied in the Coombe (two-thirds of all claims including all yearly and lesser tenants were declared ineligible), the arbitrators awarded a total of £19,000 in compensation.[116] These excessive sums resulted from the concern shown for property rights, yet there is substantial evidence that the

[111] Ibid., p. 19; Charles Cameron, *A brief history of municipal public health administration in Dublin* (London, 1914), p. 57.
[112] *1914 housing inquiry evidence*, pp 21–3.
[113] Calculations from figures on tenement rents in *1914 housing inquiry, appendices* xxii.
[114] *Return showing particulars as to the action of local authorities in Ireland under the housing of the working classes act, compiled to the 31 March 1906* H.C. (337), 1906 xvci, 843.
[115] Dublin Municipal Council Reports, 1879, no. 239, Report of Special Committee.
[116] Ibid., 1882, no. 182.

corporation was guilty of inefficient administration and was perhaps excessively partial to the interests of tenement landlords.

An inquiry by an inspector of the local government board in 1902 concluded that there was a 'want of economy and administration in civic affairs'.[117] Public spending was inadequately supervised and schemes were not always subjected to competitive contracting, while overmanning was common within municipal departments, mainly to reward political favourites.[118] The local government board auditor uncovered many financial irregularities such as the payment of wages to non-existent men[119] and his persistent criticism led the corporation in 1906 to refuse him permission to audit their accounts and resulted in a court case which the corporation lost.[120] In response some councillors and aldermen summoned a public meeting in the Phoenix Park to protest and one member, Alderman Tom Kelly, announced himself as 'ready for a scrap with Dublin Castle'.[121]

The hostility shown to the corporation undoubtedly had political undertones. A leading article on this topic in the *Freeman's Journal* noted:

The real issue is a political and administrative one and in resolving to force it to a determination the corporation have taken a stand that was bound to be made sooner or later if the local authorities are to exercise freely rights that were supposed to have been conferred on them since the Local Government Act.[122]

The criticisms voiced by the local government board also pertained to sanitary matters. In 1906, D. Edgar Flinn, a local government board medical officer, examined the recommendations which had been made in the report of the 1900 inquiry on the city's health[123] and concluded that little action had been taken on the majority of the recommendations.[124] The 1914 housing inquiry noted a series of

[117] Dublin Municipal Council Minutes, 12 Aug. 1902. Report of local government board inspector under the equalisation of rates inquiry.
[118] Dublin Municipal Council Reports, 1902 no. 214. First report departmental inquiry committee.
[119] *I.T.*, 6 June 1905.
[120] *I.T.*, 6 Aug. 1906; *Freeman's Journal*, 2 July 1907.
[121] *I.T.*, 6 Aug. 1906.
[122] *Freeman's Journal*, 7 July 1906.
[123] *Report of the departmental committee appointed by the local government board of Ireland to inquire into the public health of the city of Dublin* [Cd 243], H.C. 1900 xxxix, 681.
[124] Surgeon Colonel D. Edgar Flinn, *Official report on the sanitary circumstances and administration of the city of Dublin, with special reference to the causes of the high death-rate* (Dublin, 1906), p. 12.

failures to implement bye-laws relating to overcrowding and the cleansing of tenements and the failure to maintain a register of tenement properties. Summarising the performance of the corporation the 1914 inquiry concluded that 'There has been a want of firmness in enforcing the public health laws with regard to housing'.[125] This failure may be regarded as due to mere incompetence, or alternatively to corruption. The 1914 housing inquiry revealed that a total of sixteen members of the corporation owned tenement properties. Three of these, Alderman Corrigan, a prominent undertaker, Councillor Crozier, who was listed in the directory as a veterinary surgeon but who apparently was active as a housing agent, and Alderman O'Reilly, a publican, owned a large amount of tenement property, and a fourth member, Alderman O'Connor, owned two tenements plus a substantial number of cottages. The remaining owners held between one and three properties.[126] The three largest owners all held third class tenements, properties defined by sanitary staff as 'unfit for habitation and incapable of being rendered fit'.[127] In 1902 a tenement house in Townsend Street, the property of Alderman O'Reilly, collapsed, killing one person and injuring seven.[128] There is no evidence available concerning the extent of tenement ownership among corporation members in earlier years but it seems unlikely to have been a new trend. In 1872 a divisional magistrate had commented in a statement concerning the non-enforcement of sanitary regulations that 'the tenement owners are a large and influential class in Dublin both in and out of the corporation'.[129]

The power of tenement owners undoubtedly militated against effective controls on slum housing. One critic of sanitary policy claimed in 1901 that no successful prosecution had ever taken place against overcrowded tenements.[130] The house belonging to Alderman O'Reilly which collapsed had been condemned as unsafe by sanitary staff, but their decision was reversed by the building inspector.[131] In 1906 Councillor P. T. Daly, a trade union member of the corporation, reported two instances of pressure being brought

[125] *1914 housing inquiry report*, p. 14.
[126] Ibid., p. 13; see also *evidence*, pp 245–8.
[127] Ibid., *report*, p. 3.
[128] *I.T.*, 11 Oct. 1902.
[129] Comments of divisional magistrate re public health legislation, (S.P.O.I., CSO/RP 1872/4713).
[130] Richard M. Kelly, 'The administration of sanitary law' in *Medical Press and Circular*, 27 Feb. 1901.
[131] *I.T.*, 11 Oct. 1902.

to bear on the public health committee of the corporation to postpone prosecutions of tenement owners. One of the owners was a member of the corporation and both postponements were urged by Sir Charles Cameron, the medical officer of health.[132] The 1914 housing inquiry revealed further irregularities involving Sir Charles Cameron and tenement-owning members of the corporation. Provision existed for granting rate rebates to tenement owners who improved their properties. The three councillors who were large-scale tenement owners were among those in receipt of rebates, despite the fact that many of the properties for which these had been granted infringed bye-laws. The responsibility for granting rebates had rested with Sir Charles Cameron.[133] Dublin was not the only city to have its administation in the hands of interests opposed to reform. The London vestrymen of the 1860s were frequently slum landlords and had proved similarly hostile to enforcing bye-laws.[134] However it seems improbable that such a degree of slum landlord influence existed elsewhere by 1914.

Admitting the bye-laws were not adequately enforced against tenement owners, it still remains questionable whether more effective enforcement particularly of closure orders would have helped the housing situation. In 1914 a total of 1,518 tenements housing 22,701 persons were judged unfit for habitation and in need of immediate replacement, while a further 2,288 tenements housing 37,552 families were on the border-lines of this condition. Only 1,516, the homes of 27,052 persons, were deemed capable of being put in good repair.[135] To have condemned and closed the homes of 60,000 people would have intensified existing overcrowding problems. The 1911 census revealed that Dublin was the most congested city in the British Isles with 22.9% of the population in one-room tenements. If one-person families are excluded from our calculations the remainder lived at an average density of over six persons per room.[136] The 1914 housing inquiry believed that 'the provision of sanitary dwellings by private enterprise has been to some extent handicapped by unfair competition with insanitary dwellings which could be let at rents that would not pay for the provision of decent houses'.[137] It was estimated that a minimum rent of 5/5 would be required to provide sanitary dwellings without a

[132] *I.T.*, 6 Oct. 1908.
[133] *1914 housing inquiry report*, p. 13.
[134] Wohl, op. cit., p. 78.
[135] *1914 housing inquiry report*, p. 3.
[136] Ibid., p. 4.
[137] Ibid., p. 14.

subsidy.[138] Few tenement residents could afford this sum given their low wages. A survey of the incomes of 28,079 families revealed that in 55% of cases the head of the family earned less than £1. A further 908 were pensioners, whose incomes were probably much less.[139] The maximum rent which such families could afford was approximately 3/-, which was not an economic rent for a sanitary dwelling. In such circumstances the response of Dublin Corporation, and of other Irish municipalities was to press for a state subsidy. The first tentative steps towards such a subsidy were taken in 1908 with the passing of the Clancy Act,[140] so called because of its sponsor, John Joseph Clancy, nationalist M.P. for North County Dublin. This measure extended the repayment period for housing loans to eighty years and granted an initial two year moratorium on repayments. The Fund for the Suitors of the Supreme Court, a sum amounting to £180,000, was invested and the interest, approximately £6,500, was divided among Irish local authorities in proportion to their expenditure on working-class housing. This measure is noteworthy in being restricted to Ireland, British working-class housing receiving no state subsidy at the time. Yet when the association of municipal authorities in Ireland petitioned the Chief Secretary, Augustine Birrell, for an increased subsidy his response was unfavourable. To suggestions that Irish working-class housing loans should receive the preferential interest rates accorded to loans for agricultural labourers cottages, the Chief Secretary explained that any concession on urban housing could not be restricted to Ireland 'but involves opening the flood-gates of public grants to the other cities of the Kingdom'.[141]

Desirable though improved housing might have been it remains questionable whether the tenements played the major role in the city's health problems that has been attributed to them. The most outstanding mortality problem was the high level of adult deaths. Infant mortality levels were broadly comparable with English levels, but mortality above the age of one year was much greater[142] and, particularly after 1900, the major cause of death was tuberculosis. By 1906, there was a general improvement in the city's death-rate but mortality from tuberculosis appeared to be on the

---

[138] Ibid., p. 2.
[139] *1914 housing inquiry, appendices*, xxiii.
[140] 8 Edw. ch. 81. *An Act to provide further facilities for the erection of houses for the working classes in cities and towns in Ireland.*
[141] S.P.O.I., CSO/RP 1913/18626.
[142] Dublin Municipal Council Reports, 1892, no. 93. Report on public health for the year 1891.

Mary Daly

increase.[143] There was a strong association between the level of mortality from tuberculosis and social class. In 1912 mortality in the general service class (i.e. working class) was 7.7 times that of the professional class and the incidence rose as one descended the social scale, though domestic servants had a comparatively low incidence.[144] There was also apparently a relationship between overcrowding and tuberculosis, particularly as overcrowding increased the risks of infection. No figures exist for Dublin, but in the London borough of Finsbury (the city's most overcrowded borough) mortality from tuberculosis among those living in one-room tenements was 3.75 times that of residents of three-room tenements and 1.6 times that of residents of two-room tenements.[145] This increased mortality may be due, not to overcrowding, but to other causes. Occupants of two or three rooms were presumably more prosperous than those living in one room and they had better food and generally superior living standards. The lower mortality may reflect differences in diet rather than in accommodation. The 1939 housing inquiry revealed that the city's overcrowding problem was actually greater than in 1914. A total of 9,117 households of four or more persons lived in one-room tenements in 1936 compared with 8,743 in 1911.[146] Yet in 1940 the city's death rate was 14.36 per thousand, compared with 20.9 in 1914. The mortality from pulmonary tuberculosis in 1914 was 2.8 per thousand, by 1940 it had more than halved to 1.31 and total tubercular mortality had fallen from 3.788 to 1.63.[147] Factors other than housing, such as better treatment of disease, or more adequate food supplies were presumably responsible. There is evidence that working-class diets in the early twentieth century were seriously inadequate. Of twenty-one families studied in 1904, and excluding the 'very poor', only six had an adequate diet and one of these families spent in excess of its income.[148]

This line of analysis seems to absolve Dublin Corporation from its role as a prime culprit for the city's social condition. Low wages, it can be argued, were responsible for inadequate diet and consequently for high mortality and also for the poor quality of the

[143] Flinn, op. cit., p. 15.
[144] 1914 housing inquiry report, p. 5. Figures related to 1912.
[145] I.T., 6 May 1914.
[146] Report of inquiry into the housing of the working classes of the city of Dublin 1939–43. R/75/1 (Dublin, 1943), para. 9.
[147] Report of registrar-general 1940. T/3/20 (Dublin, 1941), p. xv.
[148] T. J. Stafford, 'Note on the social condition of certain working class families in Dublin', in Report of the royal commission on the poor laws and relief of distress. Appendix vol. x, minutes of evidence on Ireland. Appendix IID, p. 350, [Cd 5070], H.C. 1910, 1, 195.

city's housing. Low wages were to some extent the responsibility of the city's employers and the labour troubles of 1913 have a bearing on this question. The *Irish Times* however succeeded in reversing the analysis and held the city's housing conditions responsible for trade union unrest. 'The members of the I.T.G.W.U. live, for the most part in slums like Church Street. . . . We believe that if every unskilled labourer in Dublin were the tenant of three or even two rooms, the city would not be divided into two hostile camps'.[149] Some decades earlier however, E. Dwyer Gray, Home Rule M.P. and city councillor, argued that the city's housing merely reflected its wider economic problems. 'To provide them with decent habitation while they are still in want of food and have no means of earning regular and sufficient wages would, in a sense be something like mockery',[150] but the solution which he envisaged was the repeal of the Union in order to regenerate the Irish economy. When Dublin Corporation's housing comittee came to consider the verdict of the 1914 inquiry it favoured a similar analysis, arguing that 'the housing problem in Dublin is the out-crop of generations of vicissitudes in the political, manufacturing and social conditions of our people',[151] but it felt that the British government should bear the responsibility for finding a solution. It is however most unlikely that at any stage such government assistance would have been forthcoming. The nineteenth century was marked by major advances in social policy, but responsibility for measures relating to health and housing rested primarily with local authorities. This practice assumed the existence of expanding local finance to pay for such measures and of efficient and concerned local councillors who would implement new measures. Both these assumptions were ill-founded in the case of Dublin. The city's local taxes failed to grow in pace with the demands placed on them, while a local authority dominated by tenement owners, publicans and by a desire to assert the cause of Irish self-government was neither caring nor sufficiently competent. However it remains doubtful if men of the calibre of the Rathmines and Pembroke commissioners would have proved more effective. In the final analysis a complex interaction between local and national politics and economic and social change produced a combination of circumstances which made the city's problems well-nigh insoluble.

[149] *I.T.*, 4 Sept. 1913.
[150] *Report on the housing of the working classes, 1884–5. Minority report*, p. xvi.
[151] Dublin Municipal Council Reports, 1914, no. 120, Report of Housing Committee on interpartmental committee on housing.

Table I

POPULATION OF CITY AND SUBURBS, 1841–1911

	City	Increase %	Suburbs	Increase %	Total	Increase %
1841	232,726	—	48,480	—	281,206	—
1851	258,369	11	59,468	22.7	317,837	14.2
1861	254,808	—1.37	70,323	17.8	325,131	2.5
1871	246,326	—3.31	83,410	18.6	329,736	1.42
1881	249,602	1.33	95,450	14.45	345,052	3.45
1891	245,001	—1.85	102,911	7.8	347,912	0.83
1901		6.25				
Old[1]	260,035					
1901						
New	290,638	8.22[2]	90,854	8.63	381,492	8.7
1911	304,802	4.87	99,690	9.73	404,492	6.05

'Suburbs' in this table includes any area which by 1911 had become part of a suburban township, though in many cases it was not suburban in 1841. The suburbs which are aggregated in this figure are Rathmines, Pembroke, Clontarf, Drumcondra, New Kilmainham, Blackrock, Kingstown, Dalkey, Killiney and that part of Bray which was situated in County Dublin.

1. The city boundaries were extended in 1900 by the *Dublin Corporation Act* 63 & 64 Vict., ch. 214. The area added to the city comprised the townships of Clontarf, Drumcondra and New Kilmainham, whose populations were, until then, included in the total for suburbs. It also included a small part of County Dublin not previously included in either column. The 1901 'old' population is the population in 1901 living within the 1891 city boundaries.

2. The percentages are calculated on the population in 1891 of the areas which remained suburban in 1901.

Table II

DECENNIAL DEATH-RATES,
CITY AND REGISTRATION DISTRICT, 1864–1910

	City	Registration District
1864–70[1]	29.9	28.5
1871–80	32.8	30.4
1881–90	29.5	26.8
1891–1900	29.6	26.9
1901–10	23.9	22.2

Source: *Registrar-general, decennial summary of the births, deaths, and marriages registered in Ireland, 1871–80* [C 4153], H.C. 1884, xx, 996; ibid., *1881–90* [C 7536], H.C. 1894, xxv, 325; ibid., 1891–1900 [Cd 2089], H.C. 1904, xiv, 1085; ibid., 1901–10 [Cd 7121], H.C. 1914, xv, 15.

The Dublin registration district comprises the area designated 'suburban' in the previous Table, though in the 1860s some small areas subsequently added to Rathmines are not included.

1. Figures for the 1860s and 1870s are revised to allow for under-registration (see footnote 63).

Table III

DUBLIN CITY HOUSING 1841–1911

Houses

	First class	*Second class*	*Third class*	*Fourth class*	*Total*
1841	10,171	8,289	1,494	155	20,109
1851	10,827	9,693	1,680	44	22,244
1861	10,688	10,456	1,740	21	22,905
1871	10,459	11,455	1,891	91	23,896
1881	9,067	13,061	2,064	14	24,206
1891	8,720	14,638	2,391	7	25,756
1901	8,637		23,413[1]	11	32,061
1911	8,688		26,785	4	35,477

Accommodation

1841	5,605	8,412	12,297	23,197	49,511
1851	5,604	9,345	14,330	28,039	57,318
1861	5,158	9,815	16,163	27,290	58,426
1871	5,033	10,523	16,819	25,952	58,327
1881	4,692	11,013	16,660	23,360	55,725
1891	4,694	13,279	14,536	19,342	51,851
1901	4,635		33,199	21,429	59,263
1911	4,599		37,202	20,564	62,365

The classification of a house depended on the extent, number of rooms, quality and number of windows. The fourth class house was one room plus window. Third class 2–4 rooms plus windows. Second class 5–9 rooms plus windows. First class was anything larger. First class accomodation was one family in a first class house. Second class accommodation was one family in a second class house, or 2–3 families in a first class house.

Third class was one family in a third class house, 2–3 in a second class house, or 4–5 in a first class house. Fourth class was one family or more in a fourth class house, two or more in a third class house, 4 or more in a second class house, or more than six in a first class house.

1. The 1901 census combined second and third class houses and second and third class accommodation.